FOREIGN INVESTMENT, TRANSNATIONALS AND DEVELOPING COUNTRIES

Also by Sanjaya Lall
Foreign Private Manufacturing Investment and Multinational Corporations: An Annotated Bibliography

Also by Paul Streeten
Economic Integration
Value in Social Theory (*editor*)
The Crisis of Indian Planning (*editor with M. Lipton*)
Unfashionable Economics (*editor*)
Commonwealth Policy in a Global Context (*editor with Hugh Corbet*)
Diversification and Development: The Case of Coffee (*with Diane Elson*)
Aid to Africa
The Frontiers of Development Studies
Trade Strategies for Development (*editor*)

FOREIGN INVESTMENT, TRANSNATIONALS AND DEVELOPING COUNTRIES

Sanjaya Lall
Institute of Economics and Statistics, Oxford

and

Paul Streeten
Queen Elizabeth House and Institute of Commonwealth Studies, Oxford

© Sanjaya Lall and Paul Streeten 1977
All rights reserved. No part of this publication may be reproduced or transmitted, in any form or by any means, without permission

First edition 1977
Reprinted 1978, 1980

ELBS edition first published 1980

Published by
THE MACMILLAN PRESS LTD
London and Basingstoke
Associated companies in Delhi Hong Kong Lagos Singapore

ISBN 0 333 16898 4 (hardcover)
ISBN 0 333 27340 0 (ELBS)

Printed in Hong Kong

The paperback edition of this book is sold subject to the condition that it shall not, by way of trade or otherwise, be lent, resold, hired out, or otherwise circulated without the publisher's prior consent, in any form of binding or cover other than that in which it is published and without a similar condition including this condition being imposed on the subsequent purchaser

To the memory of my mother
                              S.L.

Contents

Preface   xi

PART I: TNCs AND DEVELOPING COUNTRIES

1 INTRODUCTION   3
   The Unsettled Background
   Foreign Investment and Transnational Corporations: Scope and Definition

2 THEORIES OF FOREIGN INVESTMENT AND TRANSNATIONAL BEHAVIOUR   16
   Introduction
   Economic Theories of Direct Foreign Investment
   Motivational Aspects of TNC Behaviour
   Organisation and Management
   Salient Features of TNCs

3 WELFARE OF HOST COUNTRIES: TNCs AS OLIGOPOLISTS   47
   Introduction
   A Digression on 'Welfare'
   Provision of Capital
   Organisation and Management
   Technology
   Marketing
   Bargaining and Political Power
   Concluding Note

4 WELFARE OF HOST COUNTRIES: FOREIGN INVESTMENT AS A 'GENERAL' INFLOW OF CAPITAL   81
   Introduction
   Macro-economic Approaches
   Micro-economic Approaches

PART II: THE COUNTRY STUDIES

5 THE BACKGROUND TO THE SAMPLE FIRMS AND GOVERNMENT POLICIES 89
    The Conduct of the Research
    Nature of the Sample
    The Environment of Sample Countries for Foreign Investment

6 AN ANALYSIS OF THE SAMPLE FIRMS' ACCOUNTS 99
    Relative Size of Sample Firms
    Selected Measures of Performance
    Financing Patterns
    Profitability

7 'DIRECT' BALANCE-OF-PAYMENTS EFFECTS 130
    Overall Direct Balance-of-payments Effects
    Exports
    Capital Inflows and the Cost of Servicing Foreign Investment
    Import Dependence
    Technical Payments
    Profits and Transfer Pricing

8 'TOTAL' BALANCE-OF-PAYMENTS AND 'SOCIAL' INCOME EFFECTS: METHODS OF EVALUATION 156
    The Analytical Approach
    Alternative I: The Little–Mirrlees Procedure
    Alternative II: Financial Replacement
    Alternative III: Most Likely Local Replacement

9 'TOTAL' BALANCE-OF-PAYMENTS AND 'SOCIAL' INCOME EFFECTS: THE RESULTS 169
    Alternative I: The Little–Mirrlees Model
    Alternative II: Financial Replacement
    Alternative III: Most Likely Local Replacement

10 'SOCIAL' INCOME EFFECTS: EVALUATING THE EVALUATION 181
    Introduction
    What We Have Learnt about 'Social' Costs and Benefits
    Practical Limitations of 'Social' Cost–Benefit Analysis

Conceptual Limitations of 'Social' Cost–Benefit Analysis

PART III: HOST GOVERNMENT POLICY

11 REGULATION AND BARGAINING 191
   Introduction
   Regulation
   Evaluation
   Bargaining
   Conclusion

12 THE IMPLEMENTATION OF POLICY 219
   Introduction
   Limitations on Willingness
   Limitations on Ability

Notes 225
References 251
Index 273

Preface

This book brings together many years of work on foreign investment and transnational corporations (TNCs). We have both been concerned with the impact of TNCs, particularly in the manufacturing sector, on the economies of less-developed countries (LDCs), and we have both come increasingly to realise that the conventional tools of economics, narrowly conceived, are inadequate to deal with issues which are much broader than those of 'private foreign investment'. What is at stake is the transformation of political, social and economic structures, and what is needed is political economy in the broadest sense. Unfortunately, political economy is an underdeveloped art, and this book reflects our difficulties in dealing with the enormous issues in hand without proper tools. Although we stay largely within the realms of economics as conventionally defined, it also reflects our disquiet with the use of the tools of conventional economic theory.

Part I of the book concentrates on the general questions of the growth of TNCs and their implications for the welfare of host LDCs. Part II draws upon research conducted for the New York office of the United Nations Conference on Trade and Development (UNCTAD) on the balance-of-payments and income effects of a sample of foreign investments is six LDCs. Chapters 7 to 10 present the main findings of these studies; Chapter 6 gives the results of some later work on the data collected for these studies on various aspects of the sample firms' performance. Part III discusses policy measures for host governments and outlines the difficulties in formulating and implementing policy. It is hoped that each part will in its own way prove useful to students and practitioners in this field.

The empirical part of the book was the work of Lall; the analytical sections were prepared jointly. Most of the drafting was done by Lall, but we collaborated in so many ways that it is difficult to separate our ideas and our contributions.

We owe gratitude to so many people that it would be impossible to name them all here. The secretariat of UNCTAD, and in particular Sidney Dell and Gerry Arsenis, deserve our greatest thanks for having

Preface

financed the initial research project and encouraged and commented on our work. Several people worked on the research teams; of these we should especially like to thank Andrew Elek, Daniel Chudnovsky and Kenneth Mayhew.

Those who helped us in the field must, of necessity, remain anonymous, but we are deeply grateful to them all for their co-operation and kindness. Harikleyia Bacon did valuable statistical work in the final stages of preparing the book. Of those who helped to form our ideas (though they may not agree with them) and who commented on the manuscript, we wish to thank Max Corden, Gerry Helleiner, Robert Mabro, Ajit Singh, Frances Stewart and Constantine Vaitsos. We should like to acknowledge the secretarial assistance of Valerie Boulton, Caroline Carr, Judy Chance, Margaret Ko, Karen Exley, Muriel Payne and Karen Popham.

September 1976
SANJAYA LALL
PAUL STREETEN

Part I
Transnational Corporations and Developing Countries

CHAPTER 1
Introduction

THE UNSETTLED BACKGROUND

We have now reached a stage of profound disillusionment with development economics. The days of optimism, when the problems of the poorer countries were thought to be fairly well understood, and when the solutions, though not easy, were thought at least to be amenable to the conventional tools of economic analysis, are almost past. There was a time when certain views on economic development were held with the conviction and clarity of Victorian morals: development meant, or at least was measured by, the growth of national product per head; governments could adopt generally agreed-upon policies to provide such development, by planning (balanced or unbalanced) economic growth and by encouraging international aid, trade and investment; there was often the implicit assumption of a fundamental harmony of interests both between different classes or groups within the poor countries and between different nations; the transfer of the most advanced technology and knowledge from the rich to the poor countries was considered desirable and necessary; and, more generally, there were purely 'economic' answers to problems of underdevelopment. The main conflict was seen to be neither between classes nor between nations but an intertemporal one: between consumption now and more consumption later, as a result of the savings effort. The maximum feasible savings ratio, combined with a largely technically determined capital–output ratio, yielded the target growth rate. The role of international 'co-operation', including foreign investment, was to supply missing components, in the form of extra savings, foreign exchange or skills, so as to accelerate the government-organised march of the people towards 'take-off'.

As with Victorian morality, the façade hid many unpalatable facts and contradictions. With the passage of time, some of these have become more obvious, partly as a result of the patent failure of conventional economic policies in many countries and partly as a result of changing values and a growing awareness of the largeness and complexity of the problems involved. Thus, new development literature reveals a number of 'unconventional' views: per capita growth of gross national product (GNP) hides growing inequalities of income, wealth and opportunity; governments do not or cannot always act to promote the well-being of the majority of their populations, and class or group interests do often conflict (and influence policies); external economic relations may lead to a 'dependent' form of development, and the wholesale transfer of technology may aggravate the employment, distribution and scientific problems of backward areas; non-economic factors are usually inseparable from economic ones, and the arbitrary division imposed by economists is unwarranted and misleading. These are all deep and extremely controversial issues which raise serious methodological problems for development economics. It is, for instance, no longer very clear what is meant by 'welfare' in less developed countries (LDCs) – or, much less, for the world as a whole – or even how the lines of 'economic' analysis are to be drawn. We are forced increasingly to question the values, concepts and definitions that we have been taught to use – a difficult process, but, as Gunnar Myrdal has argued in the Prologue to *Asian Drama* (1968), one which is necessary if as social scientists we are not to fall into the traps of irrelevance, implicit bias, or straightforward ideological pleading.

The topic of foreign private investment in LDCs raises all such problems with a vengeance. There are few subjects which arouse so much controversy and such a variety of interpretation and valuation (see Lall, 1974a), and certainly it is a field in which both the reality and the perception of it are changing rapidly. The heresies of yesterday are today's conventional wisdom; what was seen not very long ago as a competitive world of foreign investors acting as neutral agents of capital and technological transfer is seen now as a highly oligopolistic world of transnational corporations (TNCs) possessing great commercial and economic power, and posing a challenge to national policy and economic independence (see Streeten, 1973, and Vernon, 1971). Our own researches into the balance-of-payments and income effects of foreign manufacturing investment, which began in 1969 and ended in 1973, reflect this sort of change.[1] We started with what we considered adequate tools to analyse certain effects of a sample of foreign investments in selected LDCs, and we finished with results which, though of great interest, did not in our view convey the larger implications of the significance of TNCs for development. The value of our work thus lies not only in what we did discover but also in what we *did not*, and *could not*, discover with the tools at hand and within the framework set by the questions to which we initially addressed ourselves.

In this book we first try to analyse in general qualitative terms the nature of transnational manufacturing firms and their economic effects on host developing countries; we then describe the main findings of the UNCTAD project and show its merits and weaknesses; and we finish with a discussion of the implications for government policy. We have thought it best to keep the analytical sections separate from those on the project results, because in many ways they have different purposes. We shall touch upon problems of defining welfare and of evaluating various 'non-economic' factors; no doubt our arguments will mirror some of the confusions of the present state of the 'science'.

FOREIGN INVESTMENT AND TRANSNATIONAL CORPORATIONS: SCOPE AND DEFINITION

In spite of the recent flood of literature on TNCs and the various investigations undertaken by national governments and international organisations, data on the extent and nature of foreign private investment are still sadly inadequate. There are inherent problems in measuring foreign investment, particularly when the investment takes the form of machinery or capitalised technological contributions and when inflation renders book values of investments (which are generally the only figures available) largely meaningless. If, moreover, a distinction has to be drawn between investments where the effective control lies with the foreign firm, and so constitutes foreign investment *proper*, and those where it lies with a local entity, and so constitutes simply a form of payment for technology or some asset transferred, there arise difficulties in determining how, and to what extent, control is exercised. A majority shareholding by the foreign firm is not necessary for it to exercise control; in appropriate circumstances, and even without an explicit management contract, a particular investor can exercise control with an equity share as low as 10 per cent.

Quite apart from these conceptual difficulties, there are great gaps in the statistics available, from both investor and recipient countries, on foreign investment. Partly as a result of business secrecy and partly owing to a lack of official scrutiny, most developed countries do not publish comprehensive information on the foreign operations of their firms. Even the United States, which has by far the best coverage of all aspects of business activity, is found wanting: thus, the massive study recently prepared for the US Senate's Committee on Finance (US Tariff Commission, 1973), with almost 300 tables of detailed statistics on US transnationals for 1966 and 1970, had to rely for its 1970 data on a sample of 298 parent companies, which were then used to extrapolate figures for the entire group of some 3400 companies with foreign investments for which data had been obtained for 1966. Furthermore, data on foreign operations were available only for majority-owned affiliates, leaving out a substantial proportion of operations abroad which were in fact controlled by US TNCs. A study of the effects of UK investment overseas (Reddaway et al., 1967–8) had to depend almost entirely on sample data, while most LDCs have (with the possible exception of India in our sample countries) the scantiest idea of the real value of foreign investment in them.

Bearing these problems in mind, let us look at the available figures. The most comprehensive collection of data on foreign investment in LDCs is contained in the recent study by the UN Department of Economic and Social Affairs (UN, 1973), which has managed to glean an illuminating – but admittedly imperfect – set of tables from an amazing variety of sources. The *total book value* of foreign private investment held by the market economies came to $165 thousand million in 1971, with the US accounting for 52 per cent of the total, the UK 15 per cent, France 5 per cent, and West Germany, Switzerland, Canada and Japan about 3 to 4 per cent each. This had risen by 53 per cent from $108 thousand million in 1967, when the respective shares of the leading three investors were 55 per cent, 16 per cent and 6 per cent, and of West Germany 3 per cent, Switzerland 4 per cent, Canada 3 per cent and Japan only 1 per cent.[2]

The *developing countries* as a whole accounted for $33 thousand million of the estimated stock of investment (32 per cent of the total) at the end of 1967, the last year for which the UN study provides estimates.[3] Of this stock, the US accounted for 50 per cent, with the bulk of its investments concentrated in Central and South America; the UK for 20 per cent, with Africa and Asia taking large and almost equal shares; France for 8 per cent, mostly in Africa; the Netherlands for 5 per cent, mostly in South America; and the others for 4 per cent or less. A separate estimate by M. Emerson of the OECD Secretariat puts the value of the stock of direct investment in LDCs at the end of 1970 at $39 thousand million,[4] a rise of 15 per cent from his estimate of $34 thousand million for the end of 1967; however, the share of LDCs in the

Introduction 7

total stock of direct investment ($153 thousand million) is seen to decline to 25 per cent of the total.

The sectoral distribution of the stock of direct investment in LDCs, taken from the UN for the end of 1967 and from Emerson for the end of 1970 (in parenthesis) is as follows: petroleum 33 per cent (33), mining 11 per cent (10), manufacturing 29 per cent (31), and other 27 per cent (26). The corresponding geographical distribution is: Africa 20 per cent (20), Middle East 9 per cent (9), Asia 15 per cent (14), Latin America and other 56 per cent (57). Thus, both these distributions show very little change, with the exception that manufacturing registered a slight increase over the three-year period (manufacturing accounted for 41 per cent of the world total and for 47 per cent of the total for developed countries at the end of 1969).[5]

TABLE 1.1
Industrial Composition of US Foreign Manufacturing Investment, 1970
($ million)

Industry	Value of investment	Percentage of total
1. Chemicals and allied products	6858	22·2
2. Transport equipment	5131	16·6
3. Non-electrical machinery	3798	12·3
4. Primary and fabricated metals	2619	8·5
5. Electrical machinery	2613	8·5
6. Paper and allied products	2007	6·5
7. Food products	1853	6·0
8. Instruments	1345	4·4
9. Wood products	1296	4·2
10. Stone, clay and glass	1046	3·4
11. Rubber	974	3·1
12. Textiles and apparel	625	2·0
13. Printing and publishing	138	0·4
Other	602	1·9
Total	30915	100·0

Source: US Tariff Commission (1973), p. 407.

Within the manufacturing sector, US foreign investment, and to a lesser extent UK investment (see below), is concentrated in chemicals, machinery, electrical products and transport equipment. These are 'skill-intensive' industries in which the role of research and development

(R & D), product differentiation and marketing is particularly important. West German and Swiss investment also exhibits this pattern, while Japanese investment is directed at relatively light and low-technology industries, such as lumber, pulp, textiles, steel and non-ferrous metals. In view of the predominant positions of US and UK investment, let us look at their industrial composition in slightly greater detail. Table 1.1 shows the value and percentage breakdown of net fixed assets of foreign affiliates (majority-owned only) of US firms for 1970,[6] with the industries ranked (except for 'other') by size of investment.

The importance of 'skill-intensive' industries is apparent from this table, though exactly what this skill consists of is not clear and will be discussed later. The US Tariff Commission also compares the domestic importance of the largest foreign investors, and concludes that 'generally the rankings indicate that these industries which are strongest in terms of domestic investment in the United States also are stronger in terms of their foreign direct investment positions, while the weaker domestic investors also are the weaker foreign investors'.[7] This point is one of great importance in understanding the nature of TNCs as a whole and is borne out by many studies;[8] it is discussed in greater detail in the next chapter.

The composition of UK manufacturing investment at the end of 1971 is shown in Table 1.2, the figures being for the 'book value of net assets attributable to the United Kingdom'. It may be noted that the total value of all such assets came to £6667 million, with 72 per cent going to developed and 28 per cent to less-developed countries, and that manufacturing investment comprised 59·0 per cent of the total for all countries, 65·9 per cent for developed countries, and only 41·2 per cent for LDCs. Some differences between the American and British investment patterns are immediately obvious. Whereas chemicals, transport equipment and electrical and non-electrical machinery account for 60 per cent of US investment, they account for less than 40 per cent of British investment; the greater importance of textiles, food and tobacco, relatively old and non-technological industries, in the latter (about 36 per cent) than in the former (only 8 per cent) is also significant.

So much for the general picture of foreign investment. What is the role of *transnationals* in all this? And, before we proceed any further, what exactly is a 'transnational corporation'? Though it is now common parlance in economics to talk of 'multinational', 'international', 'transnational' or 'global' corporations (or firms, companies or enterprises), the exact meaning of these terms has not been clearly defined.[9] Many authors use them interchangeably for the same thing, while others

Introduction 9

TABLE 1.2
Industrial and Geographical Composition of UK Foreign Manufacturing Investment, end 1971
(£ million)

Industry	Value of investment			Percentage breakdown		
	Total	In developed countries	In LDCs	(1)/overall total	(2)/(1)	(3)/(1)
	(1)	(2)	(3)	(4)	(5)	(6)
1. Food, drink and tobacco	1104	840	264	28·1	76·1	23·9
2. Chemical and allied	684	571	113	17·4	83·5	16·5
3. Electrical engineering	498	417	81	12·6	83·7	16·3
4. Textiles and footwear	298	233	65	7·6	78·2	21·8
5. Mechanical engineering	263	236	27	6·7	89·7	16·3
6. Paper, printing, publishing	262	239	23	6·6	91·2	8·8
7. Metal manufacture	143	126	17	3·6	88·1	11·9
8. Rubber	134	93	41	3·4	69·4	30·6
9. Motor vehicles	93	70	23	2·4	75·3	24·7
Other	455	343	112	11·6	75·4	24·6
Total	3934	3168	766	100·0	80·5	19·5

Source: UK Government, Department of Industry (1974), Part II, Table 37.

differentiate among them in order to distinguish differences in the attitudes or national composition of management, the spread of ownership or level of organisation, or even to imply differences of a political kind. It is natural at this stage to have such a looseness of definition, since the phenomenon is a relatively new one, and different people analyse it with different ends in mind. As the tradition in economic analysis has been to think in terms of small firms operating in competitive environments, with some exceptions in the case of (domestic) oligopolies, and to conceive of foreign investment simply as a part of 'capital flows' (direct and portfolio) between nations, the emergence of gigantic firms dominating world markets, trade and investment, and operating as integrated units across national boundaries, has led to new definitions being framed as contrasts to the traditional concepts.

In order to characterise the TNC, we can distinguish three areas in which such contrasts are emphasised: we may term them 'economic', 'organisational' and 'motivational'. The *economic* definition stresses the *size, geographical spread* and *extent of foreign involvement* of the TNC. It brings out the difference between the TNC and (a) a large domestic firm which does little investing abroad, (b) a domestic firm which may invest abroad but remains a small economic unit, (c) a large firm which invests abroad but only in one or two countries, and (d) a large portfolio investor who does not seek to control his investments or to take entrepreneurial risk.

This sort of definition has been used by the Harvard Multinational Enterprise Project, which, on the basis of their having six or more foreign subsidiaries, has selected from the 500 largest US industrial firms 187 TNCs in manufacturing.[10] The US Tariff Commission has suggested that 'a typical multinational company is one with net sales of 100 million dollars to several [thousand million] dollars. Direct foreign investment in manufacturing facilities usually accounts for at least 15 to 20 per cent of the company's total investment. "Direct" is generally thought to mean at least a 25 per cent participation in the share capital of the foreign enterprise, i.e. a large enough share to imply operational control of the enterprise rather than portfolio investment.'[11] Similarly, a recent work by Parker classifies 613 of the largest manufacturing firms in the world into MPE2, MPE1 and not-MPE (MPE standing for 'multinational producing enterprise'); the first are firms 'which are clearly international in character', and have more than five foreign subsidiaries or more than 15 per cent of total sales produced abroad, the second are 'less globally orientated' and have two to five subsidiaries or 5–15 per cent of sales produced abroad, and the rest are not-MPEs.[12] On these criteria, 349 (57 per cent) of the total are in the MPE2 category, eighty-eight (14 per cent) in the MPE1 category, and 175 (29 per cent) are not-MPEs.[13]

The *organisational* definition generally takes the size and spread of TNCs for granted and analyses factors which make some *more* transnational than others by virtue of the nature of their organisation, their centralisation of decision-making and authority, their global strategy, or their ability to act as one cohesive unit under changing circumstances. This sort of definition, used more by organisation and

Introduction

business schools than by economists, highlights the difference between the relatively loose, independent and unco-ordinated structure of small foreign investors and that of complex, hierarchical and well-knit transnational ones. A 'truly' transnational company thus (a) acts as an organisation maximising *one overall objective* for all its units, (b) treats the whole world (or the parts open to it) as its operational area, and (c) is able to co-ordinate all its functions in any way necessary for achieving (a) and (b).

The *motivational* definition, usually of interest to management specialists, pays greatest attention to corporate 'philosophy' and 'motivation' in laying down criteria for 'multinationality'.[14] Thus, 'true' multinationality is generally indicated by a lack of nationalism, or a concern with the firm as a whole rather than with any of its constitutent units or any country of its operations. The best known approach of this sort, propounded by Perlmutter (1969), distinguishes between 'ethnocentric' (home-oriented), 'polycentric' (host-oriented) and 'geocentric' (world-oriented) firms, on the basis of attitudes revealed by their executives.

Each of these ways of defining TNCs, 'transnationality' or multinationality' is useful in its own context, and we shall see below how each is relevant to analysing the welfare and policy implications of TNCs for developing countries. As our study is not directed at quantifying and evaluating TNCs as such, it does not matter very much how precisely we define them.[15] In general, we may think of them as very large firms with widespread operations—MPE2 class in Parker's terminology—acting in a cohesive manner to achieve maximum profits or growth. The motivational aspect does not concern us directly, except in so far as it affects their investment behaviour, which we come to later. We may distinguish TNCs from 'other' foreign investors, smaller and less significant, ignoring the inconvenient grey area in which firms are in the process of becoming 'transnational'. Such fine distinctions are not germane to our analysis.

What, then, is the significance of TNCs? It lies in the simple fact that they overwhelmingly dominate not only international investment, but also international production, trade, finance and technology – so much so that any analysis of the present structure of international economic relationships which does not take them into account, and, indeed, concentrate its attention on them, runs the gravest risk of being unrealistic and irrelevant.[16] Let us consider some recent indicators of their relative importance.

(a) *Foreign investment*. While figures are not available for the exact proportion of the total accounted for by TNCs, it is instructive to note the extent of concentration in investment abroad by the leading capital-exporting countries. About 250–300 firms account for over 70 per cent of the United States' total foreign investment; about 165 firms account for over 80 per cent of the UK's; and eighty-two account for over 70 per cent (the nine largest for 37 per cent) of West Germany's.[17] Within the group of large firms themselves there is a considerable concentration of resources. Thus, fifteen US firms, each with foreign assets of over $100 million, accounted for 35 per cent of total US foreign manufacturing investment in 1957, and forty-six UK firms accounted for 71 per cent of UK foreign manufacturing investment in 1962.[18] There is no reason to believe that the pattern of concentration has changed; indeed, 'there are strong indications that the multinational corporations have grown dramatically, especially during the last decade. As a result, *both their absolute and relative size has expanded.*'[19]

(b) A glance at *production* data shows a similar pattern of concentration. With the growth of overall concentration in production *within* the leading capital-exporting countries,[20] the structure of production internationally has also come to be increasingly dominated by a relatively few large firms. Thus 'the value-added of all multinational corporations, estimated at roughly 500 [thousand million] dollars in 1971, was about one-fifth of world gross national product, not including centrally planned economies',[21] and value added by each of the ten leading TNCs exceeded $3 thousand million in 1971, greater than the GNP of over eighty countries. Within the TNCs as a group, moreover, production was fairly highly concentrated: of the 650 largest industrial TNCs, the four largest accounted for 10 per cent of total sales and the 211 largest (32 per cent of the total number) for about 70 per cent.[22] Comparisons of economic size between countries and companies, very popular now, must, however, be made with caution. Not only is there a problem of double-counting – value added by TNCs is part of the GNPs of countries – but, in addition, the analytical point of such an exercise is itself not clear. In many respects nation-states and private corporations are not really comparable units, so that, unless the problem being studied is specified (say, that of bargaining power, or political strength, or the sharing of benefits), a simple balancing of size of product can be misleading;[23] this being said, it must be granted that the sheer size of the leading TNCs today *is* amazing, and certainly worth bearing in mind when analysing their effects and policies to regulate them.

(c) In terms of *international trade*, the role of TNCs has increased steadily, despite their expansion of production abroad. The US Tariff Commission found that in 1970 US TNCs (broadly defined) and their affiliates accounted for about *25 per cent of world exports of all commodities* and about *20 per cent of world exports of manufactures*; the relative importance of these firms has grown recently, since the rate of growth of TNC exports in 1966–70 (69 per cent) was greater than that of world exports (53 per cent). For the US alone, these TNCs (which *exclude* foreign TNCs operating in the US) accounted for 62 per cent of exports and 34 per cent of imports of manufactured goods.[24] In terms of numbers, an estimate for 1965 shows that 123 firms exported just over 40 per cent, thirty-nine firms about 30 per cent, of total US manufactured exports.[25] Similarly, recent data for UK exports show that 80 per cent of total exports in 1971 and 81 per cent in 1972 were accounted for by firms with foreign parents or foreign affiliates (28 and 29 per cent respectively by subsidiaries and associates of foreign enterprises); of the 1738 large exporters (with exports of £8026 million) in 1972, 153 firms (9 per cent) accounted for 69 per cent of exports, and twenty-four firms (1·4 per cent) for 37 per cent.[26] In passing, it is interesting to note that Sweden, a highly advanced country with relatively small overseas investments, also has its trade dominated by international firms: research undertaken by the Swedish government[27] shows that 75 per cent of exports originated in firms that had affiliates (parent or subsidiary) abroad, and that 35 per cent of this originated in large TNCs with activities in at least ten countries. Given the similarity in the patterns of TNC growth in the advanced capitalist economies, it is very likely that anything from one-third to three-fourths of total trade in manufactured products in these economies is directly accounted for by transnationals.

Data on the role of TNCs in the trade of LDCs are rather meagre. What little there is[28] shows a wide variation. In countries like India and Pakistan, with relatively low proportions of foreign capital in their manufacturing investments and with economies where trade is relatively unimportant, TNCs play a minor role in the export of manufactures, accounting for less than 10 per cent of the total. In some more 'open' economies with strong indigenous industry (for instance, Hong Kong, Taiwan, South Korea and Colombia) TNCs contribute about 15–30 per cent of manufactured exports,[29] while in some with a large foreign presence, (for example, Brazil, Argentina, Singapore, Mexico and various Central American countries) they account for higher proportions. The growing integration of the developing economies into an international economy dominated by transnationals will probably lead to an increasing share of their manufactured trade being handled by these firms; we shall return later to the issue of exports and TNCs.

(d) The role of TNCs in *international finance* is very unclear now because of the recent flood of oil money. However, information for the end of 1971 reveals that 'as a group, private institutions on the financial scene controlled some 268 [thousand million] dollars in short-term liquid assets . . . and the lion's share of these assets was under the control of multinational firms and banks headquartered in the United States . . . [This] was *more than twice the total of all international monetary institutions in the world* at the same date.'[30] Although this estimate includes banks, it may be noted that transnational banking has grown hand-in-hand with transnational industry and maintains close links with it, so that the amount of liquidity under the *effective* control of the latter is, though not as much as $268 thousand million, still quite large – certainly more than enough to pose grave threats to potentially weak currencies.

(e) The concentration of *technology and research* in the hands of TNCs hardly needs stressing. In the USA, TNCs account for over 80 per cent of R & D expenditures in the high-technology industries,[31] with the expenditure fairly highly concentrated in the leading firms in each sector. As Table 23 of the OECD (1970a) study *Gaps in Technology* shows, the twenty largest firms in all the OECD countries with the exception of Japan accounted (in 1963–5) for around 50–70 per cent of total industrial R & D in each country, while the 100 largest accounted for 70 to over 90 per cent (52 per cent in Japan). More recent data on the USA, published annually by the National Science Foundation under the title *Research and Development in Industry*, confirm the stability over time of this concentration of R & D expenditures. There are various reasons why R & D has become concentrated in this way in the highly industrialised countries, particularly in the high-technology sectors, though the evidence is unclear on the *relative* research intensity and productivity of the very large as compared to the medium-sized firms.[32] When one considers too that the leading innovators are generally the leading transnationals, and that R & D is for the most part located in the home countries of these firms,[33] it becomes apparent that TNCs produce, own and control the bulk of the most advanced technology in the world (which control may increase over time) and that the LDCs as a whole are almost entirely dependent on them for access to such technology.

This concludes our survey of the background to the present situation of international investment. In brief, we can say that the TNC has come of age. We are now heading towards a world of rapidly increasing international production, dominated by a few hundred private enterprises from the developed countries, with investment, trade and technology all coming under their aegis. 'It is beyond dispute', in the view of the US Tariff Commission, 'that the spread of multinational business ranks with the development of the steam engine, electric power, and the automobile as one of the major events of modern economic history.'[34] How such a historical phenomenon affects the development of the poorer countries is immensely difficult to say; a great deal depends on what we conceive of as 'development' and how well we can decipher the large but subtle social and economic changes wrought by the growth of TNCs. As the Group of Eminent Persons appointed by the United Nations says, not without some dissent, 'Fundamental new problems have arisen as a direct result of the growing internationalisation of production as carried out by multinational corporations. We believe that these problems must be tackled without delay, so that tensions are eased and the benefits which can be derived from multinational corporations are fully realised.'[35]

In order to proceed with a sensible discussion, therefore, we must first examine the character of the TNC and then define as well as we can what we envisage the 'welfare' of LDCs to be. This will enable us to put the two together and discover, at least within the context we have set out, what the effect of the former on the latter is likely to be. Unless we do this, we end up in the unsatisfactory state of most such discussions, which either go into detail about the motives and features of the firms while accepting a conventional (usually business-oriented) definition of the host countries' welfare, or else explain their concept of development at great length but so oversimplify the nature of the transnationals as to render policy-making impossible. Within the confines of this book, however, we cannot pretend to be able to do more than lay the foundations for analysing this vital subject.

CHAPTER 2

Theories of Foreign Investment and Transnational Behaviour

INTRODUCTION

The description of TNCs advanced in the previous chapter may already have suggested many of their prominent characteristics. Such a description is, however, not sufficient to provide an explanation of why firms expand abroad and are concentrated in certain industries, nor of how they react to each other's moves and to the demands of increasing size. It will be useful for our purpose to review briefly the existing literature on this, using the classification of approaches – economic, organisational and motivational – adopted in the last chapter, and to highlight their main features, which to a large extent determine their effects on developing host economies.

There is an enormous amount of writing on the causes and explanations of foreign investment, especially by TNCs,[1] and our survey must of necessity concentrate on those aspects which are particularly relevant to LDCs. This chapter is laid out as follows: we start by discussing the economic theories of direct investment abroad and of the dominance of transnationals in it; we then proceed to describe the motivational and organisational aspects of transnational expansion and behaviour; and in the concluding section we present the salient characteristics of TNCs as indicated by the preceding analysis.

ECONOMIC THEORIES OF DIRECT FOREIGN INVESTMENT

We have already noted that, in the present international economy, direct foreign investment is mostly the preserve of large firms operating in monopolistic or oligopolistic markets. In analysing the causes of direct investment, or the behaviour of the main transnational investors, it is therefore necessary to take explicit account of the actual nature of factor and product markets and of the internal structures of the firms which do the investing. There are two types of 'pure' economic theory – that of international trade and that of the orthodox theory of the firm – which in their 'rigorous' neoclassical form may be relevant to the analysis of foreign investment. However, their assumptions about the nature of markets and the size of firms renders them rather unhelpful in understanding the actual phenomenon of TNC growth.

The 'pure' theory of international trade, in its familiar Heckscher–Ohlin form, generally assumes perfectly competitive markets, identical production functions in different countries, and international movements of capital in response to differences in interest rates. While its result accords with the general fact that rich countries, presumably 'capital-abundant' in this model, invest in poor countries which are 'capital-scarce' (with risk sometimes included as a modifying factor), it hardly provides a complete explanation of foreign investment as distinct from foreign borrowing or portfolio investment, of the growth of firms possessed of considerable monopoly power, of rich countries' interpenetration of each other by their large firms, or of the transfer of other productive factors (technology, management, marketing) which are just as great a part of TNC investment as the transfer of capital. Exponents of neoclassical trade theory have recognised the need to modify very 'pure' theory to accommodate the realities of transnational investment,[2] and in the following discussion we shall concentrate on the new explanations that derive very little from 'pure' theory.

The 'pure' orthodox theory of the firm faces similar handicaps. To the extent that it assumes that firms are in perfect competition (and so have equal access to all productive factors, do not exercise market power, and reach an 'optimum' size set by long-term diminishing returns to scale), it is not very useful in analysing the behaviour of TNCs which grow in extremely 'imperfect' markets, do not show marked signs of having reached limits to their growth, and are subject to various interdependencies. It could be argued that the very fact that firms need to be of a certain size and to possess certain advantages (discussed below) in order to invest abroad successfully implies that the orthodox theory is deficient in certain important respects when applied to TNCs. Certain aspects of the theory, such as its postulate of profit-maximising behaviour, may of course be relevant (with suitable modifications[3]), though even here some argue that the rise of managerial capitalism' in large corporations calls for a different analysis of firms' motivations. As this is not germane to the main purpose of this book, we shall not enter into these debates here (we shall consider later the specific motivation of TNCs to invest in particular areas), but it is clear that 'pure' theories do not offer us a suitable key for understanding transnational firms.

Recent theories of direct foreign investment, and in particular of TNC growth, have therefore turned to explanations based on 'imperfections', oligopolistic interdependence, and the possession of monopolistic advantages. These theories, which may broadly be labelled 'oligopolistic' explanations of direct investment, draw upon a variety of different fields of study (new theories of the firm, monopolistic competition, industrial structure, location, innovation, and so on) to produce a much more realistic and comprehensive, if relatively unrigorous, view of the actual process under discussion.[4]

The essence of the oligopolistic theories is that firms operating across national boundaries and over long distances suffer an intrinsic disadvantage — caused by difficulties of communication, linguistic and cultural differences, lack of knowledge of local market conditions, and so on — which, for transnational investment to prove profitable, must be sufficiently offset by some sort of special advantage over potential local competitors. In idealised competitive conditions no single firm can, by assumption, have access to any sort of special advantage which is not equally available to other firms that do not suffer from the intrinsic disadvantage of transnational operations. Direct investment cannot then take place. A local firm can simply borrow capital abroad if it needs to, at the same rate of interest as any other firm; and, since all other factors of production are equally distributed, there is no economic rationale for a foreign firm to invest in facilities which it owns and has to run from abroad. It is, therefore, *a necessary condition of direct investment that the investing firm has some monopolistic or oligopolistic advantage* not possessed by potential local competitors.

Since the explanation of TNC growth relies heavily upon factors which give rise to concentration and large size, there is an obvious similarity between the above theories and those which deal with *domestic* market structures in the advanced capital-exporting countries. The forces which lead to the growth of firms — by internal expansion as well as by merger and takeover[5] — and to increasing concentration within the leading capitalist economies, and which preserve and strengthen the dominance of particular firms — the barriers to entry of new competitors – also, to a large extent, account for the international spread of large firms and the growing concentration of international production. The recent work of some economists following Hymer's lead (see, in particular, references to works by Caves, Horst, Baumann and Stevens) has made this almost commonplace in the literature, but it must be noted that the more conventional analyses of foreign investment, based on neoclassical trade theory, wandered for a long time in the sterile reaches of high abstraction without being able to say very much about the actual process of transnational growth. The essential identity between the evolution of internal industrial structures and the export of capital was, of course, analysed much earlier by Marxist thinkers (see the surveys cited in note 1), who saw the 'imperialistic' growth of international production by large monopolistic enterprises as the 'highest stage of capitalism'. Some of Hymer's later writings combine in an interesting manner his industrial-organisation approach and his Marxist analysis of the effects of TNCs on developing countries, and show how such an unlikely synthesis can yield useful results.

To return to theories of direct investment, it should be clear at the outset that, while the existence of some oligopolistic advantage is a necessary condition for direct investment abroad, it is certainly *not sufficient*. The existence of such market imperfections characterises *all* industries in which international investment occurs, but it is also marked in some where it does not. Clearly, some sources of oligopolistic advantage are more significant in this respect than others; furthermore, even with these sources present there may be reasons for international investment not to take place at certain times or in certain places. Let us, therefore, first look at the nature of oligopolistic advantages that foreign investors may have over local ones (Step 1), and then see why they may lead to foreign investment rather than to other forms of their exploitation, such as exporting (Step 2) or separate sale of these advantages (Step 3).

The sources of monopolistic advantage may explain two things: first, why a *foreign* firm invests rather than a local one, and, second, why (in appropriate cases) a *large* foreign firm – a transnational – invests rather than a small foreign one. Clearly, such advantages are more significant the more monopolistic is the industry concerned, and, in general, they may be taken to comprise the reasons for the growing predominance of TNCs over *all* other potential investors in all areas of their operation. Some sources are more important as *permissive* factors in overseas investment than as *actively causal* ones, while some others emerge as a *consequence* of expansion and serve to reinforce the earlier advantages.

In what follows we shall try to indicate which, in our view, fall into which of these broad categories.

Step 1: Sources of Oligopolistic Advantage
(a) *Capital.* The foreign investor (or TNC) may possess a larger or cheaper source of capital than a local (or smaller foreign) competitor, by virtue of the financial strength of the parent company. There can be three main reasons for this: the parent may possess large internal resources for which its opportunity cost in terms of alternative outlets may be quite low; it may have access to capital markets in developed countries (both equity and loan) which are not open to, or at least more costly for, its competitors; and it may obtain favourable terms or priority in raising capital locally, because of its established credit rating or because there are branches of transnational banks operating locally which have prior relations with the parent firm. While this sort of advantage has been noted as an important factor in the expansion of US TNCs, especially in Europe (access to local and Eurodollar markets becoming particularly significant after the imposition of controls by the US government on capital flows abroad), the availability of finance serves mainly as a permissive factor in foreign investment. It is unlikely that, in the absence of other oligopolistic advantages, the mere access to (cheaper or more) finance will act as an inducement to direct, as opposed to purely financial (portfolio), investment, though theoretically it is possible that this by itself may facilitate expansion via takeover or merger. Even a takeover, however, is likely to require the existence of some other advantage besides finance, such as greater risk-taking propensity, or economies of scale by merging, or technological/marketing economies.[6] Conglomerate mergers between firms in completely unrelated industries are a possible exception, but such mergers are still comparatively rare in the field of international investment.[7]

(b) *Exchange risk.* It has been pointed out by Aliber that, because of the existence of exchange risk and the relative hardness of the currencies of capital-exporting countries, 'the pattern of direct investment reflects that source-country firms capitalize the same stream of expected earnings at a higher rate than host-country firms', partly because 'the market demands a premium for bearing uncertainty about exchange risk' and partly because 'the market does not attach a currency premium to the foreign income of the source-country firm'.[8] However valid such an explanation may be for direct investment in developed countries

Foreign Investment and TNC Behaviour 21

(which is where Aliber intends it to apply), it does not seem to be particularly relevant to direct investment in LDCs with highly imperfect or non-existent capital markets and with heavily regulated foreign exchanges. In so far as it boils down to a superiority of the TNC to raise local equity capital, it is useful as an adjunct to item (a), but even for developed countries it is a particularly incomplete and unsatisfactory explanation: it does not explain the pattern of cross-penetration of these countries by their respective TNCs, and it fails to account for the continued growth of US and UK TNCs, given the weakness of the dollar and the pound in some recent years.

(c) *Management.* The TNC may have the advantage of superior management, which may take the form either of greater efficiency of operation as compared to a similar operation performed by a local firm, or of a greater entrepreneurial ability to take risks, or to seek, locate and carry out viable ventures in the uncertain world of business.[9] This advantage may arise from the greater experience of foreign or TNC managers, or better training, education or higher standards of recruitment; in the context of LDCs, it may reflect the historical and cultural fact that most of these countries simply do not have an entrepreneurial–managerial class in industry. It may also arise from the different organisational forms that the very large TNCs have adopted in order to facilitate efficient and rapid decision-making across diverse and widespread units (considered in more detail below). It is difficult to know how to classify such a diffuse factor. Certain types of 'entrepreneurial' ability (in the Schumpeterian sense) are clearly causal factors in domestic and foreign expansion: a uniquely dynamic business leader, or one with a major technological innovation to exploit, may by himself lead a firm to greater success than someone else would be able to do. Certain types of organisational and managerial efficiency which are said to characterise TNCs (though there is an element of mythology in this)[10] may, on the other hand, be permissive or consequential factors in growth and not cause it, though their existence may well give TNCs an additional advantage over other firms.

(d) *Technology.* The TNC may possess superior technology as compared to a domestic or small foreign firm. By 'technology' we mean not the knowledge of the relevant sciences, which may be available in some disembodied form more or less equally to all countries, but the ability to translate this knowledge into practical, commercial use. It is patently obvious that TNCs have in many industries a superiority in 'technology' in this sense;[11] indeed, most countries want their presence precisely in order to obtain this particular superiority. We must, in order to analyse their effects, probe into this item slightly more deeply.

We noted in the last chapter that the production of technology, as measured by R & D expenditures, is highly concentrated in the developed countries, especially the USA, and within these is highly concentrated in a few firms, most of them transnational. It is these firms which are responsible for producing the bulk of marketable innovations in the non-socialist world, and it is they who, in order to protect their innovations, take out the vast majority of patents in almost all countries, developed or otherwise[12] (added to which they take various steps to keep their innovations secret or unusable by competitors). The key word is 'marketable': the highly innovative firms do not merely have to do a great deal of R & D: they must do it in order to increase their output of saleable and profitable products. This is clear enough, but its implications are less so. The vast bulk of R & D expenditures by industry goes into 'applied research and development'; in the USA, in 1973 for instance, less than 3 per cent of total R & D spending, including Federal government financed expenditures, went into 'basic' research (defined as research without a practical application in view).[13] The greater proportion of the remainder was for 'development'[14] (with the Federal government providing about 40 per cent of the funds, mostly in the aircraft and electrical equipment industries).

The distinction between 'applied' and 'development' research is hard to draw, and it is not useful for our purposes to pursue it here. What is worth remarking on, at the risk of some oversimplification, is that such R & D efforts, taken broadly, serve three different functions in the framework of oligopolistic competition which characterises international investment. These are as follows.

(i) Discovering *new processes* (more efficient methods of doing existing jobs) and *new products* (more efficient ways of meeting market needs). This is the normal meaning of 'technical progress' in conventional economic usage, and corresponds to the Marxist conception of 'raising the productive forces' of society.[15] It is also the sense in which 'technology' is generally used (with implicit approval) when the role of TNCs in the 'transfer of technology' to LDCs, or the role of technology in promoting economic growth, is considered. In terms of a firm's behaviour, it may be classified as 'offensive' innovation strategy[16] and may involve a substantial amount of internal 'basic' research, a close monitoring of basic research done in the relevant scientific establishments, and a considerable ability to undertake design-engineering and development ('problem-solving') work to bring new scientific ideas to productive application.[17]

(ii) *Product differentiation.* This covers the introduction of slight variations (in presentation, appearance and performance) in products manufactured by a firm itself or by its competitors.[18] As manufacturing industry grows more oligopolistic, and especially when particular technologies 'mature', the role of such 'marketing-oriented' R & D becomes more and more important. It must be admitted that it is often difficult to distinguish between new and differentiated products or processes, and a series of marginal changes may sometimes add up to an important innovation in the long run: a great deal depends on the criteria used for judging 'novelty' in relation to need, and conceptual problems arise when the 'need' itself is created by the new product. However, most analysts of innovation, as well as businessmen themselves, do draw this distinction, and Freeman notes that 'Several surveys . . . have shown that even in the United States, most industrial R & D is "defensive" in character concerned primarily with short term horizons and "improvements". . . . Defensive R & D is probably typical of most oligopolistic markets and is closely linked with product differentiation.'[19] Thus, several industries with heavy R & D expenditures tend to concentrate on product differentiation R & D, automobiles being the best example, while others, such as pharmaceuticals, engage in differentiation to extract the maximum benefit from basic R & D and genuine innovations.[20] A recent article in *Business Week* (1976a) notes that, with increasing government regulation, rising costs, scarce capital and 'the concentration of products into larger and fewer companies', US research efforts, even in highly technological industries, have become more 'defensive', relying more heavily on 'marketing innovation' and (low-risk) differentiation of existing products. While a good understanding of market conditions and a close integration between the research and marketing departments is crucial to the commercial success of *any* innovation, the relative importance of these two functions varies from industry to industry, and within each industry over time with the evolution of market structure and the stage of technological maturity.[21] It is arguable that marketing-oriented R & D is extremely significant and growing more so. It is important, however, to note that the normal usage of 'technology'[22] *masks this vital difference between genuine innovation and product differentiation*, a difference which, as we shall argue later, is of particular relevance to understanding the effects of TNCs on host LDCs.

(iii) *Various support activities.* A part of the expenditure on R & D does not fall into either of the above categories and can be classified only as 'support' activity for other innovation. This comprises some forms of market research not undertaken by the marketing departments proper (especially in high-technology capital and intermediate goods industries); 'scouting' the R & D work of rivals and buying up the results of research done by other (generally small) firms;[23] and taking out patents internationally (though this is not a research activity in a direct sense).

What then are the technological advantages of TNCs over other firms? We may distinguish six such advantages. First, where the minimum scale of R & D required for successful innovation is very high and there are economies of scale involved, only a very large firm will be able to undertake it successfully. Second, where the technological threshold as such is not high, but a very extensive marketing framework is needed in order to sustain profitably a stream of innovations, large size and widespread outlets will be a vital advantage.[24] This is so not only to spread the fixed costs of innovation over a broader sales base, but also to test more ideas, to promote and market innovations more successfully and to spread risks more widely. Third, where continuing R & D needs outside financial support, it is the very large firms which are better able to attract government and private finance. Fourth, because of the expense of taking out and defending patents internationally, it is the TNCs who are most protected by the patent system (though recent US Department of Justice rulings on IBM and Xerox show that the very largest firms can be successfully attacked by smaller — but still very large — TNCs).[25] Fifth, where the defence of a technological oligopoly necessitates (as in many 'mature' oligopolies) the use of restrictive practices, such as pricing conventions, cartels, information swaps and market allocations, it is again the largest firms which can benefit from such arrangements.[26] Sixth, where the success of a major innovation requires complementary technological advances in related industries, and where the preservation of existing technologies calls for control of competing technologies,[27] large size may be an enormous advantage in terms of co-ordination of technological activities and of directly investing in the firms or industries concerned.

Given that technology in a broad sense is one of the prime determinants of the success and growth of capitalist enterprises, and that technological innovation and size appear to interact in such a way as to lead to still greater size and concentration,[28] it should be clear why this factor constitutes *one of the prime causal forces* behind the growth of international production. Indeed, a number of empirical studies confirm the vital role of technology in the growth of transnationals, both by new investments and by takeover, and in the growth of the market power of large oligopolistic firms.[29] This is not to assert that technology is the only, or even the predominant factor; on the contrary, it is argued below that marketing may be equally important. Nor is it to deny that in a number of instances – particularly low-technology or mature industries with undifferentiated products[30] – TNCs do not go in for much technological innovation; indeed, in many such industries the role of transnationals is minimal and foreign investment may be relatively unimportant. It is, nevertheless, valid that the growth of technology offers one of the major advantages to TNCs in their expansion and also provides one of the strongest pressures for firms to grow, gain more market power and spread their operations more widely.

(e) *Marketing*. The role of marketing is absolutely vital to international investment, and constitutes a source of oligopolistic advantage perhaps even greater than that of technology. 'Marketing' has, like technology, a number of functions.

(i) *Market research*. This enables the firm to gain an understanding of buyers' needs as they evolve in various markets.

(ii) *Advertising and promotion:* the imparting of information to buyers and the reinforcement or creation of demand for particular products or brands. These two functions, need fulfilment and need creation, are distinct though intermixed: advertising and product differentiation may serve existing needs and evoke or create new and valuable needs, enriching human experience; or they may commercially exploit self-created desires, nuisances, fears or dangers – for the fulfilment of which (in the case of desires) or the removal of which (in the case of nuisances) the customer is charged. The effectiveness of advertising and promotion in creating and maintaining market power is hardly in doubt.[31] Its special place in the field of foreign investment has been noted by several of the authors cited previously, and it is becoming obvious that, where marketing can promote the brands of particular firms successfully, regardless of the technological intensity of the industry[32] and the innovative prowess of those firms, the market power created serves as a powerful inducement to international expansion.[33] As with R & D, there may be 'thresholds' of marketing effort that are out of reach of small firms, and the benefits of large-scale advertising may spill over into several markets even before TNCs have set up production facilities. The very nature of oligopolistic competition, with product differentiation and non-price competition, is crucially dependent on a system of powerful and sophisticated marketing. 'Innovation' could not succeed without promotion, and promotion could not succeed without 'new' or 'different' products. And both work towards concentration and transnationalisation.

(iii) *Distribution*: arrangements for getting products efficiently to their markets, for distributing them to wholesalers and retailers, for maintaining adequate stocks, and so on (similarly for buying inputs). This can, for obvious reasons, redound to the benefit of larger firms, or firms with multi-plant operations,[34] though it is more likely to serve as a consequential and cumulative benefit of transnational expansion.

(f) *Access to raw materials*. Particular foreign firms may have privileged access to raw materials or minerals, by virtue of their control (i) over the final markets or the transportation (generally shipping) of the product (as with some agricultural products); (ii) over processing (vertically integrated mineral and food processing); or (iii) over the production of the material itself (plantations and mines). The reasons for this sort of advantage may be historical (a development of privileges granted during colonial rule), technological (with processing and mining becoming more complex and capital-intensive), financial (with the minimum capital requirement of new projects, especially in mining, becoming extremely large), or related to marketing (with final product markets being dominated by particular brand names or retail chains). In most cases, at least as far as manufacturing is concerned, this sort of advantage can be traced to one or more of the others discussed above. The quest for stability in oligopolistic conditions may, however, cause the cumulative building up of such an advantage to become a 'pathological condition. . . . Companies may feel safer with assured access to sources of inputs and to outlets for products. In these circumstances the industry will shift from numerous firms which are small and competitive at each stage to one of a few large, vertically integrated concerns. Once started, the process acquires momentum.'[35]

(g) *Economies of scale*. The literature on barriers to competition has always noted economies of scale as an important source of the market power of large firms. Its relevance to international investment is clear: if certain facilities enjoy scale economies, this works to the advantage of those firms which have the finance and expertise to set up and operate such facilities. We should, however, note two points. First, economies of scale, either of the 'classical' type arising simply from the size of plant, or of the more recent type arising (in the case of multi-product plants in oligopolistic differentiated-product industries) from longer production runs,[36] are available to *all* firms which can reach the requisite size. They do not constitute a special source of market power for foreign firms or TNCs unless large size can be attained only by having access to some *other* special advantage, such as finance, technology or marketing. Thus, economies of scale as such can serve only as a permissive (and cumulative) factor in overseas expansion.

Second, the tendency towards increasing concentration and larger firms in many areas of manufacturing industry within developed countries has not in fact been accompanied by a trend towards larger and larger plants.[37] Firms here have grown more by using multi-plant operation than by increasing the size of plants, their strength deriving less from the technical advantages of large plants than from other factors which can be centralised (such as R & D, marketing, finance and managerial expertise) and which do yield economies to large firms. Economies of size of *firm* do constitute an important dynamic advantage to large and growing firms, but this is really a self-reinforcing combination of various other 'advantages' rather than a separate 'advantage' of its own.

(h) *Bargaining and political power.* Many TNCs may be better able to extract 'concessions' and favourable terms from host governments than are local firms, for two sets of reasons. First, they may possess some scarce resource, such as capital or technology, which local firms do not (this depends on their having some of the advantages discussed above). Second, they may have greater political leverage, either because of pressure exerted by the government of their home country (by means of 'aid', military or otherwise, diplomatic and political links, and so on) or because of pressure exerted by interested groups of officials or businessmen within the country.

We must not, however, put too much weight on this factor as an explanation of the *normal* process of TNC expansion, as many exponents of theories of 'neo-imperialism' are prone to do, since in fact home governments step in to help particular firms only in exceptional cases such as expropriation or a threat to vital supplies. The role of political factors is much more subtle. It is to 'make the world safe for free enterprise', to secure the goodwill of the host government, perhaps by paying the price of local participation, and to ensure that 'subversive' and unfavourable policy influences are minimised. This is not generally an exercise in naked power politics, but a diffuse, shifting and complex interplay of internal and external forces, with different effects in different places, yet tending over time to produce a powerful sociopolitical elite supporting 'free' enterprise.[38]

All these sources of oligopolistic growth have, we must stress, a *cumulative and dynamic* effect on the expansion of TNCs, and this in itself is a considerable advantage to them: thus, Horst (1972) finds that *size* (which may amalgamate all other 'advantages') is the main determinant of US foreign investment. Success breeds success in big business,[39] and there are several factors which may enhance firms' market power over time simply through the process of expansion. First, as Penrose (1956, 1959) has pointed out, the internal resources of a firm are just as important to its growth as external ones are. Thus, a firm which has grown rapidly within a country already possesses the sort of experience, management and team spirit which can enable it to expand abroad, and this sort of advantage may not, contrary to some orthodox theories of the firm, diminish with size. Second, there may be financial and technological advantages of widespread integration over several countries, permitting the tapping of different markets, the quick internal transfer of funds and know-how, and the avoidance of heavy taxes or official restrictions.[40] Third, there may be diminishing costs of entering new markets after a certain level, with increasing knowledge, bargaining power, confidence, 'fall-out' effects of advertising, and the spreading of risk.[41] We need not dwell very long on these points, since the case is fairly obvious and well-established.

To summarise the oligopolistic theory of direct investment so far, manufacturing investment abroad requires that the investing firm possess some source of oligopolistic advantage to offset the intrinsic disadvantage of foreign operations. There are many sources of such advantage, but the decisive ones, which in fact determine why some industries and firms go transnational while others (despite being oligopolistic, or having access to cheap capital or skilled management) do not, are *marketing* and *technology*. Other advantages merely add to and reinforce these basic ones; they cannot displace them. And superiority in marketing seems to be an even more fundamental precondition for transnational expansion than is superiority in technology, despite the strong stress laid on technology in the literature on TNCs: without a marketing advantage, high-technology industries may not expand production abroad, while, with such an advantage, even very low-technology industries may go transnational.[42]

This provides the first step in the explanation of direct foreign investment. It shows what permits certain firms to grow and invest internationally, but it does not show why the sources of market power possessed by these firms are exploited by direct investment rather than by exporting the product (Step 2) or by selling the advantages themselves (Step 3). Let us consider these now.

Step 2: Advantage of Direct Investment over Exporting

It may be argued that, if all the oligopolistic advantages of large firms showed up in lower prices, better products or a larger captive demand, these firms should be able to exploit such advantages by exporting rather than by undertaking the trouble and risk of organising manufacturing operations abroad. Indeed, many large firms, both with and without international operations, are major exporters from their home countries. What, then, affects the choice between these alternatives? We can identify five major factors.

(a) *Cost of production.* A combination of a modified theory of comparative advantage (to allow for imperfect competition and partial and selective factor mobility across frontiers) in the field of international trade, and that of location in industrial economics, provides the most obvious explanation of why firms from one country should choose to establish plants in another. Given the exchange rate, the techniques of production, the costs of transport and of transferring technology, and a range of different costs for factors of production, clearly some countries will have an economic advantage over others as manufacturing bases. If TNCs are assumed to have a truly 'global perspective', to take investment decisions mainly on rational cost calculations and not to be inhibited by government restrictions, they can also be assumed to allocate their resources in a commercially efficient manner among different countries.[43] Whether or not this also promotes the *welfare* of the societies concerned is a different matter, which will be discussed in the following chapter; at this stage it need only be noted that business and social welfare coincide only under special and restrictive assumptions (too often taken for granted in conventional theory, especially in the analysis of foreign investment).

In fact, the production-cost explanation of foreign direct investment accounts for a relatively small, but probably growing, proportion of TNC investment in LDCs. It is certainly the explanation for the growth of TNC 'sourcing' activities, which have been noted in the context of both developed and less-developed areas.[44] 'Sourcing' refers to the production and interchange of specific components, processes and services by geographically dispersed units of a TNC, the aim being to minimise the costs of the total process; the dispersion of IBM units in Europe and the location of electronic plants in Hong Kong, Taiwan or Mexico provide excellent examples.[45] It also accounts for certain export-oriented industries based in low-wage areas, in which entire facilities are transplanted to LDCs (particularly in special duty-free zones set aside for such activity) and the output is transported to high-cost consuming countries. This is mainly the case with certain low-technology industries, such as clothing, sports equipment or footwear, and is more the preserve of small foreign investors or buying groups (made up of retailers) than of the real transnational manufacturer. Taken together, however, such investments are still not very large in less-developed areas. Production and transportation costs have a larger part to play in explaining the growth of TNCs in the developed world, though their influence is difficult to disentangle from that of the factors mentioned below, and varies with the state of competition, the maturity of the technology and the behaviour of other firms.[46]

(b) *Government policy.* One of the most important reasons (though neither a necessary nor a sufficient condition) for undertaking foreign investment is the existence of tariffs or direct and indirect restrictions on imports, or the threat that the host country will impose them. It is generally accepted that the import-substitution strategies followed by most LDCs have been largely responsible for inducing foreign firms that used to export to them from their home countries to set up manufacturing facilities there. Of course, for such investment to occur, the conditions laid down in Step 1 must have been fulfilled: the investing firm must have some advantage over potential local competition. As foreign firms have not usually had to compete in open world markets, however, they may have operated, or at least sold their output, at costs and prices above those obtaining at home, the exact extent of the excess being determined by the amount of protection given by the host governments.

While the threat of restriction or discrimination, and so the loss of a market, is a prime factor in causing firms to establish operations abroad, we have to bring in two additional factors to explain, first, why some firms invest abroad *without* such a threat and in countries without a particular production-cost advantage, and, second, why some relatively open markets tend to attract a host of TNCs with investments of uneconomical size rather than a few with more 'rational' investment behaviour.

(c) *Importance of marketing.* Many TNCs expand abroad in relatively unprotected economies (for instance, TNCs from developed countries investing in other developed areas) not just in order to exploit cost advantages, but also in order to service the local market better. Since it is precisely the marketing factor which constitutes the chief commercial advantage of transnational firms, it is only natural that it should also prompt them to exploit and protect this advantage to the full. We should, therefore, expect to find that, in industries where product differentiation, rapid model changes, advertising and retailing are of great significance, the leading firms do their utmost to satisfy *local* tastes and requirements.[47] In many industries, especially those with mature technology, this calls for local manufacturing facilities rather than simply for export outlets; rightly or wrongly, many firms feel that managers of plants within a particular geographical or cultural area will respond better to market conditions there than will those stationed outside it.

The distance and difference in perspective of the home country is, of course, also relevant: for example, US automobile manufacturers, faced with a pattern of demand completely different from that pertaining in the United States, may feel it imperative to invest in England to produce cars suitable to English tastes (and take advantage of lower costs), while German manufacturers (despite higher wage costs) may not, and Japanese ones, making more or less suitable cars, may be able, despite the geographical distance, to conquer the marketing barrier by aggressive and highly developed marketing tactics. Industries with a very high R & D content, such as the aircraft industry, will not embark on foreign investments, because the advantage of local marketing compared with home-based marketing is small relative to the advantage yielded by new technology. The decision whether to export or to invest will depend on the relative weights attached to, on the one hand, the costs of controlling and co-ordinating a network of affiliates, and, on the other, the costs of being out of touch with the market and incurring increasing marketing costs through exporting rather than producing locally.

(d) *Oligopolistic reaction.* Even if none of the above factors are in existence, the move abroad of one firm in an oligopoly may prompt its rivals to do the same.[48] The very structure of oligopolistic competition and equilibrium is such that none of the participants can afford to ignore what the other is doing; a move abroad may be, and usually is, interpreted as a threat to the *status quo*, and, as such, as necessitating counter moves by the others. The speed of the reaction will differ from industry to industry, depending on the extent of concentration, the stability of the oligopoly, and the product range. Knickerbocker suggests that oligopolistic reaction increases with the level of concentration (except at very high levels, where the structure is more stable) and decreases with the diversity of product. He also finds that 'the few leaders of each industry, those that react swiftly to one another's moves, tend to ignore scale considerations when they invest abroad', which has important implications for their productive efficiency, and that 'the profitability of overseas manufacturing industry is positively correlated to entry concentration . . . particularly in the case of the very prompt interaction'.[49]

Thus, while foreign investment may prove both feasible and profitable *ex post*, very often the move is not made until one oligopolist sees fit to start the ball rolling. The first move may be prompted by government action or by something else, but the subsequent pattern cannot be interpreted in terms of the profit-maximising behaviour of the individual firm, independent of the actions of rival firms. This accords well with some recent Marxist analyses of international capitalism as a growing worldwide battle of competing giant firms, forced to extend continually the scope of their activity.[50] It also lends some support, though Knickerbocker himself is careful to specify offsetting influences, to Hymer and Rowthorn's conclusion that 'the cross penetration implied by the simple oligopoly model we have just described has as its *logical* end a stable equilibrium where all the dominant oligopolists have a similar world-wide distribution of sales'.[51]

(e) *Product cycle.* The 'product-cycle' model, long familiar to business schools and introduced to academic economists by Hirsch and Vernon,[52] provides a particular explanation of how the various factors mentioned above interact over time to determine production, export and foreign-investment patterns of oligopolistic enterprises. While this model does not introduce a new factor into our discussion, it is worth considering separately because of the special *sequence* it postulates, and because of the way in which it combines, and assigns varying roles to, technology, production costs and marketing factors.

The first stage of the model begins when an innovation is introduced. It is argued that new products will be invented, produced, and sold in countries with the highest incomes and skills (mainly the USA). The *invention* and *selling* of new products and processes in rich countries is easy enough to understand: these countries have the financial, organisational and intellectual resources to undertake the requisite research (the 'supply' exists), and they have large numbers of consumers with high incomes and adventurous tastes to test new products on, and the greatest pressures of competition, high wage costs or scarce materials to spur innovation (the 'demand' for innovations is high).

The *production* of new commodities in these high-cost countries needs more explanation. After all, the new techniques could be used (assuming international investment were unhindered) in more economical locations to sell in the high-income markets. Two reasons for producing near the markets are advanced. First, new products are not very price-sensitive, and the temporary technological monopoly which the innovating firm enjoys (perhaps with the help of patents) can enable it initially to disregard such cost considerations. Second, and perhaps more important, the need exists to co-ordinate the production process (especially in its 'teething' stages) with, on the one hand, the R & D function, and, on the other, the marketing function (the need to adapt production specifications quickly).[53] Clearly this reasoning applies best to cases where there is a *major* technological change.[54] If the 'innovation' is minor, of a product-differentiating type within an established technology, the need to couple production geographically with the scientific and marketing departments is less significant (the model does, in fact, perform best in explaining the rise and maturing of major changes).

If the product is successful in the rich markets, production expands, new markets are cultivated and exports develop: this is the second stage of the cycle. In this stage the innovator still has a technological lead, but competitors are attracted by its success to work on imitations or to develop similar products. The third stage commences when sufficient competition has developed, and the technology has become standardised enough, for cost and local-marketing considerations to become important. The innovating firm then seeks to maintain its profits by making more intense marketing efforts (both by promotion and by differentiating its original product) and by investing abroad in cheaper locations and nearer to foreign markets, so exploiting its technological quasi-rents to the utmost. Production shifts in location down the income scale, say from the USA to Europe, and from Europe to LDCs, until the product is 'mature' and any rents that accrue arise from marketing rather than from technological advantages. At this stage, the fourth and final, the LDC may be used as a base to export back to more developed countries, and the product may be manufactured by several firms besides the TNC originator. The importance of marketing in both *realising* the rents before maturity and *maintaining* profitability and large market shares after maturity is vital, but its role relative to technology increases as the product matures, and market dominance may shift over the cycle from firms that lead in innovation to those that lead in marketing.

The product-cycle model was never intended to serve as a *complete* explanation of trade and investment patterns, and Vernon himself goes on to say that 'the model is losing some of its relevance for those enterprises that have long since acquired a global scanning capacity and a global habit of mind'.[55] It is most useful in understanding some *initial* moves of TNCs abroad following upon major innovations; it is less so in explaining government-policy or oligopoly-induced moves, in explaining the new pattern of 'sourcing' investment, or in accounting for the spread of TNCs which have little technological advantage or are not particularly innovative. However, as long as the basic postulates of the model – innovation in high-income areas sustained and spread by worldwide cost considerations and marketing – are valid, as they certainly are, it is valuable in understanding some crucial forces in TNC expansion: the importance of maintaining monopolistic leads, the changing roles over the cycle of technology and marketing, the nature of oligopolistic rivalry, and the timing of introducing new products and techniques into LDCs.

Step 3: Advantages of Direct Investment over Licensing
A firm possessing a particular advantage could exploit it by selling or renting that advantage by itself, without the paraphernalia of direct investment. It could license rather than export or set up subsidiaries – 'licensing' being used broadly to denote the sale of technology, brand names, patents, management services, or other, similar assets. In many cases it is clearly preferable for firms to license, since there does exist a brisk trade in technology, brand names and other services, both within developed countries and between developed and less-developed ones (in this context a foreign 'investment' that takes the form of a very small, non-controlling equity participation may be counted as a licensing agreement rather than as direct investment proper).

Among the factors that influence the choice between direct investment and licensing are the size of the market, the riskiness of investment, the secrecy and novelty of the technology, the threat to other markets from licensing, the policy of the host government, the management and strategy of the firm, the industrial market structure and the range of technologies and products involved.[56] In general, the more attractive and (politically) stable the market, the newer and more tightly controlled the technology involved, the larger and more internationally involved the firm in question, the more broadly based its sources of market power, and the lower the 'absorptive' capacity of the potential licensee for the assets to be transferred, the more will direct investment be preferred over licensing. On the other hand, the more widely diffused the technology, the smaller and riskier the market, the more inexperienced, risk-averse or nationally-oriented the firm, the more specific its particular 'advantage' and the more capable the potential licensee, the more will licensing be preferred over direct investment. This is a terse and simplified description of a complex situation, and many intermediate positions are possible between investment in wholly-owned subsidiaries and licensing to unrelated firms; but the factors just mentioned cover the most significant determinants of this sort of choice. Why is this?

Where the first group of factors is relevant, the rents arising from exploiting the advantages of a promising market (or the costs and risks involved in doing so) via direct investment are likely to be far higher (lower) than via licensing. In many LDCs the possibility of licensing advanced technology to a local enterprise simply may not exist, but, even if it did, an established transnational firm will be extremely loth to sell new and secret technology for a licence fee. It will, by doing so, not only threaten its future profitability elsewhere, but also be unable to profit from its marketing and other (financial and organisational) sources of market power. The oligopolistic dominance of TNCs results precisely from their ability to *combine* several advantages into one profitable 'package'. A licensee is likely to want only one or two elements of such a package: thus, the fee it is prepared to pay, based on the expected returns to these elements, can never match the profits that the licenser can expect to earn itself on the whole combination. Once the package exists, moreover, the marginal cost of using it in a new area is relatively low, and can be kept to a minimum by the TNC's changing the major components of the package as little as possible. The marginal cost, in terms of profits forgone, of licensing is, however, likely to be very high.[57] Where the second set of factors is applicable, we are more likely to find TNCs licensing some (probably older) technology, or small firms active in selling technology or other specialised services, or large firms with a specific asset (Coca-Cola, for instance) selling it widely for royalties.

The matter is not just one of the preferences of the TNCs. Many of the advantages of TNCs *cannot* in fact be sold to other firms, either because they are inherent to the organisation or because they are so diffuse that they are impossible to define, value and transfer. A TNC's managerial and organisational capabilities, the experience and spirit of its executives, its standing in financial markets, or its contacts with various officials and other firms, can hardly be sold to outside firms, even if it is willing to co-operate. Moreover, since many of these advantages grow *cumulatively* with size and international expansion, successful TNCs would want to internalise their benefits rather than dissipate them by licensing. It is only when particular licences do not impinge on the profitability of the firm as a whole (as with selling old or peripheral technology, undertaking management contracts, or subcontracting particular processes without losing control of secret know-how), or when host government policy makes it effectively impossible to profit from a direct investment package (take, for instance, the case of the Soviet Union's purchase of a Fiat plant), that a TNC may prefer to sell a licence.

We now have before us a fairly complete explanation of the economics of the massive foreign expansion by TNCs, and also, by implication, of the limited expansion of smaller foreign investors.[58] This will allow us, in the next chapter, better to enumerate and to comprehend in detail their effects on developing host countries. It also allows us now to discuss some motivational and organisational aspects of TNC behaviour, which will be relevant to an understanding of the implications for the policies of host governments.

MOTIVATIONAL ASPECTS OF TNC BEHAVIOUR

Some of the main motivating forces of overseas expansion – the oligopolistic structure of industry and the need to exploit technological/marketing rents – have been considered already and need not be mentioned again; here we shall only discuss briefly some of the other factors which are seen by the firms themselves, or are attributed to them, as attracting them to direct investment. There are two main ways in which this question has been approached: the survey method, relying on answers given by the executives of the investing firms; and the econometric method, using statistical techniques on available data to determine the most important factors. A large number of studies have been conducted along these lines, and have tested a variety of explanatory variables, mainly for US enterprises.[59]

The survey approach seems to suggest that the most important considerations affecting investment decisions are the host government's attitudes, political stability in the host country, the prospects of market growth and the threat to established markets. Different surveys attach different weights to these factors, as is only to be expected, but they all agree that such factors as cost considerations, threat of local competition, tax incentives or short-term strategic gains are of relatively minor significance. The dangers posed by threats of political action, expropriation or arbitrary changes in ownership or remittance policies, and lengthy bureaucratic procedures, are, on the other hand, significant deterrents to investment in particular areas. There is little doubt that TNCs prefer a stable if somewhat restrictive environment to a freer but unstable one; if large modern corporations are, as Galbraith (1967) so forcefully argues, dependent for their survival on long-term planning and control of their environment, certainly in the context of their expansion in LDCs they would *aim for predictability* and reject unpredictable environments.[60] Thus, whereas TNC investment in joint ventures with, and technology sales to, various socialist countries are increasing (since these countries offer clear and firm conditions – and no threat of nationalisation!), TNCs will often end their involvement with countries that are ideologically less alien but show marked signs of political trouble. Some TNCs, however, especially highly technological ones, prefer not to enter countries where a sharing of ownership is required; this is discussed in the following section.

The econometric approach has two branches: one that investigates the behaviour of individual firms and one that studies general investment patterns. The former has tested for significance variables suggested by the theory of the firm (such as liquidity, profitability, risk, capital–stock adjustment, diversification, or maximisation of market value), as well as variables peculiar to the emerging TNC phenomenon (such as exchange-risk, international tax differences and the 'investment climate'). The outcome is not at all clear, since different variables appear to perform well in different tests; the general impression conveyed is that the foreign-investment decision is governed by a variety of factors, of which the most important are growth of sales and some measure of profitability (perhaps adjusted for risk and tax differentials) or of maximisation of the firm's market value.[61] Liquidity does not show up as a particularly important variable, either in survey or in econometric studies, except as a constraint in particular cases; it sometimes acts as an inducement to the expansion of affiliates through the availability of reinvestible profits.

The more general econometric tests of investment flows, mostly studying the patterns of US investment in the EEC, suggest that the growth of the recipient countries' national income has been the strongest attraction to foreign capital, with profitability, tariffs, and the formation of the Common Market being relatively less significant.

The best survey of these various studies is by Dunning, who also points out the intrinsic shortcomings of such exercises in estimating the influence of factors which are not really properly captured by the quantifiable variables. For instance,

> the rate of profit earned by affiliates may inadequately express their contribution to the organisation of which they are part. . . . Moreover, the more vertically or horizontally integrated [a multinational enterprise] becomes, the less meaning can be attached to the market size or potential of the country in which production is based . . . finally, the data on which the analyses of investment are based are rarely disaggregated by type of economic activity. Because of this, it is impossible to assess the extent to which different types of overseas operations are influenced by different variables.[62]

For what they are worth, however, they imply the following for less-developed host countries.

First, a *large, politically stable, and growing market* offers the greatest attraction to TNCs, despite restrictions on ownership or the specific requirements imposed by host governments. However, there is obviously a point, differing from firm to firm, beyond which such conditions would become unacceptable.

Second, *fiscal incentives* are not *per se* very effective in drawing foreign investors, unless they are the only difference between alternative locations.[63] They may, therefore, be important for small countries or for 'footloose' investors seeking export-processing zones.

Third, a large part of TNC investment behaviour is determined by such factors as oligopoly, technology, marketing, and so on (discussed previously), which are *internal to the firm*, and not under the control of host countries. However, an understanding of such factors may lead the host country better to exploit its bargaining strength.

ORGANISATIONAL ASPECTS OF TNC BEHAVIOUR

We may consider the organisational aspects of TNC expansion and behaviour in four parts: the internal structure of management and control; the strategies of financing and transfers; the attitudes to joint ventures; and the implications of the evolving structure for the distribution of power.

(a) *Internal structure.* The international expansion of business firms calls, on the organisational side, for parents and subsidiaries to co-ordinate various functions in such a way that the overall objective of the firm is promoted most efficiently without damaging the day-to-day operations of the various units. Clearly, such co-ordination requires different organisational structures as firms grow larger and more diversified and as their activities spread over greater distances. If we conceive of the organisation as 'a hierarchy of authority and responsibility',[64] as all business must be in order to function at all, its transnationalisation calls for a rearrangement of the hierarchy to cope with the diffusion of power and the complexity of international and internal communication implicit in growing size. There is a vast amount of literature on this subject,[65] into which we shall not go here; it will suffice, for our purposes, to point out the main trends in this rearrangement.

Let us start with the organisation of domestic firms as they grow larger. Organisation theorists classify the development of firms into three stages. Stage 1 refers to the owner – manager firm. Stage 2 refers to the firm which has functional departments (responsible for sales, production, marketing, finance, and so on), each directly responsible to the president; it breaks down the initial leadership role, unified in the Stage 1 entrepreneur, into several component parts, each with its own organisation and separate hierarchy. Stage 2 organisations can reach very large sizes, but are generally representative of industries in which the product range is narrow and the technology is stable (for instance, steel and paper). In Stage 3 the organisation is reordered in such a way that a number of Stage 2 organisations are set up to deal with separate products or areas (or some combination of product and area), but with *some vital co-ordinating functions centralised at the apex of the firm.* These functions concern the efficient operation of the entire enterprise as one commercial unit, and so must monitor and control the relevant parts of the functioning of each of the product/area divisions: the allocation of finance, strategic planning of investment and marketing, and sometimes the direction of R & D. The exact nature of the centralisation depends on the nature and history of particular firms, but it would seem that some such process is essential for growing and diversifying firms.[66]

In the sphere of foreign investment there is a parallel development. The subsidiary starts in Stage 1 with a fair amount of autonomy, which is progressively reduced as the operations grow larger and the parent develops a 'global perspective'. The usual development is the setting-up of an international division to co-ordinate all foreign activities, rather similar in concept to a functional Stage 2 division (though an international division is also sometimes used in firms with domestic Stage 3 structures). As the international division grows there are pressures to break it down into a Stage 3 'global' structure, with product strategies being devised for the whole world market, or for large areas. This 'global' structure is being further developed into a 'grid' structure, still nascent, in which functions are co-ordinated in various novel ways to achieve optimum control and communication.

The tendency, if we may generalise somewhat freely, is for TNCs to knit the structure of organisational power into tighter hierarchies, with the most important decisions taken at the centre and the more routine ones left to the subsidiaries. Given the necessity of long-term and flexible central planning, the need to maximise the benefits of diverse and far-flung sets of operations, and the nature of oligopolistic competition,[67] it is inevitable that such structural changes should occur, and that they should be accompanied by corresponding changes in corporate philosophy, attitudes of executives, group loyalty, and so on, which are psychologically necessary for their implementation.[68]

(b) *Financial strategies.* With a centralisation of financial control and the need to operate across several different political, currency, tax and control regimes, TNCs are developing particular financial strategies which can maximise their global profits in, and reduce global exposure to, different conditions and risks.[69] These strategies involve the following.

(i) *Capital financing.* TNCs prefer to commit a small amount of their own capital for the initial investment and to raise the bulk of their requirements locally. Thus, it has been noted for US TNCs in manufacturing that in the period 1966–70 the amount of equity investment by the parents was only 12 per cent of the total expenditures on investment and remittances: some 35 per cent came from local borrowing, 27 per cent from profits and 26 per cent from depreciation allowances.[70] Such a policy not only minimises the parent company's exposure to various sorts of risk, but also enables it to 'gear' its capital very highly to local borrowing and so maximise the returns earned.

TNCs sometimes also often find it more advantageous to expand by acquiring going concerns than by setting up new ones.[71] The US Tariff Commission (1973) notes four advantages of acquisition: first, it may allow rapid market entry; second, it may yield proprietary control over a body of technology; third, it may offer an efficient operating plant and skilled personnel; and, fourth, it may cost less than its true worth (in the eyes of the TNC). In LDCs the last two reasons are particularly significant; the addition of prestigious brand names, new products and aggressive marketing to a going concern can do wonders to its earning capacity. Despite the reluctance which many host governments exhibit towards foreign takeovers, we find that almost 65 per cent of 2904 subsidiaries of 187 US and 209 other TNCs on which there is information had, by the end of the 1960s, been acquired by this method in LDCs.[72]

(ii) *Financial transfers.* A closely integrated framework of financial relationships between different units of the same firm provides a variety of channels through which funds can be transferred between them, openly or otherwise, with relative ease.[73] Some of these channels, such as transfer prices, royalties, fees, interest and similar payments, are now well known in the literature, and are discussed later. Others are more devious, and are perhaps worth noting. One of the less publicised findings of the Watergate investigation, reported in *The Times* (1974), is as follows:

> American Airlines, for example, 'laundered' its $55,000 (about £22,000) contribution to the President Nixon campaign by channelling cash through a New York bank to the private Swiss bank account of a Lebanese agent, who in turn sent the money to the re-election committee via a different New York bank. The expense was charged by the company to the agent in connection with a used aircraft to Middle East Airlines. Ashland Oil made its illegal $100,000 contribution to the same cause by charging the expenses of an undeveloped leasehold held by its subsidiary in Gabon, Africa. . . . The Goodyear Tire and Rubber Company also made use of Swiss bank accounts, charging its $100,000 to the President's campaign to volume discounts from suppliers of the company's foreign subsidiaries . . . Gulf Oil made its contribution of over $125,000 through a subsidiary

registered in the Bahamas, charging it off merely as a miscellaneous expense.

The purpose of this particular case does not concern us: what does is the *existence* of such means of transfer, which are in practice difficult, if not impossible, to check from outside the firm. The amazing, and seemingly endless, disclosures about illegal and semi-legal payments to foreign governments and agents made by several TNCs (and large military equipment manufacturers which are not transnational in their manufacturing operations), now appearing almost every day in the press, have revealed so much about the potentialities for hidden transfers that it would take a major research project simply to analyse and classify them. As a *Financial Times* correspondent notes, these may only be 'the tip of the iceberg', and 'the Comptroller of the Currency [in the USA] has tacitly admitted [that] the American tax authorities have neither the manpower nor the expertise to track down all these channels'.[74] The 'iceberg' may, of course, contain various US (and non-US) TNCs not yet subject to investigation.[75]

(iii) *Asset/liability management.* An appropriate management of assets and liabilities in different currencies, including the leading and lagging of payments, can serve to minimise TNCs' exposure to exchange risk, and, in some cases, to speculate actively against weak currencies.

All such strategies are in the process of evolution and refinement, and different TNCs use them actively to different extents. Obviously, it is unrealistic to think of TNCs achieving any sort of 'optimum financial planning' in a world of great complexity and uncertainty; 'however, as the pressures of world-wide competition mount, the U.S. multinational enterprise will find it more essential to explore all the financial tools at its command to achieve an optimal outcome'.[76] In other words, the process of growth and competition will *itself* necessitate a more 'rational' use of all such devices, to go together with increasing control of rent-yielding advantages and their worldwide exploitation.

(c) *Joint ventures.* These considerations also go a long way towards explaining TNCs' attitudes to joint ventures, and particularly to holding minority or locally controlled positions. In general, TNCs prefer to retain control of their affiliate operations and to expand via wholly-owned subsidiaries rather than dilute their ownership to other (local) firms. Thus, the UN study reports that 'at least 80 per cent of United States affiliates and 75 per cent of United Kingdom affiliates are either wholly-owned or majority controlled. In terms of stock of investment, these two countries have placed about 90 per cent in affiliates which are at least majority-owned.'[77] Similarly, Vernon provides data on the ownership patterns of 187 US and 209 other TNCs for 1968–70, in LDCs only, which show that, out of 1407 US subsidiaries on which information was available, 50 per cent were wholly-owned, 18 per cent majority-owned and 32 per cent minority-owned. For 1349 non-US TNC subsidiaries, these ratios were 24, 28 and 48 per cent respectively.[78] Thus, of the total of 2726 subsidiaries, 59 per cent were either wholly- or majority-owned, with US TNCs revealing a much more marked preference for such a position than did the TNCs of other countries. In addition, a substantial, but unknown, proportion of minority-owned affiliates were under the effective control of TNCs. In view of the recent policies of most LDCs, to have local majority ownership of foreign investments, these figures testify to the bargaining strength and entrenched positions of the TNCs in them.

It is clear why TNCs prefer to retain control of and maximise their equity stake. Since the very essence of going transnational is to exploit the commercial rents yielded by applying a marketing and technology 'package' at relatively low marginal cost, a TNC would not wish to share these rents with local shareholders who can offer little in return. Furthermore, the rationalisation and centralisation of authority increasingly tends to make a sharing of control difficult and cumbersome.[79] The more 'global' a firm's outlook, the more tightly knit its organisation and the more subject to technological – marketing change the industry, the more does local participation impinge on its ability to adapt and to maximise the rents it earns on its package.

This is not to say that TNCs never accept joint ventures. Obviously they do, for several reasons: first, because government policies in many LDCs make this the only method of entry;[80] second, because local partners may sometimes provide valuable local marketing knowledge and government contacts, or the opportunity, where the local partners are already active in distribution or production, to extend oligopolistic control over some part of the manufacturing, technological or marketing process; and, third, in order to tackle particularly large or risky projects. In this case they may join with other TNCs[81] or, where the technological demands are very high (as with INTELSAT),[82] with governments as well. However, the most important reason for the growth of joint ventures in LDCs is simply that in many such countries the joint venture has become the only means by which TNCs can establish a presence there.

This sort of reasoning also makes it apparent why *some* TNCs, and many small foreign investors, will be less hostile to joint ventures. The less-centralised transnationals, or the small firms, may be content to give their subsidiaries a fair amount of autonomy, may be dependent on local capital or may be particularly risk-averse. In some cases they may simply have a low-rent yielding package which reduces their bargaining power and makes them less reluctant to share it. It is important, when formulating policy, to bear this in mind.

(d) *Distribution of power.* It is an extremely difficult task to assess the distribution of power in large organisations, and even more so in complex, modern societies; obviously it is not a subject that we can tackle at any great length here. Yet it is useful for our purposes to have a general idea of the direction of change implied by the growth and evolution of TNCs. We shall postulate two trends which strike us as being true in very general terms, though there may be exceptions and deviations from them.

First, as regards the internal distribution of corporate power (within TNCs), it seems that the rearrangements of the hierarchy implied by organisational changes has led to an increasing concentration of power at the apex, the home office, of the transnationals. In most cases this power is exercised by nationals of the home country, who are united by a common language and culture, and who are usually also shareholders in their respective organisations. In some firms there is some transnationality of ownership and power (as with cross-country mergers in Europe), but the process of cross-national development necessitates centralisation, and this process tends to exclude people who come from different cultural or linguistic backgrounds. This is perhaps not as significant as the fact that *LDCs are more or less excluded from participation* in the centralised use of power in TNCs, so that for them its sharing among different nationalities, say in Europe, is really irrelevant.[83]

Second, as regards the distribution of power in society, it is widely argued that the growth of TNCs has posed an increasing challenge to the traditional power of national governments[84] and that new forms of political and economic control are needed to cope with it in the future. It is less generally admitted that there may be some association of changes in the distribution of socio-political power with the growing economic power of these corporations. Many radical as well as other observers have argued that the rise of large corporations (monopoly capital) has led to the subtle, but very real, formation of a 'super elite' in developed

Foreign Investment and TNC Behaviour 45

societies, wielding enormous influence over their functioning, policies and foreign relations.[85] This must *not* be taken to mean that particular firms or even the super elites always dominate policy (though they sometimes do), nor that governments or various sections of society are happy to part with effective power to large private corporations, nor, indeed, that bigness is not feared and resented.

What it does mean, in our opinion, is that fundamentally governments of the developed free world acquiesce in and support the general direction of development of capitalistic enterprises (in their present 'monopoly capital' form), since these comprise the mainstay of their economies, and that, despite occasional checks and shifts in the balance of power, they will continue to follow policies which provide these enterprises with a conducive environment.[86] Furthermore, whether or not the internationalisation of business increases confrontation between individual developed states[87] (we think such confrontations are superficial), from the point of view of LDCs as a group it seems fairly likely that any serious challenge to its spread into their economies will lead to various subtle or overt pressures from developed countries' governments to 'liberalise' in favour of private enterprise. We have already remarked that (with a few exceptions) this is not a major factor in the growth of particular TNCs, but its importance in fashioning the environment should not be lightly dismissed. Pressures may not always succeed, of course. Much depends on the configuration of pressures and interests *within* the LDCs, and how these react to the changes in the developed capitalist world and to the growth of TNCs. We shall touch upon this question in a later chapter.

SALIENT FEATURES OF TNCS

Let us now draw upon the preceding analysis to highlight some of the most important features of TNCs.

First, TNCs are heavily predominant in certain industries characterised by the importance of marketing and technology and by an oligopolistic or monopolistic organisation of industry within the developed countries.

Second, it follows from the nature of TNCs' expansion and inherent mode of operation that their products are new and advanced, and in LDCs must cater for a market which has relatively high incomes, sophisticated tastes and is responsive to modern marketing techniques.

Third, these products are generally produced by techniques which are the most advanced in their respective fields, often backed by heavy R & D, and transferred wholesale to all areas of operation in order to maximise the returns from given packages of technological/marketing advantages.

Fourth, TNC expansion tends to reproduce the oligopolistic conditions of the TNCs' home markets internationally and is marked by a search for stability, predictability and congenial environments.

Fifth, the maturing of TNC oligopolies may bring in its train various commercial practices to bolster the dominance of the market leaders, and may in the long run be supported by overt or covert policies followed by their home governments.

Sixth, TNCs are most attracted by large and growing economies which offer reasonably stable political conditions for their operation.

Seventh, their organisational evolution leads to a centralisation of certain vital functions concerning finance, location, marketing and research, and lends itself to rational worldwide strategies of financing and production.

Eighth, the nature of oligopolistic advantage and organisational needs causes TNCs to prefer complete or majority ownership of subsidiaries. It may also lead, in appropriate cases, to a preference for takeovers of existing firms and the commitment of a small dose of capital and a large dose of other 'advantages'.

Ninth, the increasing role of a few hundred TNCs in international production, trade, investment and technology, and the increasing centralisation of power within these corporations have important implications for the structure of socio-political power within developed as well as less-developed countries.

CHAPTER 3

Welfare of Host Countries: TNCs as Oligopolists

INTRODUCTION

The effects of foreign private investment on host LDCs are a subject on which there is considerable controversy and confusion. Not only does endless debate take place about the existence and magnitude of the various costs and benefits, but there is also fundamental disagreement about what constitutes 'cost' or 'benefit'.[1] It is not uncommon to find different writers accusing each other of 'bias', 'prejudice', 'subjectivity' or even 'extremism' when discussing the welfare effects of TNCs, each implying that his own approach is in some way more neutral and objective. No normative analysis (dealing, in this case, with judgements about what is 'good' or 'bad' for society) *can* be value-free and objective, and certainly economics, despite the pretensions of several 'rigorous' practitioners, does not provide us with neutral, scientific tools for tackling welfare problems.[2] One may be consistent or inconsistent in welfare arguments or be more or less persuasive – but ultimately there is no scientific test of right or wrong. For this reason there cannot be a final objective judgement on the welfare implications of TNCs for developing countries.

While such problems arise for all forms of applied economics, there are several reasons why TNCs raise particularly difficult problems for normative analysis, and why there is a special lack of consensus on their effects on LDCs.

(a) There are great gaps in information about their activities. Certain of these (for instance, with regard to their practices on transfer pricing, the effects of their marketing practices on tastes and demand, and their attempts to influence policy and politics) can, in principle, be filled through more research and monitoring.

(b) There are also a number of unknown factors that by their very nature, are unknowable. Among these are the effects of large (non-marginal) changes in foreign investment, the potential suppression of domestic entrepreneurship, the diffuse socio-political–cultural effects of a large foreign 'presence', and several other kinds of 'externalities'.

(c) The emphasis given to various effects can be very different, even within the conventional framework of economic analysis. Different 'theories' of development have variously emphasised different 'missing components' (such as savings, foreign exchange, technology, entrepreneurship and skills)[3] that can be provided by foreign investment.

(d) The value judgements on which the welfare analysis is based may differ significantly, so much so that we may find different welfare paradigms being applied,[4] with completely different specifications of what constitutes social welfare.

(e) Finally, the 'alternative situations'[5] assumed may be very different, with some analysts taking only marginal changes in foreign investment into account, some thinking in terms of nationally-owned private firms replacing large areas of foreign investment, and others considering a totally different political–economic structure, with no role for private investment at all.

Taken together, these deficiencies and differences in emphasis and values may become extremely significant, and the form of the debate may range from mild acrimony to hostile incomprehension. In so far as the differences arise simply from lack of information or from attaching different importance to different factors, further research and argument may help to resolve conflicts and advance knowledge. However, in so far as differences arise from more basic disagreements, over values and alternatives, reconciliation may be more difficult, sometimes impossible. No particular standpoint is more legitimate than any other, and none is defensible on ultimate principles.

It is important to be aware of these problems when discussing the welfare effects of TNCs. While we cannot, by our own reasoning, make a claim to 'objectivity' in the following analysis, we can, in providing a general summary (if not a comprehensive one, for the literature is enormous) of the debate, attempt to point out *where* the major differences in opinion arise. The attempt may help clarify the sources of conflict and show why so many protagonists in this field seem to 'talk past' each other without making real contact.[6]

The following section discusses some problems encountered in analysing the effects of TNCs with conventional welfare tools. The succeeding sections describe these effects under several of the headings used previously to analyse the particular 'advantages' of TNCs over other investors. Since these oligopolistic 'advantages' comprise the most significant differences between transnationals and alternative forms (local and foreign) of investment, a discussion of how they affect host LDCs seems the best way to understand the role of TNCs. In the next chapter we shall revert to the more conventional method of analysing foreign investment as a 'general' inflow of capital.

A DIGRESSION ON 'WELFARE'

While a chapter on the effects of foreign investment on LDCs is hardly the right place to launch into a discussion of welfare economics, it has become increasingly apparent to us that it is extremely difficult to describe these effects within the conventional welfare framework. A short digression on the elements of the conventional paradigm may, therefore, help to clarify what these difficulties are, and why the introduction of value judgements and assumptions not contained in this paradigm may be necessary in order to conduct an analysis.[7]

The neoclassical welfare paradigm, in its dominant Paretian form, may be seen to have three basic components which are essential to its application to the assessment of welfare in a capitalist society:

(a) *The ideological base.* The fundamental assumption which enables a conceptualisation of the welfare of capitalist society as a whole, and without which it would be meaningless to talk of 'social' costs and benefits (or to proceed from individual to social welfare and *vice versa*), is that there is a *basic harmony of interests in society*, and that, in particular, there is no conflict, along Marxian lines, between those who own the means of production and those who do not.[8]

(b) *The individualistic premise.* This is composed of the assumptions that the individual attempts to maximise his own welfare, and knows best what this is, and the value judgement that this is the welfare which ought to be maximised in order to maximise social well-being.[9] The individualistic premise provides the ultimate datum of welfare analysis – the fulfilment of individual 'preferences' – beyond which the economist cannot venture very far. Given the ideological base, which presumes that individual or group interests do not conflict in any fundamental manner, it is quite valid to proceed with such a definition of 'social welfare', with some relatively minor qualifications for preferences which have to be expressed collectively or for interdependence in some forms (but not based on class conflict) of individual preference.[10] Furthermore, given the liberal philosophy underlying the individualistic premise, the economist is not required to question how the preferences are formed (they are taken as exogenously determined) nor to assess whether the fulfilment of some preferences is more conducive to social well-being than is that of others. Minor exceptions are sometimes admitted – tastes may be affected by advertising, and 'merit' wants may deserve to be met before others – but these are exceptions to rules which are considered otherwise sound.

(c) *The political premise.* The state is assigned a specific role in conventional welfare economics. It is taken to be neutral between different classes or groups in society; to be the repository of 'social welfare', often equated to the 'national interest'; and to be essentially in harmony with other states with which it has economic relations. The neutrality and national-interest attributes are based on the ideological premise – clearly, if there were a fundamental conflict of interest in society, the state could not be neutral, and could not represent the (fictional) 'national interest'.

The combination of these three elements enables economists to analyse the conditions under which social welfare is maximised, and to recommend policies to the government that enhance it in actual circumstances. As anyone familiar with elementary economics knows, the ideal conditions are those under which free and perfect competition (with perfect foresight) can obtain. The distribution of income raises difficulties: welfare may be 'optimised' for any given distribution, and the paradigm itself prevents one from saying anything definite about the desirability of particular distributions. The general procedure is then to treat distribution as a 'political' problem, to be resolved by a neutral government on non-economic grounds, though recently some development economists have begun to incorporate specific (non-Paretian) value judgements and to recommend policies to reduce inequalities where these are found to be very large.[11]

In the field of international economics, welfare optimisation within this paradigm calls, with relatively minor qualifications (for 'optimum' tariffs or taxes, scale economies, 'infant' industries and some forms of market 'imperfection'), for free movements of commodities and capital (unskilled and semi-skilled labour is generally taken to be immobile between countries). There is a basic presumption that *foreign investment*

TNCs as Oligopolists

raises incomes and social welfare in recipient LDCs unless the 'optimum' conditions are significantly distorted by protection, monopoly and externalities. The growth of oligopolistic control of trade and production in international markets is generally ignored, or else taken as a constraint which LDCs can do nothing about, while externalities (of the sort considered relevant in this paradigm) are generally taken to be more favourable than unfavourable to foreign investment. This leaves domestic monopoly and protection as possible detractors from the welfare gains conferred by TNCs. Both are treated as 'policy' problems. The host government is assumed to be free to adopt measures to reduce the incidence of monopoly (by encouraging domestic and foreign competition) and of protection (by promoting freer trade); TNCs are simply neutral providers of capital and various other 'advantages', and any welfare loss from their operations – with the major exception admitted being the misuse of transfer prices (discussed later) – must *necessarily arise from misguided government policy*.[12] The division of welfare gains between the host government and the TNC is, however, admitted to depend, at least in part, on their relative strength in bargaining over terms and their skill in improving upon the initial bargain, rather than simply upon given market prices; but the scope for such bargaining is greatly reduced by the assumption that any measure that reduces the returns to the foreign company will also tend to reduce its investment, so that the host government has to weigh the advantages of its bargaining terms against the advantages of more investment. This implies an assumption about the absence of monopoly or oligopoly rents.

If the effects of TNCs are judged only by the criteria of conventional welfare theory, it is difficult to arrive at any other sort of conclusion: a large part of the answer is implicit in the premises and the method. Thus, in the absence of other welfare tools, economists tend to start by assuming that TNCs raise welfare (by satisfying individual preferences expressed in the market, income-distribution being a 'non-economic' matter), and then to proceed, usually qualitatively, by adding a number of extra benefits (superior technology, marketing, management, export and competitive performance) and subtracting some costs (tax evasion, restrictive practices). Such a procedure undoubtedly provides useful information and insights, but its premises limit it in important ways when the particular problems of TNCs in developing countries are considered. These limitations arise as follows.

(a) Conventional welfare economics cannot draw general distinctions between preferences on grounds of their social or ethical desirability. All preferences deserve to be fulfilled if they are expressed in the market; only a few exceptions are admitted (in the case of collective or non-market goods, 'merit' wants, and obviously harmful demands, prohibited by law). If the pattern of market demand is considered undesirable, it is usually traced to the structure of income distribution, and so reduced to a distinct non-economic 'policy' problem.

(b) Similarly, economists cannot inquire into the factors which shape preferences, and so cannot distinguish between those which express 'genuine' needs and those which result from education, demonstration, ostentation, advertising and other 'learnt' factors. It is a tenet of conventional economics that such distinctions are not drawn, and that economists, being 'objective', cannot pass value judgements on this score *qua* economists.[13]

(c) The difficulties (already noted) that welfare economics faces when dealing with income distribution lead it to push distribution into 'political' or 'moral' spheres. If one kept to the strict principles of Paretian welfare economics, one would not be able to evaluate differences between income gains accruing to, say, the very rich as opposed to the very poor. Many economists do find ways of introducing political and moral judgements, and some directly attack the assumption of class harmony which underlies neoclassical economics — in all this they deviate from the straight and narrow path of 'objectivity'.

(d) The usual escape route of welfare economists when faced with such ethical problems is to 'leave it all to the government', the final repository of the 'national' interest. If, however, the assumption of government neutrality is challenged, and a theory of the state introduced in which political power in some way reflects the configuration of economic power (with classes or groups not being in essential harmony), the fiction of the 'national' interest has to be abandoned and it has to be investigated *whose* interest is in fact being promoted (or compromised with other, conflicting interests). This has, to put it mildly, serious implications for normal welfare economics, but these cannot be pursued here.

Many of these limitations have been criticised by economists of all types, but some of the strongest challenges to the conventional paradigm have come from those who work on development problems, particularly those concerned with international investment. And it is in the area of development economics more than in any other field that neoclassical economists and neo-Marxian economists have engaged in a dialogue.

TNCs as Oligopolists

The discussion in the remainder of this chapter will illustrate the nature of the departures from the conventional paradigm. The essential purpose of these departures has been to challenge the reasoning which leads to the bland conclusion that TNCs increase the welfare of the host country unless the government has adopted wrong policies. Even if it were accepted that TNCs raise national product at 'undistorted' prices, *it would not follow that economic welfare in the host country is increased, unless a number of other conditions are also satisfied.*

A great deal of the confusion and controversy about this subject arises from the acceptance and specification of these 'other' conditions. Those who accept the conventional paradigm *in toto* usually deny that their reasoning has any value judgements or ideological elements; they dismiss the inclusion of any 'other' conditions as subjective, biased and unscientific. Even if they accept that their argument is based on a 'vision' of society (what Schumpeter called the 'pre-analytic cognitive act') and contains value judgements, they argue that their vision is more correct and their values more acceptable (or widely accepted). The critics can easily reverse these charges, with predictable, and regrettably bitter, results. Further, since much of the debate is conducted at a polemical level, without adequate effort to clarify what the differences are and why they arise, the controversy is sometimes confounded by misunderstanding and by the participants 'talking past' each other.

This digression into conceptual issues has set the stage for the introduction of different value judgements and assumptions into the discussion of the welfare effects of TNCs. We do not hope to have spiked the guns of those who disagree with our particular perspective (which will become clear in the course of the following discussion). On the contrary, we hope to sharpen the debate by evaluating the weaknesses of each side, the critics and the supporters of TNCs, and to act as 'translators' (who help bridge the gaps between conflicting paradigms in an instance of Kuhnian 'paradigm change'[14]) by tracing the source of their differences. Let us now discuss the effects of TNCs under each of the main headings which constitute their advantages over other investors.

PROVISION OF CAPITAL

The world's largest enterprises can command enormous financial resources for investment, both internally and by tapping various external capital markets and financial institutions. Not only do TNCs have access to finance: they often have *privileged* access, and can obtain funds on better terms than other firms (certainly as compared with firms from LDCs, most of which cannot on their own raise long-term funds in international markets at all). Furthermore, with the expansion of transnational banking into several LDCs, TNCs which have long-established links with the parent banks can extend these links to their subsidiaries, and enable them to raise credit on favourable terms.

Besides the benefits that TNCs can offer in terms of *direct* provision of capital, they can also stimulate it *indirectly* in three ways. First, a transnational investor wanting to set up an exceptionally large plant may invite other TNCs to contribute to its financing (and to share in the risks). The incidence of such multinational consortia has risen quite noticeably in recent years, especially in Eastern Europe and the Middle East, and in industries with scale economies and stable technologies. Secondly, the free entry of private capital may stimulate, indeed sometimes may be a condition for, the flow of official aid from the home countries of the TNCs (as well as from international aid agencies). Thirdly, foreign firms may mobilise local savings, which would otherwise remain idle or be used in less productive activities, by offering attractive investment opportunities on domestic capital markets.

As against these benefits that TNCs can offer in terms of filling the savings and foreign exchange 'gaps' in LDCs, we can set several *costs*.

(a) Direct private investment is a relatively expensive way to acquire foreign capital, and investment by the large transnationals tends to be more expensive than investment by smaller firms. There is little doubt that the rate of profit of TNCs is significantly higher than the long-term rate of interest in international capital markets and that TNCs are more profitable than other firms;[15] our own studies confirm that host economies do not gain much financial benefit from foreign direct investment, and would be seen to gain even less if hidden remittances in the form of transfer pricing were fully known. Two points must, however, be noted. First, the main advantages offered by TNCs are supposed to be not finance, but technology, marketing and superior management, and these are presumably reflected in the higher cost of the finance (whether or not the host LDC receives genuine 'welfare' gains from the other advantages is another matter, and must be judged on different grounds from case to case). Secondly, aid and foreign borrowing are not generally substitutable for foreign direct investment by an LDC; they are, if anything, complementary. On the other hand, the host country can always divert foreign exchange from other uses if extra aid is not available. The proper economic calculation would be to compare the cost of servicing TNC investment with the opportunity cost of providing the capital domestically plus the cost of buying the other components of the TNC package. This is on the assumptions, of which neither may be correct, that the 'other' components are wanted and are for sale at acceptable prices. The assessment would depend on the particular circumstances.

(b) The actual inflow of capital provided by the TNC may not be very large. We noted in Chapter 2 that US parent TNCs as a whole provided only 12 per cent of the total value of expenditures on capital investment and profit remittances in 1966–70 (for sample figures see Chapter 6), the remainder coming from *locally earned and reinvested profits* and *local savings*. As far as reinvested profits go, the amount of the investment may legitimately be considered as a foreign-exchange inflow as long as the funds could have been repatriated by the foreign firm. Though many critics of TNCs, especially in Latin America, complain that this somehow represents a misuse of local resources to finance foreign profit-bearing investments, the reasoning is invalid – at least, so long as one accepts the legitimacy of profit. A more valid criticism may be that the profits earned are 'too high', because of the market power of large TNCs; but this is irrelevant to the above argument, which is concerned not with the level of profits but, apparently, with the ethics of the private-enterprise system.

As far as the use of local savings is concerned, we must distinguish between local equity (which earns profits) and local borrowing (which earns interest). Local equity shareholders get the same return on their capital as do foreign shareholders in the TNC (unless transfer pricing is used against the former so as to remit profits clandestinely to the foreign parent), and there is little ground for objecting to TNCs raising local capital in this form, as long as the investment as such is considered desirable. On the contrary, since the TNC usually has sources of market power beyond the reach of local firms, such financing, if the TNC can be persuaded or obliged to accept it, is a good way of capturing a part of its rents domestically.

Local financing in the form of loans is different, for two reasons: (i) it raises the rate of profit on foreign capital which is 'geared' with domestic loans,[16] and so diverts domestic savings from other uses only to benefit the foreign investor; and (ii) it may lead to foreign subsidiaries being preferred as clients by financial institutions, by virtue of being part of transnational businesses, and so to local firms having less credit than they otherwise would. The first may be regarded as socially undesirable, as long as the funds would have been used equally productively elsewhere in the economy. Several governments in LDCs seem to take this condition for granted, and restrict the amount of long-term loans that foreign firms can raise locally.[17] If their assumption is reasonable, it follows that capital should, as far as possible without harming present and future relationships with TNCs, be provided to them in the form of equity rather than loans. The second point, concerning the status of foreign subsidiaries as privileged borrowers, is often mentioned in the literature but is difficult to verify empirically. Our own sample data (see Chapter 6) do not indicate that foreign firms gear themselves more highly than domestic ones, though this does not, of course, establish that they are not favoured borrowers. If it *were* the case that TNCs were given preference – and this seems likely on *a priori* grounds – it could lead to a socially undesirable pattern of lending, and there would be a strong case for the redirection of credit to help deserving local entrepreneurs.

(c) The capital contribution of a TNC may be in the form of machinery or capitalised intangibles (know-how, goodwill, and so on) rather than cash. The valuation of such contributions is difficult, and may be quite arbitrary. Thus, in order to raise its equity share in an investment, the TNC may assign a high value to, say, used machinery or a brand-name, the value of which most LDC governments normally would not check closely. Furthermore, a domestic technology buyer or shareholder may knowingly collaborate in the overvaluation of equipment and intangibles so as to by-pass official control of profit and royalty payments.[18] This raises issues of transfer pricing, which we shall discuss later.

ORGANISATION AND MANAGEMENT

In the previous chapter we described the evolution of the organisational structure of TNCs, and the possible advantages that this might confer upon them. The growth of international activities across diverse ranges of products, the need to control a large number of units in a flexible yet cohesive manner, and the emergence of a 'global' view of business have necessitated major evolutions in the managerial and organisational practices of TNCs. The tendency has been, though it is by no means universal, to centralise a number of crucial functions and to delegate authority on more routine ones, reinforcing the structure with sophisticated communication systems, procedures and manuals, to ensure compliance with general policies.[19]

TNCs as Oligopolists

The *benefits* to host countries of the managerial superiority of TNCs are of three types.

(a) Managerial efficiency in operations, arising from better training, higher standards of recruitment, faster communications with the parent company and the world as a whole, and a more dynamic outlook generally.

(b) Entrepreneurial ability in seeking out investment opportunities, organising suppliers and markets, and perhaps developing new technologies to suit particular conditions.

(c) Externalities arising from training received by employees (technical, executive, accounting, and so on) who later leave the firm, and the demonstration effect on competing local firms, suppliers and even government officials who come into contact with the practices adopted by TNCs.

These benefits presumably show up in lower costs and prices, better investments, and a general improvement in managerial standards in the host country. Two qualifications may be noted. First, the sheer size and growth of TNCs is sometimes taken as evidence of their superior efficiency in operations. If this is not interpreted as a mere tautology — success defines efficiency — there is room for doubt whether the practices of TNCs are in fact more efficient than those of smaller firms, and whether their size does not, after a certain level, tend to act as a defence against threats from smaller but more efficient rivals. There is certainly some evidence (references are given in the notes to Chapter 2) that large firms are less productive of innovations per unit of R & D expenditure than smaller firms are, and the same may be true of routine management, though evidence for or against this is hard to find.[20] Second, much of the benefit of training locals in the practices of TNCs may not lead to external benefits in LDCs, because these practices may be irrelevant, event alien, to the normal methods of business operation there. In such a case, departing employees may worsen the effective standards of management in the host country, by importing practices suitable to very large, complex and impersonal institutions into small, personal and culturally different ones.

Such qualifications apart, the tightly controlled and hierarchical structure of TNCs may entail more important *costs* to host LDCs. The first may be broadly labelled the *dependence and subordination* which this structure imposes on subsidiaries in a worldwide transnational system. The centralisation of authority and crucial decisions in the head offices of TNCs, which, as we noted in the previous chapter, are staffed by the nationals of the home countries of these companies,[21] leads to a sort of imperialist system in the organisation, with the head office dictating to the 'colonies', the subsidiaries, the rules, the actions and the values to be followed. The most vivid description of this is by Hymer, who writes,

> It is not technology which creates inequality; rather, it is *organisation* that imposes a ritual judicial asymmetry on the use of intrinsically symmetrical means of communication and arbitrarily creates unequal capacities to initiate and terminate exchange, to store and retrieve information, and to determine that extent of the exchange and the terms of the discussion . . . [The result is that] a regime of multinational corporations would offer under-developed countries neither national independence nor equality. . . . It would turn underdeveloped economies into branch-plant countries, not only with reference to their economic functions but throughout the whole gamut of social, political and cultural roles.[22]

Two points are immediately obvious about Hymer's argument. First, the conventional welfare paradigm has been totally rejected. The scope of inquiry stretches far beyond the narrowly economic, and value judgements (about independence, autonomy, dignity, equality and subordination) are introduced which have no role in the conventional scheme. Second, the 'alternative situation' implicitly considered is not of a marginal change in foreign investments – in that case, the social, political and cultural factors would hardly change – but of a radical change in all the external relations of LDCs, with TNCs being a leading, but not the only, representation of these relations. Neither of these points is, as such, a criticism of the substance of Hymer's argument.

We have little to say on the non-economic aspects of the case: it is incontestable that TNCs are among the most powerful external forces affecting social and cultural attitudes in LDCs[23] and that they directly or indirectly influence political currents in host countries (we discuss this later); whether this is a 'good thing' or not is a matter of preference. As for the economic aspects, while it is plain that the growth of TNCs has an effect on the technological, consumption and other patterns of host countries, and that this has several undesirable features, it is not clear that it is *organisation* that is the main causal element, with the others being merely passive. It may be argued that the hierarchical form which the organisation takes is a product of growth compelled by technological factors or by oligopolistic competition more generally. The sort of inequality and loss of autonomy which Hymer is attacking is inherent in the entire structure of international economic relationships between developed and less-developed areas,[24] and there is little analytical purpose served by selecting one manifestation.

The second type of cost arises from the *financial practices* which a tightly-knit organisational structure facilitates. An important facet of the international growth of firms has been that a number of transactions between different countries now take place between units of the same firms. These cover sales of technology and services as well as of commodities of all kinds, and the valuation placed on these, particularly the last, has given rise to the well-known problem of *transfer pricing*.[25]

The problem arises from the fact that transfer prices, being under the control of the firm concerned, can be put at levels which differ from prices which would obtain in 'arm's-length' transactions, and so can be manipulated to shift profits clandestinely from one area of operations to another. If the different units of a TNC behaved like independent firms, clearly the problem would not arise. However, given the growing extent of intra-firm trade,[26] it is the *centralisation of authority* and the growth of a *global business strategy* that creates fears on the part of governments (both host and home) that they are losing legitimate tax revenue.

We must be careful not to exaggerate. There are indications that different TNCs have different policies with regard to transfer pricing, and a prominent business-school text points out that many firms are losing 'millions of dollars' through 'sub-optimal' use of the various financial devices open to them.[27] On the other hand, the very process of organisational rationalisation and increasing intra-firm trade that accompanies transnational growth (and, of course, the advice tendered by business specialists) tends to increase the ability of TNCs to handle complex international pricing strategies, and the increasing concern expressed by governments about the regulation of transfer-pricing practices shows that the problem is acutely felt.[28] The examples of flexibility of pricing manipulations mentioned in Chapter 2, the evidence on transfer pricing in Colombia presented in Chapter 7, and the existence of several thriving tax havens[29] should warn us against treating the phenomenon lightly.

The *inducements* to TNCs to use transfer pricing have been amply discussed in the literature,[30] and here we need mention them only briefly. They may be grouped under two headings. Those that arise from the desire (directly) to *increase global post-tax profits* are: international differences in tax and tariff rates, multiple exchange rates, quantitative restrictions on profit remission, existence of local shareholders, exchange-rate instability, and the overstating of apparent costs as a means to obtain higher protection against imports. Those that arise from the need to *reduce risk and uncertainty* over the long term are: present or anticipated balance-of-payments difficulties, political threats to profit repatriation (or to survival) in a particular country, trade-union pressures, and the risk of attracting competition from other (mainly transnational) firms. In general, it seems plausible to argue, as Lall (1973) has done, that many LDCs, with their combination of exchange problems, pressures for local shareholding, political risks and tendencies to socialism, will offer substantial incentives to TNCs to keep a 'low profit profile' and so use transfer pricing against them. The incidence may differ from country to country (those with the political machinery to implement an all-out capitalist strategy may feel more secure) and from industry to industry (low-technology industries with standardised inputs being less vulnerable), but the danger is certainly present and cannot be ignored.

These are the external factors which may cause a firm to use transfer prices to move profits out of a host country. Actual transfer-pricing policies may be affected not only by these, but also by *constraints* which are set by external (checks by tax and customs authorities) and internal (the need to monitor and control subsidiaries) factors. Firms make a great deal of the fact that, because of external checks, they are unable to manipulate transfer prices, and it is certainly true that, with a growing awareness of the problem, several governments have tightened their procedures for regulating intra-firm transactions. The following points should, however, be noted.

(a) The monitoring of prices charged on intra-firm transactions is a difficult, complex and extensive task with which most administrations in LDCs are ill-equipped to deal.[31] Furthermore, the two sets of authorities which are normally concerned with these prices may act in conflicting ways: customs authorities want to set high prices on imports to increase tariff revenue, while tax authorities want the opposite, to increase taxable profits.

(b) While there are serious administrative problems in checking whether firms are charging correct market prices, there are far more difficult problems which arise when the goods are *specific* to the firm and *do not have* market (or comparable arm's-length) prices. Many of the commodities exchanged in intra-firm trade are of this type, and there are severe practical as well as theoretical problems in deciding what a correct reference price should be. The greatest difficulty arises in

TNCs as Oligopolists 61

allocating such fixed costs as R & D, administration and marketing expenses incurred by the parent company to individual items produced by it and 'sold' to affiliates. For research-based TNCs this involves determining not only how fixed costs of successful as well as unsuccessful innovations should be spread over particular items, but also what a 'fair' reward is for risk in doing research and what it is 'fair' to charge subsidiaries in countries which do not benefit from major areas of its research. Clearly there cannot be a *correct* solution (in the absence of actual competitive arm's-length prices); any price set within a range is bound to be arbitrary. In such a situation, it will not be costs that determine price but 'what the market will bear'—and this will be determined by the bargaining strength of the parties involved (in this case the TNC and the governments of host and home countries).[32] It is likely, however, that, given this indeterminacy and the relative administrative weakness of host governments in LDCs, the transfer-pricing tool will be used more to the advantage of the sophisticated TNCs than to that of the host LDCs. It is also likely that the incidence of transfer pricing will be higher the more highly technological the industry and the more firm-specific the goods involved; the fact that the bulk of the evidence comes from the pharmaceutical industry tends to support this hypothesis (see Chapter 8 below).

(c) Most of the official action taken recently to regulate transfer pricing has in fact occurred in the developed countries, despite the publicity which has been given in the literature to attempts by the Andean Pact. The US government, under section 482 of its Internal Revenue Code, is probably the most rigorous and experienced in dealing with this problem;[33] it uses three methods for determining arm's-length prices, the actual outcome in most cases being determined by a negotiation (bargain) between the company and the authorities. Its example is being followed by many European countries,[34] which are also setting up procedures for international exchange of price data on TNC trade. The Andean Group's attempts, while yielding valuable fiscal benefits, are still not very comprehensive; other developing countries have still to make a start in dealing with transfer pricing.[35] If it is the case that official checks evolve faster and more stringently in the developed world, the effect would be to *tilt the balance further against the less-developed countries*, with the fiscal authorities of the former gaining at the expense of the latter.[36]

The costs to host LDCs from transfer pricing accrue not only to the authorities which lose tax revenue (net of any gains made in tariffs), but also to local shareholders who lose part of their legitimate profits, workers who lose if low declared profits retard wage increases, and consumers who pay higher prices if TNCs are able to obtain greater protection and charge higher prices.

The internal constraints to transfer pricing arise from the need to exercise proper financial control over subsidiaries and to offer proper incentives to the management of subsidiaries which might otherwise be required to show low profits or losses. While it may be true that some firms operating internationally do find these constraints important (thus the variety of practice noted above), it is difficult to believe that, with a centralisation of pricing decision-making, sophisticated accounting and communication techniques, and the ease of keeping different accounts for different purposes, they will continue to be important for the majority of TNCs. Certainly the evidence on financial manipulations (referred to elsewhere in this book) does not indicate that such constraints are by themselves very binding.

The final cost of the managerial and entrepreneurial superiority of TNCs is the *suppression of domestic entrepreneurship*. It is often argued[37] that unrestricted entry of TNCs into an underdeveloped economy with a weak national entrepreneurial class will cause all the dynamic sectors of industry to be taken over by the transnationals, with the domestically owned industrial sector relegated to subsidiary role of the provider of ancillary inputs. There is certainly good reason to expect this. Even a developed economy with strong entrepreneurial resources (for instance, Canada) can find it difficult to prevent the leadership in the main branches of industry from passing to foreign TNCs; a backward economy with far weaker defences faces a much greater threat.

There may be two reasons for regarding this as a cost. First, on 'purely' economic grounds, the domination of an economy (or of many of its leading industries) by TNCs may be *economically detrimental* to the long-run development of the host country (taking 'development' now to stand simply for the growth of GNP at market prices) on three counts.

(a) It may lead to a lower rate of accumulation domestically because a proportion of the profits is repatriated rather than invested locally. This would be the case, however, only if local investors earned the same rate of profit as foreign ones (essentially if they have the same technology and managerial skills), if they did not also send part of their profits abroad, and if conditions in the host economy (politically as well as economically) were such that the foreign investor chose to repatriate rather than enlarge his investments.

(b) Similarly, it may lead to higher (open or hidden) charges for technology or other services, a greater incidence of undesirable practices such as transfer pricing and export restrictions, or a lower degree of national control over monetary and fiscal policy. Again, the final economic cost of this depends upon whether the technology or other services would have been available in the alternative situation, whether affiliates were in fact charged more than unrelated buyers of technology, and whether a relatively 'open' economy (with respect to exchange rates, capital flows, and so on) is not more efficient than one which is more insulated from international market forces.[38]

(c) Its effect on the market structure may be to induce a very high degree of oligopolistic concentration, and so to impose the costs of diminished price competition, excessive product differentiation, possible cartelisation, and so on. This assumes that a nationally owned industrial structure would be different, and that domestic oligopolists would behave differently.[39]

On 'purely' economic grounds, therefore, there are clearly a number of potential costs of foreign domination, but it is difficult to assess how important these may be without specifying a number of conditions – about various political and economic factors affecting foreign investment, about the availability of technology, about the capabilities of domestic entrepreneurs and the efficacy of national policies which go against 'free' market forces, about alternative market structures during industrial development, and so on – which are in practice almost impossible to assess. Several of these points are touched upon elsewhere, so we shall not labour them here.

The second reason for regarding domination by TNCs as a cost is based upon 'non-economic' considerations. Such considerations may be grouped into four views, ranging from that of mild nationalism to that of radical socialism: first, national ownership of means of production may be regarded as desirable *per se*; second, foreign ownership may impose costs in social, political and cultural terms; third, it may distort the pattern of development, inhibit local technology and primarily serve to enrich a small section of the population; and, fourth, it may block the road to socialist reforms in the future.[40] The first represents an undercurrent of feeling contained in much of the criticism of TNCs, especially in the 'American Challenge' sort of reaction which was popular in Europe in the 1960s. The second is common in many developing countries, but in a 'pure' form (i.e. without other ideological connotations) is perhaps best seen in the Canadian resentment of US transnationals. The third is the sort of mixture of socialism and nationalism which many Latin American writers of the 'structuralist' and 'dependence' schools display, while the fourth is explicitly Marxist.

It is difficult to separate the 'economic' arguments from the 'non-economic' ones, and we do not wish to draw a very firm distinction or to suggest that one is more legitimate or objective than the other (thus the inverted commas). Indeed, we ourselves introduce, as we noted before, explicitly 'non-economic' judgements into our discussion of welfare effects. The foregoing analysis is mainly intended to illustrate, once more, how differences in assessment of the virtues of national enterprise reflect differences in interpretation of (and gaps in) information, differences in value judgements, and differences in the desired 'alternative situations' with which the actual one is compared.

TECHNOLOGY

The 'transfer of technology' has now become perhaps the predominant issue around which discussions of TNCs and their dealings with developing countries revolve.[41] Indeed, concern with the control and regulation of TNCs as a whole seems to have become increasingly subsumed under a consideration of policies for transferring technology on terms favourable to the receiving developing countries, and under conditions that are in some sense appropriate to their social and economic needs. It is not difficult to understand why. 'Technology', defined widely to mean the human ability to handle the means of production, and 'innovation', the production of new technology, are the lifeblood of economic growth, accumulation, trade and even changes in the organisation of social relations and the relations of production. In this general sense, the transfer of the ability to produce most efficiently is held to be the key to progress in the poor countries, and is the attribute which they demand most from TNCs.[42]

While in this very general sense technology is certainly a vital component of economic progress, it has, however, come to be increasingly recognised that the *particular form* that technology takes at a given time and in a given context is heavily influenced by the socio-economic environment for which it is produced. It cannot, in other words, simply be assumed to be a neutral factor which has to be transferred wholesale to completely different environments 'to raise productivity' and 'welfare'.[43] An evaluation of the real welfare effects of technology transferred by TNCs must be based upon an understanding of the context in which TNCs produce their technology, the market and institutions which govern the transfer of this technology to LDCs, and the social and economic effects of the transfer.

We have already described the main elements of the context in developed countries in which the bulk of modern technology is produced. Let us reiterate the main points. The production of new technology (as measured by the distribution of R & D expenditures or patents taken out) is very highly concentrated among the most advanced capitalist countries, and within these among a few leading (mostly transnational) firms. With the growing oligopolistic nature of manufacturing industry, in 'low' as well as' high'technology sectors, a great deal of technological innovation (directed at the *rich* markets which account for the bulk of sales, and based on competitive and cost pressures in *developed* countries) is aimed not at discovering new processes and products, but at product differentiation. The balance between 'real' technological advance and 'marketing-oriented' innovation varies from one industry to another, depending upon the scientific base of the industry, the stage of maturity of the ruling technology, the stability of the oligopoly, and the nature of the market, with some sectors (such as computers) being heavily science and 'real'-technology based, and so spending relatively little on marketing innovation,[44] and others (such as processed foods) being heavily market based, with relatively little 'real' innovation and a stable and widely diffused technology.[45] While it obviously is difficult to draw a firm line between the two sorts of innovation, the distinction between them is widely recognised, and it is vital for our purposes to bear it in mind.

The most important force behind the transnational growth of the leading oligopolistic firms has been the possession of a 'package' or combination of these technological and marketing advantages and the pressure to capitalise on these in larger markets. Within the present structure of manufacturing industry (and growing more so over time), the production of new technology is in many industries inextricably linked with, and dependent upon, the process of product differentiation and the use of a highly sophisticated, widespread and effective marketing structure. Technological innovation could not survive without marketing, and marketing would not succeed without a constant stream of new or differentiated products. Thus, only a part of what is normally termed 'innovation' goes towards the production of genuinely new processes and products ('raising the productive forces' in Marxist terms, in order to raise the rate of surplus value); the rest is broadly defensive and marketing-oriented (for 'realising' surplus value in the process of capitalist competition).

This is the background to the production of the technology which is relevant to our discussion. Let us now briefly examine the nature of the market (and supporting institutions) and the socio-economic context of recipient LDCs, in order to assess its welfare effects.

Technology Markets and Institutions
The technology 'market' has several peculiarities which distinguish it from a normally functioning market for commodities.[46] These peculiarities arise from the fact that it deals with knowledge, which, once produced, costs little at the margin to sell (in unlimited quantities), yet can be very expensive to produce and commercialise, and, mostly because of this, is extremely concentrated in its ownership. Since private production of marketable knowledge must earn a suitable reward for effort and risk, the intrinsically social (or 'public-good') nature of the product must be counterbalanced by secrecy and legal rights (both of which have limited durations) and by its embodiment in a suitably marketed branded commodity (which may have a fairly long remunerative life). And since the buyer of knowledge is, especially when he buys the whole 'package' of direct investment by a TNC, very imperfectly informed of what he is buying, the usual assumption of an 'informed buyer' acting in a competitive market does not hold.

If we add to this the consideration that LDCs have little capacity to 'go it alone' in many fields of advanced technology and that they often lack even the information or the ability to shop around for alternative technologies and sources of supply, it is easy to see why 'The situation is quite different from that of an "equilibrium price" reached in a competitive market. It is more like that of a bilateral monopoly or oligopoly where bargaining theory applies',[47] a situation where, we may add, the developing countries often find themselves at a grave disadvantage. If we disregard for the moment questions of appropriateness and concentrate on the direct financial costs of buying technology in this market, the following points may be made about technology transfers through TNCs.

First, there are several *sources of technology* besides large transnational companies – from consultants who have no interest in directly owning and running manufacturing enterprises, and smaller firms which may license the technology or undertake direct investments, to official and international agencies which can provide technical assistance without charge or for a small fee, and enterprises from socialist countries. The relative importance of TNCs in this spectrum depends on how technology-intensive an industry is, how rapidly the technology is changing, and how far the commercialisation of technology needs organisational and marketing know-how (and export markets). Clearly, the more advanced and dynamic the technology, and the more difficult its commercialisation, the greater the hold of TNCs.

Second, within the sector of the market dominated by TNCs (which in fact comprises the main part of technology transfers in manufacturing), there are *several ways* in which technology can be bought: ranging from the outright purchase of a design or patent, via several intermediate arrangements requiring technical collaboration and /or equity participation by the TNC, to direct investment in a wholly-owned subsidiary.[48] The choice of form is strongly influenced by the policy of the host government, but it depends also upon the sophistication and secrecy of the technology, the monopoly power and corporate policy of the seller, the absorptive capacity of the buyer, and the need for continuous and close co-operation to keep abreast of latest developments.[49] A powerful TNC in a high-technology sector will usually demand – and get – high equity participation or complete ownership in a subsidiary; a TNC in a low-technology sector facing a capable recipient may well sell a licence or settle for a minority position.[50]

Third, the *price set* will depend greatly on the form of transfer chosen and the bargaining skills of the parties. A wholly-owned subsidiary may not pay royalties or technical fees separately, since the benefits of technology accrue, in any case, to the parent, in the form of dividends; if it does pay royalties, the purpose would be to minimise tax payments in home or host countries. As the percentage of equity held by the TNC declines, the price charged rises, so that the local partner pays proportionately for the benefit he receives in the form of higher profits; at the other end, in the case of an outright sale, the TNC gets all its returns from royalties unless it can realise profits from charging high prices for selling machinery, intermediates and services to accompany the technology.[51] The importance of *bargaining* can hardly be overstressed. The acceptable price to the seller may lie between the marginal cost of transferring the technology (which would be very low or nil unless the future threat to markets were also included) and the price which would compensate it for the alternative of direct investment (which would be higher, since the TNC would profit from a package of several 'advantages', not just superior technology) if this were feasible, or a price which would drive the buyer to other sources of technology. The price to the buyer, correspondingly, may lie between zero and the net (after allowance for profit) discounted stream of benefits it expects from the new technology, or the net cost of finding alternative sources of technology (including, at the extreme, the cost of developing the technology locally). The range within which bargaining can occur may be fairly wide, especially where the technology is scarce and the different parties have differing assessments of values and alternatives.

Fourth, the *conditions attached* to the transfer of technology, reflecting to some extent elements of the sale (such as future threat to export markets) which cannot be readily included in the price, can substantially modify the benefits that are transferred with the technology.[52] These conditions may restrict the freedom of the licensee to buy and sell commodities related to the technology transferred, and may sometimes stipulate how the benefits of future technological advances by the licensee are to be exploited, how the contracts are to be terminated and where disputes are to be arbitrated. A great deal of the current argument about 'international codes of conduct' for technology transfers revolves around the legitimacy of these restrictions, but there seems to be emerging agreement that they should be minimised and strictly regulated.

Finally, the institution of the *patent system*, as embodied in the Paris Convention and national laws, has come in for a great deal of criticism in recent years,[53] and it seems likely that, under the initiative of UNCTAD, many developing countries will modify their laws on patenting and tighten up their administration of them. The main arguments of the critics have been that, while the granting of patent protection by LDCs to TNCs which produce innovations mainly for the developed world does not offer any significant benefits, either in terms of stimulating R & D or in terms of promoting foreign capital and technology inflows, it does entail some significant costs: since the great majority of patents taken out are foreign and are not used for production within the country, the effect is to block the domestic market from cheaper imports and to prevent domestic firms from using the patented (or relevant competitive) technology. Furthermore, the sale of patented technology is often hemmed in by restrictive clauses and backed by the sale of intermediate and capital goods on which transfer pricing can be used.

It *is* widely accepted that patents granted by LDCs do not significantly stimulate innovation, and that the existence of patent protection does not, except indirectly as a sign of goodwill towards private enterprise, by itself attract foreign capital.[54] As for the costs, there is certainly *some* truth in the allegations noted above. However, we

TNCs as Oligopolists   69

should be careful in interpreting the evidence. As Penrose (1973) points out, a number of the abuses may be found in technology transfers even in the absence of patents: there may be good economic reason for not using patents for production in particular LDCs, so that 'non-use' is not really an abuse of patent protection; other abuses (such as restrictive clauses) may well accompany the sale of non-patented technology (this is noted for India in Chapter 7); and alternative imports or technology may simply not be available, so that it would be unfair to blame patents for the high price of technology.

There are other reasons for not putting too great an emphasis on the role of the patent system in the transfer of manufacturing technology as a whole.[55] With the growing importance of unpatented know-how in the application of new technology, with rising minimum scales of production and with the growing importance of marketing *vis a vis* technology in securing the market power of the leading oligopolistic firms, *patents have become relatively insignificant for a number of important transnational industries*, especially the engineering, electrical, food-processing and transport industries. The main sector for which they continue to be important, and which, consequently, is in the forefront of all battles to protect and extend patent protection, is fine chemicals—in particular, pharmaceuticals. Here the innovation is relatively easy to copy without recourse to unpatented know-how and there are sources of cheap imports from non-patent-observing countries such as Italy (though Italy seems to be in the process of adopting EEC patent laws). The bulk of evidence on patent 'abuse' thus comes from the drug industry and it is here that LDCs can gain most by opting out of seriously modifying the system (with a qualification about possible loss of exports). The evidence thus far is more indicative than definitive, and it may well be that patents remain significant for innovations by small firms in other sectors of developed countries; however, as far as LDCs are concerned, it seems fair to say that the main reforms should concentrate on minimising the costs of the patent system in a few selected sectors where patent-generated monopoly has significant independent effects.[56]

What, then, are the costs and benefits of buying technology from TNCs? The *benefits* arise from the fact that TNCs are the main producers, and in many cases the only ones, of technology in manufacturing; that direct investment by them may prove the fastest and most efficient way of getting access to the latest technology; and that they are able to provide the whole package which can enable the transfer and successful commercial application of technology. The *costs* arise because the rents TNCs can realise by virtue of their monopolistic power may be excessive in relation to the technological benefit received by the host LDC. In the case of a wholly-owned subsidiary, the host economy pays not just for the technology but also for the whole combination of 'advantages' which constitute the TNC's market power. In the case of a licensing agreement, the host economy may not pay for the whole package, but then it may not receive the latest technology, and/or it may, because of its weak bargaining position, pay too much (directly or indirectly) for the technology received, and suffer from restrictive practices. Moreover, because of administrative weaknesses, an LDC may 'over-import' technology, i.e. let several firms buy similar technology from different sources, or allow TNCs to enter sectors where domestic technology is quite adequate, and where the advantage of the foreign investors lies in their marketing superiority. We return to these problems in Part III of this book, where we discuss policy issues.

Appropriateness of Technology
The above discussion has assumed a situation where the technology supplied is 'appropriate' to the needs of the host economy; let us now assume that the cost is suitable and concentrate on the much more difficult problem of appropriateness.[57] It is here that we again come up squarely against problems of defining 'welfare'.

The question of appropriateness has two aspects: as regards the products which are made with the technology transferred, and as regards the use of factors of production. Let us start with the *appropriateness of products*. We saw in the last chapter that the rise of TNCs is, in many industries (clearly in consumption goods, but also in others whose product can be used only in certain consumer industries), crucially dependent upon their ability to produce a sophisticated, highly differentiated and heavily promoted, constantly changing and well-packaged range of commodities. This is not an attribute that is, in some sense, 'added on' to their technological or managerial advantages: it is the *very essence* of the oligopolistic competition and technological progress which are the basis of transnational expansion.

It is this tendency that is partly responsible for the excessive sophistication and over-elaboration of many products and processes and their inappropriateness for LDCs. True, part of the explanation must be found in the fact that these products have been developed in high-income, high-savings, high-investment-per-worker countries, where consumer demand is sophisticated and capital per worker is plentiful. But this is not the whole story. Companies in search of profits should not find it difficult to invent and develop cheap, mass-produced products, appropriate to the lower incomes of the masses in the poor countries. But if imitation is easy, as it is in the case of simple products and processes, and the advantage soon lost, the incentive is lacking. It is therefore in the nature of the TNC that its products and processes should be excessively sophisticated in relation to the needs of the LDCs and in relation to the chances of a favourable bargain.

What are the welfare implications of having TNC technology which has evolved in this oligopolistic structure? The conventional paradigm would tell us that – barring problems arising from income distribution, which it is for the government to resolve on 'political' grounds anyway – it is good because it 'fulfils preferences' and 'widens the range of choice'. We would argue, on the other hand, that the fulfilment of preferences expressed in the market is not the final criterion of welfare, certainly not in extremely poor countries, and that the use of scarce resources for the production of goods which are over-differentiated, over-packaged, over-promoted, over-specified and within the reach of only a small elite, or, if bought by the poor, at the expense of more essential products, is not conducive to 'national welfare'. This is not to say that all TNC technology is unnecessary in LDCs – clearly that would be absurd. But the free import of foreign capital and of the sort of technology many TNCs excel in would reproduce the pattern of the developed countries and would be undesirable. In other words, a definition of welfare based on meeting *basic social needs* would lead to a *fairly small proportion of TNC technology being regarded as beneficial*. We cannot provide *a priori* rules for judging what is, or is not, beneficial (the evaluation must vary according to the needs and circumstances of each country) but we can make a clear break from the logic which leads to the *a priori* conclusion that the free flow of investment and technology always tends to maximise welfare (unless government policy is wrong).

The issue of *appropriateness of factor use* is related to, but not identical with, the previous problem. It arises from the fact that TNCs transfer to LDCs technology which is excessively capital-intensive in relation to their factor endowments, and so cause: (a) an aggravation of employment problems; (b) a worsening of income inequalities; (c) distorting influences on technology used by other industrial firms; and (d) a bias in production towards the sort of high-income, sophisticated and differentiated products for which the technology has been developed. While the evidence on the precise extent of adaptability of modern technology and the actual adaptation of existing techniques to the labour-surplus situation of LDCs by foreign firms is far from complete, and to some extent conflicting,[58] the following conclusions may be drawn from the literature.

(a) As far as *adaptability* goes, much of modern 'high' technology cannot be changed to suit LDCs' endowments: the demands of precision, continuity, scale and complexity are too great. However, some 'low' technologies (for instance, in simple industries such as textiles) and 'peripheral' or 'ancillary' technology (for instance, transport or handling) are more adaptable. The scope of adaptability can be extended, but the cost, in terms of R & D and organisational requirements, may be quite high.

(b) As far as *adaptation* of foreign technology goes, the bulk of *basic or 'core' production technology* transferred by TNCs, both directly and by licensing, is not adapted in any significant way to low-wage conditions, though some *scaling down* of technology seems to be undertaken to adjust to smaller runs than would be appropriate in developed countries. There is evidence, however, that even a given 'core' technology can, with some adaptation, be used more intensively so as to yield higher output and/or employ more labour, and the peripheral or ancillary technologies are often adapted to more labour-intensive methods.

(c) As far as the *comparative performance* of TNCs and local or other foreign firms is concerned, the results are unclear and the method of comparison rather shaky.[59] There is not enough evidence to conclude that, compared with other firms, TNCs *as such* use more capital-intensive technology in relevant industries (though they may well be concentrated in capital-intensive industries); if anything, the evidence suggests that TNCs are *more able to adapt* given basic technologies to suit factor endowments in LDCs, especially when put under competitive pressure.

Several reasons have been advanced for the lack of any major modification of transferred technology.[60] Besides the obvious one that a range of technologies appropriate to LDCs simply does not exist in several high-technology industries, they are: inappropriate prices for labour and capital (relatively over-pricing the former); low labour productivity; lack of competition; scale requirements; skewed ('dependent') patterns of consumption favouring modern products; the danger of having technologies 'stolen' if they are too simple; lack of local adaptive R & D; the threat of labour problems; and the greater adaptability of capital-intensive plants to fluctuations in demand.[61]

TNCs as Oligopolists

In general it may be argued that, given the potentially high costs of adaptation, the reason why TNCs make so little effort to change their core technologies is precisely that *it is on the basis of the advantages of possessing these technologies that they have become transnational.* The very essence of profiting from international operations lies in the ability to apply a given package to different areas with as little costly adaptation as possible. In many important ways, therefore, the transmission of 'unsuitable' technology to produce 'inappropriate' products is the main driving force of transnational investment. And, as long as TNCs are increasingly the dominant form of production in the developed capitalist world, it is difficult to see how *any* mode of technology transfer can provide an 'appropriate' technology for LDCs that are (however imperfectly) integrated into the capitalist system. As Frances Stewart (1974) has argued, once the pattern of demand is given – and the pattern of industrial demand in LDCs is largely determined by the progress of technology in the developed world – the sort of technology needed is also defined. The advance of the capitalist mode of production in LDCs, if one likes to think in these terms, takes place via its most developed technological forms in the capitalist world; and, in so far as this is true, there is little scope for 'intermediate' technology in much of manufacturing industry (though the system *will* transfer the labour-intensive parts of complex technologies to low-wage areas). Thus, the 'costs' of TNC expansion, in this sense, are not due to inaction or intent on the part of TNCs and technology buyers; they are a reflection of a wider phenomenon.

Other Effects
The integration of LDCs into an international framework of technology transfer where there is negligible autonomous R & D conducted has far-reaching consequences for *science and research* in these countries.[62] The attitudes of subservient dependence it creates may inhibit the capacity to do even relatively minor adaptive research, or to put into industrial application processes which *have* been developed locally.[63] At a more basic level, it may bias the whole science and education policy towards over-theoretical or irrelevant curricula, and so prevent even preliminary moves towards technological 'independence'. Furthermore, the small R & D establishments which some TNCs maintain in industrially advanced LDCs may serve, among other purposes (mainly marketing innovation), as antennae to pick up and transmit abroad research done locally.[64]

Defenders of TNCs argue that notions of technological 'independence' are unrealistic and obsolete today, and that LDCs should not waste valuable resources in duplicating the enormous investments in R & D undertaken by developed countries. This is certainly valid for that part of complex, modern technology which is necessary for the well-being of LDCs,[65] but it leaves out two important points. First, as noted above, a large part of the actual process of innovation is not geared to meeting the social needs of LDCs, and, if it is to be replaced by more appropriate products and processes, may have to be replaced by indigenous technology. Second, unless one believes that countries which are at present underdeveloped will *never* make important technological contributions, there is a strong case for initiating policies which counter some of the more damaging effects of technological dependence. This is one field where 'learning by doing' and, more important, by making mistakes, is absolutely vital, and a passive acceptance of the *status quo* can prevent LDCs from ever undertaking the cost and effort of this process.

On the benefit side, the integration of LDCs into a worldwide structure of production by TNCs, with only that sort of technology being transferred to them which, given their labour and skill endowments, fits in with global cost-minimisation of these companies, may lead to an *expansion of exports* of components ('sourcing' exports, as distinct from the TNC-related exports mentioned in the following section) which would otherwise be available.[66] While there are clear advantages, in terms of foreign exchange, tax revenue and employment, that host countries can receive from 'sourcing' investments and technology, it has been noted that these benefits are not very large[67] and may be unstable over a long period. The ample opportunities that exist for transfer pricing, the use of relatively skilled labour, competition between LDCs for such investments, the 'footloose' nature of these facilities, the limited externalities that result, and their sensitivity to tax concessions, wage rates and labour conditions (they are extremely allergic to unionisation), may all reduce the final gain to the host economy.[68] On the other hand, some countries, such as Mexico,[69] that (for geographical and political reasons) have been successful in attracting a large quantity of sourcing investment, have managed to expand exports and employment on this basis for a long period (albeit at the cost of substantial foreign domination of industry, and of the types of distortion noted previously).

There are now signs that many LDCs are eager to break into this game, and it is likely that the next phase of TNC expansion into the Third World will have sourcing investment as a major component. If this occurs, TNCs may themselves act as pressure groups in favour of trade liberalisation (for the relevant manufactured products) in their developed home countries, as they have done in the past in the USA with respect to the tariff provisions for 'offshore' processing.[70] This may be counted as an important benefit to LDCs which share in this boom, to be offset against the costs of greater absorption into the TNC ambit.

MARKETING

While recent theories of direct foreign investment, trade in differentiated products and technological innovation have placed enormous emphasis on the role of marketing, there is a curious, and unfortunate, lack of empirical studies concerning the effects of the marketing practices of TNCs on less-developed host countries. The scattered evidence that exists[71] does, however, confirm that the advertising, promotion and product-differentiation practices of TNCs do serve to influence market demand strongly and create barriers to entry for smaller and less effective marketers. This is, of course, hardly a startling proposition. Few people doubt that 'advertising pays': business firms themselves attach crucial importance to marketing, and the literature on industrial organisation stresses the interrelationships of promotion, product differentiation, concentration, entry barriers and profitability.

In the context of TNC operations in LDCs, two additional points may be noted: first, there tends to be a strong prejudice in favour of foreign products and brand names, a legacy of the colonial experience and a hallmark of the socio-cultural 'dependence' that characterises most elites in developing capitalist countries; and, second, there is a considerable 'spill-over' effect of the promotional efforts of TNCs in the developed world, so that many leading brands are well known even before TNCs launch marketing drives in particular LDCs.[72] Both these factors serve to strengthen greatly the marketing power of foreign firms in LDCs.

There are two sorts of *benefits* that host LDCs may derive from the marketing skills of TNCs. First, as regards the *internal* marketing and distribution networks, the skills of foreign firms may bring about improvements in, for instance, storage and transport arrangements, leading, where this is relevant, to longer life, better quality, improved delivery and lower prices of products; closer co-ordination of supply and design with the particular specifications of products demanded, which is an important benefit in selling capital and intermediate goods to other manufacturers;[73] better information about products to consumers in general; and the provision of a wider range of products, with accompanying progress in methods of retailing, market research, and in realising the economies of large-scale distribution networks.

Second, on the *external* side, manufactured exports may be greatly increased by using the worldwide marketing outlets, skill and reputation of TNCs. The benefits to exports are, again, of two sorts: (a) the buying and retailing of relatively simple 'traditional' products which are labour-intensive in their production,[74] and (b) the marketing of sophisticated, product-differentiated, brand-name goods where heavy promotional expenditures are required.[75] (We do not include 'sourcing' exports of components – considered in the last section – here, since these are based not on the marketing skills involved in selling them abroad, but on the transfer of labour-intensive parts of complex technologies. However, many of the considerations noted for 'sourcing' also apply here.)

There are also *costs* of submitting to the powerful marketing practices of TNCs. The *internal* costs are of two types. First, there are some relatively less important ones to be set against the benefits noted above: the benefits of improved marketing may not show up in lower prices to the consumer (or may show up temporarily while local competition lasts) and may add only to the profits of the TNCs; franchising and exclusive-dealership practices by TNCs, often used for well-known branded products, may strengthen their market power but not help consumers; their advertising and promotion tactics may, similarly, increase the degree of monopoly, facilitate takeovers and add to marketing costs.

Second, at a more fundamental level, there are the social costs which arise from the product differentiation and proliferation, need and taste creation and elite consumption that are inherent in the marketing practices of TNCs.[76] Unless one held to the traditional paradigm so firmly that one regarded all market preferences as autonomous and social welfare as defined by their fulfilment, it would be very difficult to accept the obvious effects of TNCs in this regard as beneficial to poor societies where even the most essential human needs are not met. On the contrary, it can be persuasively argued that all such promotional practices which add to the unnecessary characteristics ('necessity' being defined by reference to essential human needs) of products and create a demand for them are *wasteful and undesirable* – the more so if they further raise barriers to the entry of domestic firms, lead to greater concentration and induce similar marketing expenditures by local firms.

TNCs as Oligopolists

As with most such arguments, there arises the problem of *attribution*. Is the 'blame' for excessive promotion to be attached only to TNCs, or is it inherent in the nature of modern capitalist enterprise? On the one hand, it is clear that local firms and importers advertise and differentiate. On the other, it is also clear that TNCs, being the most powerful and dynamic elements in the growth of private enterprise, in some sense lead and shape the pattern of oligopolistic marketing behaviour. Thus, while it would be illegitimate to 'blame' TNCs as such, it would also be illegitimate to regard them as passively reacting to forces beyond their control. How costs are attributed depends largely on how the 'alternative situation' is defined; no definitive answer is possible.

As far as *exports* are concerned, it is certainly true that TNCs possess advantages in marketing certain manufactures in world markets. Three qualifications may, however, be noted. First, these exports are still a very small proportion of manufactured exports for those LDCs, such as India, that are not strongly dominated by TNCs, and that have recently managed, by the efforts of domestic firms, to achieve impressive gains in these exports.[77] Second, comparative analyses of the actual export performances of foreign and domestic firms do not support a *general* presumption that the former are better at exporting than the latter are.[78] TNCs perform better than local firms in some countries and not in others; sufficient evidence does not yet exist to explain why, though the incidence of restrictive clauses as regards exports in technology transfers and the growing importance of global planning by TNCs[79] may provide part of the explanation. Third, TNCs appear to be particularly reluctant to invest heavily in export-oriented facilities in LDCs where there are signs of political hostility or instability, labour pressures, or strong moves towards local participation (though they are willing to take greater risks in import-substituting investments, which do not pose the same problems for long-term global planning). Thus, LDCs which desire large doses of export-oriented investments from abroad may well have to curtail union power and curb nationalist (or socialist) policies, and (often by political repression) toe a strict line which appeals to TNCs.

BARGAINING AND POLITICAL POWER

As far as *bargaining* is concerned, it is generally considered that TNCs, with their command over resources, markets and technology, their ability to manipulate prices and their possession of bargaining skills, are able to extract more concessions from host governments than small foreign or local firms can do. Three qualifying factors should be mentioned: first, bargaining strength would vary from industry to industry, depending upon the scarcity of the technology, the TNCs' hold upon markets, and the scale of investments required; second, it would depend upon the timing of the bargain, since the TNC would be in a weaker position once its investment had been made or once a competing TNC had entered the area; and, third, it would depend upon the political orientation of the government and the strength of the domestic industrialist class (for instance, TNCs with joint ventures with local firms may be in a stronger position in some countries than those with wholly-owned subsidiaries).

In general, however, it is probably true that TNCs have a bargaining position superior to that of other firms, and that their superiority is increasing with their growing economic power in the developed world. It is probably also true that LDC governments with vast, inefficient and corruptible administrations (and conflicting objectives to achieve), are not able to make the best use of the power they do have – though they seem to be 'learning by doing'. (These issues will be considered in Part III.) The bargaining power of TNCs may be regarded as a social *cost* to host LDCs if (a) it leads to the latter's share of net benefits being smaller than it would be with another form of investment; (b) it leads to a higher rate of protection and so raises domestic prices and distorts the industrial structure in general; (c) it is accompanied by unethical practices, such as bribery by the firms or by political pressures by home governments of TNCs (via aid, trade and military channels); (d) it pre-empts investment opportunities which would otherwise have been exploited by local firms; or (e) it causes the host government to adopt broad economic and political policies which it would not otherwise have chosen to adopt. On the other hand, it may be regarded as a *benefit* if: (a) it forces the government to adopt more rational economic policies (though the criteria of 'rationality' are open to debate); (b) it introduces more competition into protected markets; or (c) TNCs are less prone to unethical practices than local firms are.

As far as *political power* is concerned, the issues are far more controversial and ideological. There are two sorts of problems that arise. The first derives from the *theory of the state* which is explicitly or implicitly employed. Most economists of the conventional welfare school assume, as we noted previously, that the state is the 'repository of the national interest' and is able freely to pursue policies which it regards as being conducive to 'national welfare'.[80] In extreme cases the state is (implicitly) taken to be above all group or class interests, to perceive conflicts and inequities as they arise and to deal with them justly and wisely. A more realistic stand is taken by those who, while holding the state to be the ultimate repository of national interest, admit that it is open to pressures, intimidation or favouritism,[81] and so may, for some periods, pursue policies which promote sectional rather than 'social' interests. We then find a range of theories from those that treat states as predominantly elitist[82] to explicitly Marxist ones that treat political power essentially as a crystallisation of class forces concerned to maintain the capitalist system of property relations.[83] The relations between TNCs and political power in host countries can be, and evidently are, interpreted very differently according to the theory used: the differences lie not so much in the evidence as in the assumptions.

The second problem derives from the *welfare assessment* of the interaction of governments and TNCs. Even if everyone accepted that governments attempt variously to nationalise, restrict, control, regulate or encourage TNCs, and that TNCs, in their turn, attempt variously to bribe, threaten, persuade or co-operate with governments, there would be considerable disagreement about what the 'proper role' of governments is. The 'optimum' may range from a fully-integrated capitalist system with a minimum of ('economically irrational' or 'misguided') nationalist intervention by governments, to relatively autarkic LDCs pursuing 'genuine' development along socialist lines; similarly, the 'proper role' for government would then range from simply providing the basic legal, political and infrastructural framework, and appropriate macro-economic policies, for untrammelled free enterprise, to completely owning the means of production and tightly controlling TNCs when dealings with them become necessary for LDCs. The significance of what Myrdal termed the 'political element' in economic prescriptions can hardly be overstressed.

CONCLUDING NOTE

It should be obvious why we have not attempted to synthesise the preceding arguments to arrive at a net evaluation of the welfare effects of TNCs on LDCs. Instead of trying to pass 'objective' judgement on this extremely controversial issue, we have tried to show, with reference to the main 'advantages' which are claimed for TNCs, how little we actually know and why there may be valid grounds for dispute about the normative interpretation of what we do. It is far from evident what

TNCs actually do as regards transfer pricing, technology adaptation or political manoeuvring, for instance. It is even less evident what would happen to domestic enterprise, productivity, technology and consumption if TNCs were absent. But it is entirely open to question how we should normatively assess the contribution of their various possible effects, and whether we should attribute them to particular firms, to TNCs as a whole or to the workings of the capitalist system, of which TNCs are the leading force.

This chapter has concentrated on the actual (i.e. large and oligopolistic) character of TNCs, both for the sake of realism and in order to deal with issues which arouse most concern in the Third World today. In the next chapter we shall deal briefly with more traditional treatments of foreign investment, which are derived from 'pure' theory and do not specifically take the peculiarities of TNCs, as opposed to capital inflows in general, into account.

CHAPTER 4

Welfare of Host Countries: Foreign Investment as a 'General' Inflow of Capital

INTRODUCTION

The traditional method of analysing the effects of foreign investment has been to treat it as a 'general' inflow of capital from abroad, and to use the standard tools of neoclassical welfare, trade and growth theory to work out its impact on the host economy. By a 'general' inflow of capital we mean one or both of two things: first, in the narrow usage of 'pure' trade theory, direct investment inflows often are *not distinguished from other types of capital inflows* (loans, portfolio investments) from abroad, the whole being treated as foreign 'borrowing'; second, in a slightly broader sense, foreign direct investment *is* differentiated from other capital inflows—but by virtue of the fact that profits rather than interest are paid abroad, and that the risk element is rather different—but the *main distinguishing features of the large oligopolists* (which in fact dominate international investment) *are not taken into account in any significant way.*

Some economists who tackle TNCs on these theoretical lines do take note, in developing their 'rigorous' models, of 'externalities' and market 'distortions', but these are appended as minor qualifications to a theoretical approach based on competitive assumptions and, when quantitative procedures are adopted, are generally dropped altogether. We have chosen the reverse procedure, placing much greater emphasis on the peculiarly oligopolistic features of TNCs, and on qualitative but 'unrigorous' analysis, than on abstract theoretical models which serve both to obscure the most important aspects of the reality and to produce welfare conclusions which are largely implicit in the premises. The justification should be obvious.

It may, nevertheless, be useful to provide a brief review of the more traditional theoretical literature on the effects of foreign investment, partly for the sake of completeness and partly as an introduction to the next part of the book, where some of the traditional techniques have been adopted for our UNCTAD studies. We may divide the 'general' treatment of foreign investment into two parts (treated separately in the following two sections of this chapter). The first is the more theoretical and deals with its macro-economic effects; the second deals with foreign investment at the micro level and has been developed as a tool for specifically empirical, quantitative work.

MACRO-ECONOMIC APPROACHES

The usual convention in trade theory in analysing the effects of foreign capital inflow has been to treat it simply as a rise in foreign 'borrowing'. Given the existence of unemployment and shortage of savings or foreign exchange in LDCs, such 'borrowing' leads, if used productively and not offered protection, to a rise in output and income in the host country, with beneficial effects on the balance-of-payments, but indeterminate effects on the terms of trade (depending on whether the impact of increased output falls on import substitutes or exportables). It may be followed by a small loss in income owing to a worsening of the terms of trade when extra foreign exchange is required to service the foreign capital. The general conclusion is that the net final effect on GNP (and so 'social welfare') will be positive, unless there are significantly adverse effects owing to monopoly power, government interference with free market prices or externalities.

Given the definition of welfare adopted (see the second section of Chapter 3) and the usual assumption that an (undifferentiated) rise in 'borrowing' takes place under competitive conditions — monopolistic distortions are generally attributed to faulty policies of the host government and may be removed by letting in more foreign competition or by taking appropriate remedial action — a strong presumption is established that foreign investment is beneficial unless there is excessive protection or unless externalities are sufficiently unfavourable.[1] The sorts of externalities considered relevant — and we are moving into more realistic discussions of the type considered in the previous chapter—are effects on domestic savings and investment, competition, and technology, and are taken on the whole (with one major exception, noted below) to be more favourable than not to foreign investment: the latter acts as a catalyst to domestic savings, stimulates investment in related industries, introduces competition and provides access to new technology; but it may sometimes pre-empt investment opportunities, introduce oligopoly and provide inappropriate technology. However, as long as externalities remain indeterminate but not harmful, it follows that direct investment must be beneficial unless the government has done something wrong. This reasoning takes place at a relatively simple intuitive level; let us now come to more theoretical analyses.

Recent formal analysis of the effects of foreign investment in a neoclassical framework dates from an article by MacDougall,[2] who used a partial equilibrium, comparative-static approach to show how the gains from marginal increments in foreign investment (neglecting terms-of-trade effects) would be shared between labour and domestic and foreign capital. His main conclusions were that the host country would gain mainly through taxes on foreign profits, through economies of scale and through external economies, and that real wages would rise at the expense of profits because of the declining marginal productivity of capital (affecting both local and foreign capitalists). Subsequent developments in trade theory have extended MacDougall's welfare analysis in several ways, the main ones being as follows.

(a) The analysis of 'optimum' taxes and tariffs on capital inflows and commodity trade, by Kemp, Jones and others,[3] though this is not directly related to the benefits of foreign investment as such.

(b) Dynamic growth models with foreign investment and trade, using 'pure' trade theory, as with Pitchford (1970) and Brems (1970); or, for LDCs in particular, as with Bos et al. (1974) and Bacha (1974).

(c) Comparative-static general equilibrium models, as with Pearce and Rowan (1966) in their analysis of the effects of foreign investment on the capital-exporting country.

(d) Comparative-static trade theory, generally of the Heckscher–Ohlin variety, incorporating capital movements with varying assumptions about technology, skills, factor endowments, transfer costs, and so on, as with Baldwin (1970) and Chipman (1971).[4]

All these developments have taken place at a fairly high level of abstraction and have been based on models which greatly simplify reality, and in this context perhaps grossly oversimplify it. The empirical application of these models has been very limited, and, where it has been attempted,[5] has suffered from the vast number of simplifications made. While this does not in any way discredit the effort, great care has to be exercised in interpreting the results for the purposes of *normative* analysis. In particular, the unquestioning use of conventional welfare tools, and the neglect of non-marginal changes, externalities, oligopoly and various socio-political effects — all of which seriously affect the welfare of the host country, as we have tried to show — render this sort of exercise of limited use in understanding the real problems and concerns that arise in this field.

One particular controversy about the macro-economic effects of 'general' foreign investment in LDCs, concerning the detrimental effects of inflows of foreign capital on domestic savings and capital–output ratios, deserves mention. The debate has turned on whether foreign capital inflows reduce savings and raise capital intensity in recipient LDCs, so affecting growth and the pattern and productivity of investment.[6] The final statistical picture is still unclear, but, even if it were not, it is debatable whether, in view of the generality of the hypothesis and large number of other factors involved in the causal chain (from the inflow of capital, via the effect on savings, investment, and capital–output ratios, to growth of GNP), much faith could be put in the results of such computations. The latest and most comprehensive test seems to show, for what it is worth, that growth is highly significantly correlated with domestic savings and aid, but not with the *net inflows* of foreign investment; furthermore, the *stock* of foreign capital seems in general to exert a clear and significant negative impact on growth (though this relation does not hold for different regions taken separately).[7] The interpretation advanced is that foreign capital inflows generally help growth but that the structural effects of direct foreign investment tend to retard it. As this approach is open to the same sort of objection, for purposes of normative analysis, as the one which shows that foreign investment is desirable because it promotes growth in GNP, we shall not consider it at greater length here.

MICRO-ECONOMIC APPROACHES

Apart from the various detailed empirical studies of different aspects of foreign investment (referred to in previous chapters), which have used rather *ad hoc* methods for working out the costs and benefits to host economies, the main efforts at the micro level to evaluate the full welfare

Foreign Investment as 'General' Capital Inflow

implications of foreign investments have come as offshoots of recent developments in the field of social cost–benefit analysis for LDCs. The essential premise of such efforts has been that the application of 'shadow prices' approximating to a neoclassical free-trade welfare 'optimum' (but derived in practice from a partial rather than a full-blown general equilibrium model) can yield *quantifiable estimates of social welfare* from particular investments, *whether they are local or foreign*.[8] The technique of cost–benefit analysis most commonly used has been the so-called 'Little–Mirrlees method' of project evaluation, based on Little and Mirrlees (1969). Our UNCTAD studies (see Chapter 1, note 1) applied this method in evaluating the balance-of-payments and income effects of a sample of firms in several LDCs.[9]

Since we shall discuss later the methods, results and shortcomings of the Little–Mirrlees technique in its application to TNC investments, we need not go into them in detail here. However, some general observations may be useful to round off this part of the book. If one accepts the welfare paradigm on which all methods of social cost–benefit analysis are based, the Little–Mirrlees method provides *in principle* an extremely flexible tool for assessing social costs and benefits. *In practice*, however, the quantification procedure suffers from a number of limitations,[10] which lead (a) to exclude some of the most important aspects of the 'external' effects of TNC entry on tastes, technology, industrial structure and society generally; (b) to leave out of consideration 'alternative situations' which (as with undertaking the investment locally) cannot be adequately quantified because of the large number of unknowns and 'unknowables'; and (c) to deal inadequately with a number of 'world prices' which are determined arbitrarily by the TNC (transfer prices), for which 'free' markets do not exist (technology), or which are fixed only after a bargaining process.[11]

As we argued in the previous chapter, however, the more serious problems arise from the welfare premises themselves on which the valuation of 'social' welfare is based. The neoclassical paradigm finds it very difficult to accommodate judgements about taste-creation, appropriateness of products, product differentiation, and various 'non-economic' effects of TNCs, which many feel to be a necessary part of the welfare evaluation of TNCs. In such cases, it usually resorts to defining welfare with reference to 'objective functions' prescribed by the government, a solution itself fraught with difficulties if it is admitted that governments can be biased, elitist or subject to class domination.[12] We return, then, to the point made earlier that *judgements of welfare cannot be final or objective:* in the case of TNCs the subjective and ideological elements are particularly significant and should be clearly recognised as such.

Given all these limitations, is there any point in doing empirical work? We believe so — as long as the findings as regards the ultimate welfare of society are not overstressed. There is much to be learnt about the behavioural, financial, efficiency and other facets of TNC operations in LDCs, and any piece of information that helps fill the present gaps is greatly welcome. Furthermore, if the precise implications of the welfare basis of cost–benefit analysis are kept in mind, the use of shadow-pricing techniques does yield useful insights about certain effects of foreign investments, if not about the total impact on welfare. Let us, therefore, now turn to the empirical part of our study.

Part II
The Country Studies

CHAPTER 5

The Background to the Sample Firms and Government Policies

In this part of the book we shall deal with the methods used in, and the main findings of, empirical studies of the balance-of-payments and income effects of particular foreign investments in the manufacturing sectors of six less-developed countries: Jamaica, Kenya, India, Iran, Colombia and Malaysia. These studies were undertaken on behalf of the UNCTAD secretariat, and were conducted in three stages, covering two countries at a time, with the respective reports being circulated by UNCTAD over a period of three years (1970–3). The present chapter briefly describes the conduct of the research, the nature of the firms in the sample and the general policies pursued by the host governments with respect to foreign investment. Chapter 6 presents some data on the financial structure, profitability and performance of the sample firms. Chapter 7 gives the 'direct' balance-of-payments effects. The tools used to evaluate the 'total' balance-of-payments and 'social' income effects of these firms are discussed in Chapter 8, and the results obtained in Chapter 9. In Chapter 10 the merits and weaknesses of the approach used in trying to quantify the 'social' effects of foreign investments are assessed.

THE CONDUCT OF THE RESEARCH

While the research project was financed, and the terms of reference and choice of countries dictated, by UNCTAD, the team which did the field-work and processed the information obtained was based for the main part on Oxford University (at the Institute of Economics and Statistics and Queen Elizabeth House), and initially on the Institute of Development Studies at the University of Sussex. The field-work consisted of visits to the study countries by teams of two to five persons for periods ranging from five to twelve weeks, during which interviews were held with private firms, government officials, bankers and academics, and data were collected on foreign investment in general and on the operations of selected investments (both local and foreign-owned) in particular, for as long as possible. We made no attempt to gather information from the parent companies of foreign investors, relying on published and unpublished company accounts and official statistics in the host countries for our material; there are, as we shall discuss later, many shortcomings in this approach, but it is unlikely that we could have obtained more detailed or more reliable figures if we had spent time with the parent firms.

The research teams did not have any formal status either as UNCTAD representatives or as official guests. They were, in consequence, entirely dependent on the goodwill of the people interviewed, and the responsiveness of the latter varied greatly from country to country, reflecting the general environment for foreign enterprise, the requirements for publication of company accounts, the official attitudes to secrecy and disclosure, and the quality of statistics in general. In India, for instance, public limited companies were obliged to produce extremely detailed annual reports for their shareholders, and we needed only to supplement these with relatively easily obtained figures for imports and exports; it proved impossible, on the other hand, to obtain any unpublished information from official sources. In Colombia, by contrast, firms were not required to publish detailed accounts and were generally unwilling to provide us with any figures; but the government was extremely co-operative and gave us considerable assistance. In Iran and Malaysia neither the firms nor the governments were particularly helpful, while in Jamaica and Kenya both were reasonably co-operative but were not, having been visited in the pilot stage of the project, asked for very detailed statistics.

The quality and coverage of the data were, therefore, rather uneven, and this fault could not in the nature of things be remedied later. India and Colombia provided – if we bear in mind the limitations of company accounts – the best figures and the largest number of sample firms: we shall concentrate on these countries in our description of financial structure and performance, in the following chapter. The others provided sketchy information which had to be carefully supplemented and filled in later, in some cases by adjusting for obvious inconsistencies and in others by extrapolating from data provided by similar firms.

While we believe that there are no large errors which would invalidate the main findings of our studies regarding income and balance-of-payments effects, the figures are not precise enough to make it worthwhile to go into financing patterns in great detail for firms outside the Indian and Colombian samples. In any case, since these two countries provide almost 70 per cent of the total number of firms in our sample, the deficiency is perhaps not so very important.

The only country in which we could obtain, for the sample firms, information of a type that would not show up in accounts — restrictive clauses in contracts, negotiations with the government, transfer prices and the like — was Colombia.[1] For India there exists considerable published information on foreign investment in general, as well as on restrictive practices by foreign investors and technology sellers (all called 'foreign collaborators' in Indian terminology),[2] but we were unable to obtain any specific information on restrictive practices or transfer pricing by sample firms. For the other countries there were few general studies of the extent and value of foreign investments, and even less in terms of surveys of restrictive and similar practices by foreign firms;[3] in the event, our information on the practices of sample firms was limited to occasional hints dropped at interviews, which led us to believe that various restrictive practices were in use, though we could obtain little to substantiate our impressions.[4]

NATURE OF THE SAMPLE

The country samples comprise data on eleven firms in Jamaica, eight in Kenya, fifty-three in India, sixteen in Iran, fifty-six in Colombia and fifteen in Malaysia, making 159 in all. Table 5.1 gives a breakdown of the samples by the extent of foreign ownership. Of the total number of sample firms, 28 per cent are wholly foreign, 40 per cent are foreign majority-owned, 24 per cent are with foreign minority participation, and 8 per cent are wholly local. The first two categories, comprising 68 per cent of the total, are clearly foreign-controlled, and some firms in the third group (one in Kenya, five in Iran, thirteen in India, three in Colombia and two in Malaysia) may be, despite the minority foreign equity holding, bringing the probable total of foreign-controlled firms to 133 (84 per cent).[5] Though the choice of firms was not intended to represent the pattern of industrial ownership in these countries, the actual sample does in fact reflect the general picture, with wholly-foreign and foreign-majority firms predominating in all countries with the

TABLE 5.1
Extent of Foreign Equity Participation in Country Samples
(by number of firms)

Country	100%	50–99%	1–49%	Nil	Total
Jamaica	5	6	–	–	11
Kenya	5	2	1	–	8
India	–	21	24	8	53
Iran	–	9	6	1	16
Colombia	31	20	4	1	56
Malaysia	4	6	3	2	15
Total	45	64	38	12	159

exception of India, and to a lesser extent Iran. Most of the sample countries are now trying, in some cases by legislation, to promote local equity participation, but for the period covered by our study foreign ownership was predominant in manufacturing investments.

The average period for which we have data on sample firms is five to seven years, covering the period till 1968 for Jamaica and Kenya, till 1969 for India and Iran, and till 1970 for Colombia and Malaysia. The firms themselves had generally been in operation in these areas for longer periods, but were unwilling, or found it inconvenient, to provide us with data for their entire lives.

Table 5.2 shows the industrial composition of the samples. Chemicals and pharmaceuticals account for the bulk of the sample firms, followed by transport equipment, electrical products and machinery and metal products – a pattern which is fairly similar to that of US foreign manufacturing investment as described in Chapter 1. The origin of foreign capital in the 147 sample firms which have direct investment from abroad is given in Table 5.3, and its distribution conforms broadly with that of foreign investment in LDCs generally. The predominance of US firms in Colombia and of UK firms in India reflects very clearly the historical patterns of these major capital-exporting countries' investments (in Latin America and the Empire/Commonwealth respectively), while the more diverse patterns in the others reveal, in so far as one can say anything on the basis of such small samples, partly the influence of geography (Jamaica's position near the USA), partly the rise of mixed new investors in general, and partly, of course, history.

Of these 147 firms with foreign equity, some eighty-eight (60 per cent) can be classified as 'transnational' along lines suggested by Parker for

Background to Sample Firms and Government Policies 93

TABLE 5.2
Distribution of Sample Firms by Industry
(by number of firms)

	Jamaica	Kenya	India	Iran	Colombia	Malaysia	Total
Food products	3	2	—	—	—	—	5
Textiles, clothing	1	—	—	—	—	2	3
Pharmaceuticals	—	2	4	6	20	—	32
Other chemicals	4	—	7	2	16	3	32
Paper	1	1	—	—	3	—	5
Rubber	—	—	4	—	3	1	8
Electrical	—	—	10	2	7	2	21
Machinery and metal products	2	2	9	—	5	2	20
Transport equipment	—	—	19	3	2	2	26
Miscellaneous	—	1	—	3	—	3	7
Total	11	8	53	16	56	15	159

MPE2 firms (discussed in Chapter 1). Taking the country samples separately, nine firms in Jamaica, five in Kenya, twenty-one in India, eight in Iran, thirty-eight in Colombia and seven in Malaysia are affiliated to TNCs, as identified in lists compiled by Parker (1974) and the UN (1973). It may be of interest to note that of these eighty-eight firms, thirty-seven (42 per cent) are wholly foreign-owned, forty-two (48 per cent) are foreign majority-owned, six (7 per cent) are foreign minority-owned with the foreign share being over 25 per cent, and only three (3 per cent) are foreign minority-owned with the foreign share

TABLE 5.3
Source of Foreign Capital in Sample Firms
(by number of firms)

	Jamaica	Kenya	India	Iran	Colombia	Malaysia	Total
Mixed origin	—	3	1	1	8	3	16 (11%)
USA	4	1	7	5	36	1	54 (37%)
UK	5	3	24	2	2	5	41 (28%)
Canada	2	1	1	—	2	1	7 (5%)
West Germany	—	—	6	1	2	—	9 (6%)
Other European	—	—	6	4	5	—	15 (10%)
Other	—	—	—	2	—	3	5 (3%)
Total	11	8	45	15	55	13	147 (100%)

being smaller than 25 per cent. Thus, about 97 per cent of TNC affiliates are controlled from abroad, as compared with 76 per cent for the remaining firms with foreign capital. While the smallness of the sample prevents us from basing any firm generalisations on this, it is apparent that the observed pattern conforms with that mentioned in Chapter 2: i.e. TNCs prefer wholly- or majority-owned affiliates, but may, if pressed hard enough, be prepared to accept minority positions. Different TNCs may, of course, have different policies towards sharing control and the equity of their affiliates: of the nine TNCs in our sample on which we have data on more than one investment, three had wholly-owned subsidiaries in all their investments, five had different percentages of equity but kept majority ownership in all cases, and one had a majority position in one country and a minority one in another. The pattern seems completely unrelated to the industries to which these TNCs belong.

In the absence of a proper sampling framework we cannot determine how well our samples represent the total population of foreign investments in the relevant countries. We can, however, indicate roughly the size of our sample coverage in terms of sales and, where possible, net worth.

Jamaica. Sample firms accounted for 10–15 per cent of total manufacturing output in 1968; the eleven firms were among the thirty most important foreign investors in the country.

Kenya. Sample firms accounted for about 18 per cent of total manufacturing output and 8 per cent of numbers employed in manufacturing in 1966.

India. Sample firms accounted for 9 per cent of the sales of the 1044 leading manufacturing public limited companies (as covered by periodic Reserve Bank surveys) in 1966–7; the sample firms with foreign majority ownership accounted for 21 per cent of the sales of 290 foreign-controlled companies in the same period. The foreign net worth of sample firms came to 21 per cent of total foreign direct manufacturing investment in India in 1967, and to 37 per cent of such investment in the industries covered by the sample.

Iran. Sample firms accounted for 8 per cent of the output of industrial establishments in 1967, but this small coverage may be explained by the fact that the *Annual Survey of Industry* covers 161,000 'establishments', including tiny workshops. Foreign net worth in sample firms came to 36 per cent of gross foreign capital inflows in the appropriate industries during 1963–8 (the period of an upsurge in foreign manufacturing investment in Iran) and to 24 per cent of total gross inflows.

Colombia. Sales by sample firms accounted for 48 per cent of sales by 1024 manufacturing firms covered by the industrial census for 1968, while their foreign net worth came to 80 per cent of foreign capital inflows into the relevant industries, and to 60 per cent of foreign capital inflows into manufacturing generally, in 1917–66.

Malaysia. Sales by sample firms accounted for 5 per cent of the total sales by firms covered in the *Census of Manufacturing Industry* for West Malaysia in 1968; their foreign net worth came to 26 per cent of foreign investment in 152 'Pioneer Firms' in operation in 1969.

The sample was thus quite variable in terms of its coverage of manufacturing industry generally and of foreign investment in particular, but it seems fair to say that, for India, Iran, Colombia and Malaysia, on which the requisite information is available and where it seems to account for over 20 per cent of total foreign manufacturing investment, it is not too unrepresentative of foreign investment. For Colombia the coverage is exceptionally good, while for Jamaica and Kenya it may be on the poor side. The Iranian and Malaysian data are not very detailed or reliable, leaving us with India and Colombia as the best sources for more detailed examination.

THE ENVIRONMENT OF SAMPLE COUNTRIES FOR FOREIGN INVESTMENT

The attractiveness of a country to foreign investors is determined in part by its general economic and political conditions and in part by the policies pursued by its government. The former comprise (for manufacturing industry) such factors as the size and rate of growth of its market or, perhaps more appropriately, the richer sections of its market, the skill of its labour force, political and social stability and the prospects for future development. Table 5.4 presents some data on the recent economic background to the sample countries, including some data on the share of income accounted for by the top 20 per cent ('elite') of their populations. It reveals some conflicting tendencies. India, for instance, had the largest market in terms of total and elite GNP and so offered a tempting prospect to foreign investors; yet it had the lowest per capita income in 1971, and the lowest rate of growth over the period 1960–71. Jamaica, on the other hand, had the highest per capita income and a fairly good record of growth, but the size of its total markets, despite a high concentration at the top, was very small. Colombia suffered some of the handicaps of slow growth, despite a large elite market; but Iran offered reasonably sized markets, high per capita incomes and an outstanding performance in terms of growth. While exact figures are not available, it seems likely that Iran's rate of growth of foreign manufacturing investment is higher than that of any of the other countries in the sample, and perhaps one of the highest in the developing world as a whole.

TABLE 5.4
Economic Background to Sample Countries

	Jamaica	Kenya	India	Iran	Colombia	Malaysia
GNP (1971), US $ million	1370	1850	62,720	13,420	8180	4500
Per capita GNP (1971), US $	720	160	110	450	370	400
Percentage average annual growth per capita GNP (1960–71)	3·3	3·5	1·3	6·5	1·7	3·1
Percentage share of top 20 per cent in GNP (year)	62 (1958)	68 (1969)	52 (1964)	55 (1968)	61 (1970)	56 (1970)

Sources: IBRD (1973); and M. S. Ahluwalia, 'Income Inequality: Some Dimensions of the Problem', in Chenery et al. (1974).

All the sample countries offer more or less stable socio-political environments in which foreign enterprise can function. While their attitudes to foreign investment and their policies towards it differ considerably, none of them has a 'bad' record in terms of uncompensated expropriation, arbitrary discrimination or unpredictable changes in regulations with respect to foreign enterprise. Jamaica has been the most welcoming to foreign investors, India the most restrictive in controlling private enterprise (local and foreign), and Colombia the strictest in controlling foreign enterprise specifically. We cannot go into any detail on the specific policies of these countries, described at greater length in the original UNCTAD studies, but we may mention the most important features very briefly.

Investment incentives. All the sample countries offer fiscal incentives to various forms of industrial investment generally, with Jamaica and Malaysia the most generous and India and Colombia the least so; none of them offers specific inducements to foreign investors (except to export-oriented enterprises).

Taxes. India has the highest rates of taxation (over 50 per cent) while the others are moderate (35–45 per cent) and in line with the corporate taxation policies of developed countries.

Ownership. India limits foreign ownership to 40 per cent in most cases, while Iran and Malaysia generally limit it to 49 per cent. Colombia has adopted the 'fade-out' provisions of the Andean Pact[6] recently, though before 1967 it had almost no restrictions on foreign investments. Kenya and Jamaica favour joint ventures but do not require them formally; however, Leys reports that the Kenyan government has itself undertaken substantial equity participation in recent foreign investments.[7]

Entry. India has barred foreigners from investing in certain industries; it also has extensive screening and licensing provisions for prospective investors. Jamaica appears to have no screening; all the others have, but, except in the case of Colombia, where entry is becoming more tightly controlled, the procedures are inadequate and the effect minimal.

Protection against imports and promotion of exports. All the sample countries offer substantial protection to local and foreign enterprises by means of tariffs and import quotas (or prohibition). Most of them offer export subsidies and tariff drawbacks on imports used for producing exports, as well as more lenient terms all round for export-oriented firms.

Profits and technical payments. Colombia has limited profit remittances since 1967 to 14 per cent of foreign net worth, and has instituted strict regulation of technological contracts and payments. India has no limits on profit remittances but regulates royalties and limits their life and level. Malaysia has a policy of limiting royalty rates, while the others seem not to regulate profits or technological activity officially.

Transfer pricing. Colombia has recently instituted policies to check transfer prices charged by foreign firms; Kenya has employed a Swiss firm to do so, and India is trying to set up procedures to check them. The others seem not to have adopted any specific policies in this respect.

Patents. India and Colombia have recently revised their patent laws, in order to counter the most obvious abuses of patenting (in terms of creating import monopolies and permitting restrictive practices). The others appear wholly to conform to the international Paris Convention.[8]

Restrictive practices. Kenya, India and Colombia have adopted methods of checking and reducing the use of restrictive clauses of various types by foreign enterprises in formal contracts; the others have not.

Employment. All countries have requirements for local training and employment of nationals. Malaysia has a vigorous programme for the advancement of Malays, in order to achieve 'racial balance'.

In general, India and Colombia have the most comprehensive and centralised policies for evaluation and bargaining with respect to foreign investments; Kenya, Iran and Malaysia have some screening procedures but no tight central control, while Jamaica is (or has been) extremely liberal in its policies to foreign enterprises.

While India and Colombia seem to have many similarities in their policies in this field, there is one major difference: Indians are not, in their policy towards TNCs, particularly worried about 'foreign domination', and are much more concerned about the role of private enterprise as a whole, while Colombians want to promote private enterprise, but are concerned to keep it in national hands. Given the differences in foreign presence in these areas, this is quite understandable, as is the relative lack of concern with both problems in the other countries, which have much lower levels of industrialisation.

CHAPTER 6

An Analysis of the Sample Firms' Accounts

In this chapter we shall present a brief analysis of some aspects of the sample firms' performance, financing and profitability as shown by their annual balance sheets and profit-and-loss accounts. A great deal of attention is devoted in the literature to discussing how foreign investors finance their investments, how profitable transnationals are, and how they 'perform' in various respects *vis à vis* other firms in less-developed countries; yet there is still a large grey area of semi-ignorance on these matters, illuminated only by fragmentary and scattered evidence, from small samples or else provided on a highly aggregated basis by capital-exporting countries (mainly the USA).[1] Our data, pertaining mainly to the 109 sample firms from India and Colombia, can add only a little to the empirical knowledge that exists (the analysis of financial patterns, productivity and performance was not germane to the main purposes of our research and so was not pursued at great length), but it may none the less prove useful in clarifying some of the issues.

A few preliminary words of caution: declared company accounts are never a completely reliable guide to the real 'performance' of firms, and much less so when, as with TNCs, some of the important costs are determined directly by the firms concerned. These problems are discussed in other places in this book, and are mentioned here only to remind readers of the uncertain nature of even the best available data. Such uncertainty is not solely due to financial manipulations on the part of the TNCs. Some items, such as the amount of depreciation each year, are inherently subject to arbitrary valuation within a fairly wide range, while inflation, which normally is not taken into account, further distorts the value of fixed assets. Other items are liable to 'doctoring' by local, just as much as by foreign, enterprises. There are basic conceptual problems about how such items as 'capital employed' should be defined, to which convention provides a workable but not completely satisfactory answer.[2] And, finally, there are the difficulties of comparison and interpretation entailed in using data from a short period of the lives of firms of different ages facing different market conditions. There is little we can do to resolve such problems, which pervade all studies of this type, and should be clearly borne in mind.

The following discussion is divided into four parts: the first compares the sizes of different types of sample firms; the second deals with some selected measures of (non-profit) performance; the third describes their financial patterns; and the fourth analyses their profitability.

RELATIVE SIZE OF SAMPLE FIRMS

We start by comparing the sizes of the sample firms in the different countries. There are various measures – sales, value-added, capital, employment – which could be used to compare size. Each of them suffers from limitations when used on its own,[3] and ideally we should have some combination of several measures; however, our information on employment is rather scanty, and we have chosen, for reasons of convenience, to use sales and two measures of assets employed to indicate comparative sizes. We shall remark on their defects below.

Sales figures (net of resale of finished goods undertaken for parent companies) are taken for the year 1968 – 9 and converted into US dollars at the exchange rate ruling at the time. The main drawbacks of using sales for a comparison of size are, first, that sales in any particular year may be misleading, because of differing rates of capacity utilisation; and, second, that international comparisons may be affected by exchange-rate distortions. The second problem is of course inherent in any comparison of data for different countries, and cannot be remedied here. As for the first, we do not, unfortunately, have sufficiently detailed knowledge of rates of capacity utilisation for individual firms in a comparable year to supplement the comparison of sales data, so that we must assume (perhaps unjustifiably) that these were similar for different industries and countries.

Table 6.1 shows the average sales of the sample firms – overall, by country and classified into four groups (TNCs versus non-TNCs, and foreign versus locally-controlled firms). It also gives the firms' average number of years in operation. The figures show the following.

First, the average size of sales of sample firms of all types is extremely small by the standards of developed countries[4] (especially when it is noted that these firms are among the largest in the sample countries).

Analysis of Sample Firms' Accounts

TABLE 6.1
Average Size of Sample Firms' Sales, by Country, 1968–9
(US $ million)

Firms, etc.	Jamaica	Kenya	India	Iran	Colombia	Malaysia	Total sample
All firms	2·4	5·1	12·1	2·0	5·2	3·6	6·8
TNCs	2·5	4·2	21·3	1·4	6·2	5·2	8·8
Non-TNCs	1·6	6·5	5·7	2·7	3·0	2·2	4·2
Foreign-controlled	2·4	5·1	14·2	1·9	5·3	4·1	6·8
Locally controlled	–	–	8·5	3·3	2·2	0·4	6·9
Average no. of years in operation (as of 1969–70)	5	15	14	5	16	6	12

Clearly, the scale of operations of manufacturing enterprises in LDCs is determined more by the size of the domestic market than by any minimum requirements of technology or scale. This applies to TNCs as well as to other firms: in fact, with the exception of Iran, where the low age of firms may account for their smallness, the average size of TNC sales can be ranked in exactly the same order as the respective countries' GNPs (as shown in Table 5.4). A comparison of sales by industry, and of the sales of different subsidiaries of the few TNCs in the sample which have investments in two or more countries, serves to confirm that the size of the market is the most significant factor affecting size. This provides support for Knickerbocker's thesis that oligopolistic firms ignore scale considerations in their international moves to counter each other's actions, and is corroborated by Brash's findings for Australia.[5]

Second, TNCs are, on average, over twice the size of non-TNCs in all the country samples with the exception of Kenya and Iran. These two samples, with twenty-four out of the total of 159 firms, are affected by the apparently fortuitous inclusion of a few exceptionally large non-TNCs, and should not be taken to modify seriously the general finding for the other countries. This finding is certainly what we would expect from the general considerations, discussed in Chapter 2, concerning the causes and determinants of TNC growth, and from the background information on the size and importance of TNCs in the world economy, as discussed in Chapter 1.[6]

Third, the difference between foreign- and locally controlled firms follows more or less the same pattern as does that between TNCs and non-TNCs, but the size of some locally-controlled firms in India brings their average for the sample to just above the average for foreign-controlled firms. The data for the Indian sample show that foreign-controlled firms are much larger than others in electrical and chemical industries, about equal in transport, and smaller in machinery and metal products.

Let us now compare the size of *total assets* and *net fixed capital* employed (both taken directly from the balance sheets) for the Indian and Colombian samples (the data for the other samples are not reliable enough to warrant such comparisons). We have already indicated some of the problems inherent in comparing figures for assets. The value of net *fixed* assets as stated in balance sheets is not a very good indicator of their real value, because the depreciation methods used by accountants are based on arbitrary conventions and are dictated by the tax system, and because inflation is not fully (if at all) taken into account. The value of *current* assets may vary from firm to firm according to peculiar and changing market conditions, which would affect the value and quantity of stocks and the volume of trade credit receivable. It may, on the other hand, be argued that such distortions do not greatly affect a comparison of firms of roughly similar ages operating in roughly similar conditions, and that an averaging process may cancel out most individual aberrations. Bearing these qualifications in mind, let us see what the figures, presented in Table 6.2, tell us.

The general picture conveyed by the asset figures strongly confirms that conveyed by the sales figures: on average, the Indian firms are substantially larger than the Colombian ones; TNCs are larger than non-TNCs in both countries, with the size difference between them being more marked in India than in Colombia, and in the size of total, as opposed to net fixed, assets; and foreign-controlled firms in India (the Colombian comparison being meaningless because of the small number of locally controlled firms) are larger than locally controlled ones, but with the difference being markedly less than in the case of TNCs and non-TNCs.[7]

In terms of total assets, TNCs are 2·6 times larger than non-TNCs in India, as compared to 1·8 times in Colombia, and in terms of net fixed assets these ratios are 2·1 and 1·2 respectively. An analysis-of-variance test for the TNC and non-TNC groups in the two countries shows that the groupings, on both total- and fixed-asset criteria, are meaningful at a 5 per cent level *only* for India. For the Colombian sample, the higher average figures for TNCs do not in fact represent a statistically significant larger size for TNCs as a group. As for foreign and locally

TABLE 6.2.
Total Assets and Net Fixed Capital Employed by Indian and Colombian Sample Firms, 1968–9
(US $ million)

Firms		India				Colombia			
		Total assets		Net fixed assets		Total assets		Net fixed assets	
		Total value	Average per firm	Total value	Average per firm	Total value	Average per firm	Total value	Average per firm
All firms	(109)	502·1 (53)	9·5	160·8	3·0	319·5 (56)	5·7	72·9	1·3
TNCs	(59)	316·6 (21)	15·1	95·2	4·5	252·1 (38)	6·6	52·2	1·4
Non-TNCs	(50)	185·5 (32)	5·8	65·6	2·1	67·4 (18)	3·7	20·7	1·2
Foreign-controlled	(87)	340·2 (33)	10·3	113·4	3·4	314·3 (54)	5·8	72·2	1·3
Locally controlled	(22)	161·9 (20)	8·1	47·4	2·4	5·2 (2)	2·6	0·7	0·4

Note: Figures in parentheses denote the number of firms in each category.

controlled firms, the Indian figures fail to show any significance in the size of the two groups for either measure of size. It is impossible for us to say whether the lack of significant difference in size in Colombia reflects a bias in the sample or a general fact about the operations of TNCs relative to other firms in the Colombian economy. If the latter *is* the case, however, the explanation may be (a) that TNC subsidiaries are younger than other firms, or (b) that they are not very different from other firms in a small and industrially relatively backward economy, but that the differences between them in terms of size begin to show only in a larger market and a more developed economic environment. In view of the fact that TNC subsidiaries are in fact of the same age as other firms in the Colombian sample, and somewhat older than the Indian firms, the first explanation is not very apt. The second seems more convincing on *a priori* grounds; certainly, despite the low per capita income in India, the market for industrial goods is much larger there, and the industrial sector more advanced, than in Colombia.

A recent study for Australia by Parry[8] may be seen to provide support for the second explanation, that TNCs are *relatively larger* than non-TNCs in richer and industrially more developed markets. Parry finds, on comparing 223 TNC subsidiaries to 757 non-TNC subsidiaries – all in the Australian manufacturing sector in 1971 – that on average the former are 3·7 times larger than the latter. The average size of assets of the TNCs (US $30·7 million), as well as of the other firms (US $8·3 million), is greater than for the Indian sample, but the difference is much larger for TNCs than for non-TNCs. There are some problems in interpreting Parry's figures – for instance, he does not test for dispersion or significance of groupings – but the general impression gained is clear enough.[9] If we went on to look at the figures on TNCs in the leading capitalist countries, we should obtain much stronger confirmation of the tendency for TNCs to be relatively larger than other firms in more developed markets. We may, therefore, be justified in accepting the market-development explanation of the relative sizes of TNCs and non-TNCs.

A comparison of the Tables 6.1 and 6.2 shows that, while the sample for Colombia as a whole has a higher asset-to-sales ratio than that for India, TNCs in both countries seem to fare better in terms of sales to assets employed than do non-TNCs. This has implications for efficiency and capital intensity that we shall consider in more detail in the next section.

Analysis of Sample Firms' Accounts 105

SELECTED MEASURES OF PERFORMANCE

In this section we shall deal with a few measures of 'performance' that are not covered in the sections on financing, profitability and balance-of-payments effects. The measures are grouped as follows: (a) use of capital, (b) capital and labour productivity,[10] and (c) advertising. We do not discuss R & D expenditures for the sample firms, as these are nil in the vast majority of cases, and are so small where they do exist that they do not merit attention.[11] In the absence of comprehensive data on employment by the sample firms, we shall have to make do with more indirect measures of factor intensity and productivity. Needless to say, these measures suffer from various drawbacks, of a conceptual nature (as regards, say, the definition of capital, labour, productivity, and so on), and as concerns the meaningfulness of the data. We remarked earlier on the inherent defects of balance-sheet data for capital items; when these are related to such current items as sales, value-added, and wage and salary payments (termed 'personnel payments' for short), there are further problems of interpretation, (for example, owing to different rates of capacity utilisation). In addition, the period chosen (1968–9) may be untypical (India, for instance, was suffering from depression) and may be too brief for long-term tendencies to show themselves. As we do not have the resources to attempt to remedy these defects, we must accept the limitations imposed on the results and interpret them accordingly.

Use of Capital

In recent years, a great deal has been written about the choice of technology in developing countries. In the particular context of the study of TNCs, the debate has, as we saw in Chapter 3, revolved around the introduction of 'inappropriate' (excessively capital-intensive) techniques by foreign firms and the way in which this distorts the choice of technology in the developing economies.[12] Our data cannot even begin to deal with the fundamental problem of whether technologies used by sample firms have been 'inappropriate' with reference to some social optimum, since we are unable to postulate what such an optimum would be in concrete terms or whether suitable alternative technologies are actually available in the conditions with which we are dealing. Nor can we investigate whether and to what extent TNCs have adapted techniques developed in rich countries to conditions in poor ones.[13] What we can do, briefly and imperfectly, is to throw some light on the relative use of capital by various types of sample firms. We can, in the absence of employment figures, utilise two indicators of capital use: capital employed in relation to net sales (the capital–output ratio) and wage-salary payments in relation to capital employed (capital intensity). The first is not really an indicator of the choice of technology in terms of the capital–labour combination, and is affected by efficiency of capital use (which we come to later), but it still provides a guide to one important and interesting aspect of the foreign-investment question. The second is a more direct measure of the capital–labour ratio,[14] and so is relevant to the whole vexed question of the choice of technique by different sorts of firms.

Capital–output ratios. We use four measures of capital: two of total 'capital employed', one of total assets and one of net fixed assets. The two measures of 'capital employed' (which stands for net fixed plus net current assets) reflect two different definitions of net current assets: (a) the conventional one of total current assets minus short-term loans and 'other' current liabilities, and (b) an alternative one of total current assets minus 'other' current liabilities only. The point at issue is whether short-term loans (of under one year) which are 'rolled over' from period to period – as most bank loans and other short-term credits are – should not really be counted as long-term loans. If they *are*, and so are included under long-term liabilities, the value of net current assets, and so of total capital employed, is correspondingly increased. Both measures have their merits, and we leave it to the reader to pick the one that he finds most appropriate.

Table 6.3 shows the various ratios of capital and assets to sales for the Indian and Colombian samples, grouped by industry and transnationality. The main features of the table are as follows.

First, overall and for each industry, except machinery and metal products, the ratio of total assets to sales is higher for the Colombian than for the Indian sample; the same – with the exceptions here being pharmaceuticals, transport and rubber in definition (a) – is true for both measures of capital employed. In terms of net fixed assets, however, the position seems to be reversed, with the Colombian sample employing less capital per unit of sales in every industry except for 'other chemicals'.[15] The difference is owing to the relative holdings of net current assets: the Colombian firms tend to hold much higher stocks and other current assets, as a percentage of sales, than do the Indian firms. For the two samples taken together, for instance, stocks come to 37 per cent, and other current assets to 48 per cent, of sales, as compared to 30 and 24 per cent respectively for India;[16] and it is this which to a large

TABLE 6.3
Net Capital Employed, Total Assets and Net Fixed Assets as Percentages of Sales for Indian and Colombian Sample Firms, 1968–9

Industry, etc.	India				Colombia			
	Net Capital employed		Total assets	Net fixed assets	Net capital employed		Total assets	Net fixed assets
	(a)	(b)			(a)	(b)		
Pharmaceuticals	49·7	59·8	86·5	27·3	39·0	88·0	100·2	13·5
Other chemicals	32·0	36·9	44·8	14·6	69·1	109·6	119·2	42·9
Paper	–	–	–	–	65·3	88·4	96·3	53·7
Rubber	37·9	48·0	63·8	18·2	32·6	61·4	74·0	15·3
Electrical	60·7	89·2	118·2	40·0	82·5	140·3	160·9	14·2
Machinery	56·0	89·0	125·5	40·6	56·9	99·6	107·9	17·7
Transport	42·4	55·8	85·7	27·5	9·3	108·1	109·2	9·1
Total	43·4	58·9	78·5	25·1	51·7	99·2	110·2	25·1
TNCs	41·6	53·4	70·9	21·1	45·7	95·3	106·4	22·0
Non-TNCs	47·9	72·5	96·9	34·5	78·2	114·5	126·7	38·8

Note: For the number of firms in each industry, see Table 5.2.

extent accounts for the Colombian firms' higher capital–output ratios. It is not clear why this occurs: perhaps inflation creates an incentive to hold larger current stocks; perhaps more credit per unit of sales has to be given to buyers in Colombia than to those in India; or perhaps it is simply a difference in business practice. In addition, for the Colombian firms there is a far greater divergence between the two definitions of capital employed than there is for the Indian firms: this is due to the Colombian firms' much larger reliance on short-term loans (see next section).

Second, in both the samples TNCs have lower capital–output ratios, by every measure, than non-TNCs have. Furthermore, a comparison of the Indian sample TNCs with larger samples for Indian manufacturing firms again shows that the former perform much better in this respect.[17] This may have one or both of two explanations: first, that TNCs are as efficient as other firms in terms of utilising their capital for production, but are using techniques which need less capital per unit of output; and, second, that they use the same techniques but are more efficient in achieving higher turnovers on capital employed ('efficiency' in this sense may also be taken to include economies of scale). We do not have the kind of information necessary to test the first hypothesis, though below we do examine the choice of technique in the context of capital–labour ratios. As for the second hypothesis, in the next sub-section we test for measures of capital productivity (value-added in relation to capital).

Whatever the explanation, it seems at first sight that the ratios reveal that the TNCs' performance is superior to that of the other firms. To some extent, the possibility that TNCs use *less capital* per unit of output than other firms do is contrary to expectation: TNCs do undoubtedly lead in the use of new technology, which usually (but not always) tends to increase the use of capital per unit of output; they are relatively predominant in capital-intensive industries; and there is little evidence that they adapt their 'core' technologies to different environments. The possibility that they are *more efficient* seems more plausible: they are clearly larger than non-TNCs in the sample and so may reap economies of scale, and their management techniques may be superior to those of other firms. However, before we read too much into the data, we must note the following.

First, there is little *a priori* reason to expect that, regardless of the *industrial* composition of the sample and of the particular characteristics of the *managements* of the different firms in question, TNCs *as such* would be significantly different from non-TNCs in matters of technology and efficiency. The discussion below shows that industrial groupings are in fact very important in efficiency and choice of technology.

Second, analysis-of-variance tests for the TNC–non-TNC groupings for India and Colombia for all the above ratios *fail to show any significance* even at a 10 per cent level. While the treatment means all confirm the general result that TNCs have lower capital–output ratios by the various measures, the only test which shows a faint significance (at the 15 per cent level) is for Indian and Colombian samples combined, for the ratio of fixed assets to sales. The average findings shown in the table cannot, therefore, support any strong statement about TNCs and non-TNCs in general.

Capital–labour ratios. The relationship between capital and labour is shown here by total personnel payments (PPs) as percentages of total assets and fixed assets for the Indian and Colombian samples (Table 6.4). The ratios may be taken to be an indirect measure of capital intensity, with lower PPs per unit of assets (especially fixed assets) denoting higher capital–labour ratios. In general, the fixed-asset data confirm the impression conveyed by Table 6.3 that, except in the case of the 'other-chemical' group, Colombian firms are less capital-intensive than Indian firms are, while the total-asset data show that they use generally more current assets than Indian firms do. The comparison of

TABLE 6.4
Personnel Payments as Percentages of Total and Fixed Assets for Indian and Colombian Samples 1968–9

Industry, etc.	India		Colombia	
	Total assets	Fixed assets	Total assets	Fixed assets
Pharmaceuticals	22·8	70·8	15·1	112·6
Other chemicals	21·3	75·9	10·1	28·0
Paper	–	–	8·0	14·4
Rubber	18·0	62·8	20·4	94·1
Electrical	10·8	31·1	10·1	113·8
Machinery	12·7	36·0	15·2	92·6
Transport	12·3	37·8	5·3	64·5
Total	14·9	47·5	11·7	51·2
TNCs	16·3	54·1	12·1	58·4
Non-TNCs	12·5	35·1	10·2	33·2

TNCs and non-TNCs is more interesting: as with the capital–output measures, both ratios seem to indicate that PPs per unit of assets employed are higher, and capital intensity is lower, for TNCs than for other firms. Similarly, a comparison with the larger samples for Indian manufacturing shows that sample TNCs have higher PPs–assets ratios than other firms have.[18] In other words, TNCs appear to be generally *less capital-intensive*, in *both meanings of the term* (i.e. capital–output and capital–labour ratios), than non-TNCs are.[19] This assumes that wage rates for given kinds of labour in the two groups are similar. We have little information on this, but impressionistic evidence suggests that TNCs may pay somewhat higher rates; whether or not this is sufficient to account for the overall difference, we cannot say.

As with capital–output ratios, however, statistical tests for the various ratios show that the TNC–non-TNC grouping is *not meaningful*, either for the Indian or Colombian sample as a whole, or for individual industries within these samples.[20] Of the other tests attempted, the following show interesting results.

First, groupings by *industry* (regardless of transnationality) show significance for both country samples. For the Indian sample, with the fifty-three firms grouped into four industries, we find that the PPs–fixed-assets ratio is significant at the 10 per cent level, with the groups, in descending order (ascending capital intensity), being: machinery and rubber; chemicals and pharmaceuticals; electrical; and transport. Similarly, for the Colombian sample we find the following (again in order) significant at the 5 per cent level: pharmaceuticals; paper and rubber; electricals, machinery and transport; and other chemicals. The PPs–total-assets ratio is significant for Colombia at the 5 per cent level, but not for India, with the ordering being very similar to the one just given.

Second, for both samples, groupings by *size* of firm (measured by total assets) are barely significant at the 15 per cent level. A division of the firms into three size groups seems to show that the largest firms are the least, and the medium-sized firms the most, capital-intensive (in terms of fixed assets), with the smallest firms coming between them. The order is the same for both countries.

What can we conclude about capital intensity from this brief analysis? Transnationality as such does not have a discernible impact; the industrial category is very significant; and size does not seem to have a strong and uniform inflence – though the largest firms seem to be the least, and the medium-sized firms the most, capital-intensive.[21] The nature of the data precludes a much more refined analysis, but it would appear justifiable to conclude that, *once industrial influences are accounted for, there is no decisive difference in technology arising from the origin of the investment.* This is hardly surprising, as local firms are almost entirely dependent on foreign technology; furthermore, this general statement is not incompatible with the possibility that TNCs have more *modern* technology, or influence local firms' *choice* of technology (neither of which propositions can be tested by the data at hand).

Capital and Labour Productivity
Table 6.5 shows various ratios involving value-added (VA):[22]
(a) VA – total assets and (b) VA – fixed assets may be seen as measures

TABLE 6.5
Various Value-Added Ratios for Indian and Colombian Samples

Ratio	India			Colombia		
	Total	TNCs	Non-TNCs	Total	TNCs	Non-TNCs
(a) VA – total assets	32·8	35·8	27·4	29·4	27·3	37·0
(b) VA – fixed assets	102·4	119·0	77·0	128·9	132·0	120·9
(c) VA – sales	32·4	29·1	46·9	25·7	25·4	26·6
(d) VA – PPs	251·2	226·2	364·9	219·8	219·8	219·3

of capital productivity; (c) VA–sales may be seen as a rough indicator of the income-creating capacities of firms, a very general measure of efficiency; and (d) VA–PPs may be taken as a measure of labour productivity, though it may, under certain assumptions, also be a measure of capital intensity. The figures for each industry are not shown in the table, but they are mentioned relative to the results of statistical tests.

As far as capital productivity is concerned, the VA–total-assets ratios seem to show conflicting tendencies for the two countries, but the VA–fixed-assets ratios seem to support the tendencies suggested by the capital–output ratios above (that TNCs are more efficient and use less capital than non-TNCs). As before, however, analysis-of-variance tests for the TNC–non-TNC, and for the foreign- and locally controlled, groupings fail to show the slightest significance, either for country samples or for individual industries within those samples, again confirming that this particular factor does not have an independent effect on productivity.

The industrial groupings as such (regardless of multinationality) are, however, significant at the 5 per cent level for both countries, and the results show up far better for fixed- than for total-assets ratios. The rankings for VA–fixed assets are as follows: for India, the highest capital productivity is shown by (1) chemicals and pharmaceuticals, followed by (2) machinery and rubber, (3) transport and (4) electricals; for Colombia, the highest is (1) pharmaceuticals, followed by (2) electricals, machinery and transport, (3) paper and rubber, and (4) other chemicals. Size groupings are entirely insignificant for Colombia, but for India they are significant at the 10 per cent level, with the largest firms having the highest VA–fixed-assets ratios, followed by the smallest and the medium-sized firms. The general conclusions regarding the capital-intensity measures may therefore be taken to apply here as well.

In both countries, non-TNCs seem to perform better than TNCs for VA–sales. The grouping fails to show statistical significance for India, but for Colombia the non-TNC groups are significantly different from the TNC groups at the 5 per cent level. However, all other groupings turn out to be insignificant, casting doubt on the validity of the single finding for Colombia.

The labour-productivity ratios do not show any significant difference between TNCs and non-TNCs for India, but, surprisingly, do so at the 10 per cent level for Colombia, showing TNCs to have a *lower* ratio than non-TNCs (against the ranking shown by the weighted averages). This may well, in view of the lack of significance of other, similar ratios, be an accidental result. The industrial groupings are significant for both countries at the 10 per cent level, with rankings being as follows. India: (1) transport, (2) chemicals and pharmaceuticals, (3) machinery and rubber, and (4) electricals. Colombia: (1) paper and rubber, (2) electricals, machinery and transport, (3) other chemicals, and (4) pharmaceuticals.

If we discount the two apparently accidental significant results for Colombia for the TNC–non-TNC groupings, we are left with very little solid evidence, on the basis of the measures tried, on the relative performances of these groupings. *The figures certainly do not support any strong allegations for or against TNCs as regards their relative efficiency, choice of technique or productivity.* Industrial factors seem to be quite important, but several others which we have not tested may equally well be significant in determining these patterns. If we had had better data and greater resources, we might have been able to uncover some interesting tendencies; but, as matters are, we must remain agnostic.

Advertising

The only country for which we possess comprehensive detailed information on advertising expenditures is Colombia, where the sample as a whole spent on this item 6·6 per cent of its value of sales. The industry with the highest advertising expenditure was pharmaceuticals (11·3 per cent), followed by machinery and metal products (10·0), transport (8·8) and paper (6·8); other industries spent between 3 and 6 per cent on advertising. While individual firms' advertising expenditures showed some variation around the relevant industry means this was especially so in machinery and metal products, an analysis-of-variance test shows, at a 5 per cent level, that the pharmaceutical firms as a group spent significantly more than other industries. This is entirely expected, of course, since the drug industry in developed countries is known to indulge in heavy promotion expenditures, and derives much of its market power from this source.[23]

What is perhaps a trifle unexpected is the finding that TNCs as a group do not appear to spend a significantly larger proportion of their sales on advertising than non-TNCs do. The treatment means of the two groups come to 7·8 and 5·5, which is as we should expect, but the grouping is not significant even at the 10 per cent level. There is thus little empirical support, from an admittedly limited sample, for the proposition that TNCs are prone to spend much more on promotion than are other firms; the differences that exist are, if anything, due to industrial characteristics. This does not, however, disprove that TNCs may be *better at marketing* (conceived broadly to include product differentiation, packaging as well as advertising) than other firms and may devote a larger part of their total expenditure to this; neither does it take account of the strong possibility that TNC subsidiaries benefit from the widespread *promotional efforts of the parent systems* and so may not themselves need to spend more than local competitors. It is also possible that TNCs influence the level of advertising by local firms, but we have no means of checking this.

FINANCING PATTERNS

The financial structure of the Indian and Colombian sample firms, as shown by their balance sheets for 1968–9, is summarised in Table 6.6. The usual net asset and liability figures do not show the total accumulated sources and uses of funds, since depreciation allowances are deducted when stating net fixed asset values, and, as they do not add to the net worth of the firms, are not counted as a liability. Such allowances do, however, constitute a substantial source of funds for reinvestment, and in Table 6.6 we have included them both under 'sources' and under 'uses'. We should note that this is not the normal type of 'sources and uses' table, showing the *flows of funds* over a specified period: it is more a description of total *accumulated* sources and uses from the start of a firm's life. The main difference between the two lies in the fact that the normal flow table also shows distributed profits on both sides of the flow.[24]

The balance sheets from which the table has been derived contain a wealth of information which could be analysed to discover liquidity ratios, financial practices, and so on; though dear to the heart of the financial analyst, however, such analysis would not add greatly to our understanding of the *economic* functioning of the firms. We have confined ourselves to a few selected features, given in the ratios of Table 6.7, which seem most relevant to the financial problems debated in the TNC literature. What do these ratios show?

First, the two country samples as such reveal interesting differences. The level of *internal* financing (equity plus depreciation and reinvested profits) as a whole is higher for India than for Colombia, while the level of total *foreign* financing (foreign share of internal financing plus foreign loans) is much lower. This reflects in part the high average level of foreign shareholding in Colombia (87 per cent for the sample as a whole) as compared to India (51 per cent), and in part the much greater use of

TABLE 6.6
Financial Structure of Indian and Colombian Sample Firms, 1968–9
(percentages)

	India					Colombia		
	Total	Foreign-controlled	Locally controlled	TNCs	Non-TNCs	Total	TNCs	Non-TNCs
Sources (total 100%)								
Equity	23·3	25·5	18·1	24·9	20·5	18·4	15·7	28·2
Foreign	11·8	15·5	2·6	14·8	6·1	16·0	14·7	20·7
Local	11·5	10·0	15·5	10·1	14·4	2·4	1·0	7·5
Reserves	14·5	15·1	13·3	14·7	14·3	13·3	14·2	10·4
Depreciation	15·9	18·3	10·0	16·9	14·1	12·4	11·8	14·8
Long-term loans	8·6	5·4	16·7	7·6	10·0	9·4	8·1	14·0
Foreign	1·3	1·4	1·0	1·7	0·6	3·9	2·6	8·6
Local	7·3	4·0	15·7	5·9	9·4	5·5	5·5	5·4
Short-term loans	16·6	15·4	19·7	14·9	20·7	37·8	41·1	25·8
Foreign	0·7	0·8	0·7	0·8	0·6	16·7	19·6	6·5
Local banks	13·4	12·0	17·0	11·5	17·1	9·8	10·5	7·6
Other local	2·5	2·6	2·0	1·6	3·0	11·3	11·0	11·7
Other current liabilities	21·0	20·4	22·2	20·5	20·4	8·7	9·2	6·9

TABLE 6.6 (cont'd)

| | \multicolumn{4}{c|}{India} | \multicolumn{3}{c}{Colombia} |
	Total	Foreign-controlled	Locally controlled	TNCs	Non-TNCs	Total	TNCs	Non-TNCs
Uses (total 100%)								
Gross fixed assets	42·3	45·5	34·3	41·2	44·3	32·4	30·1	40·9
Depreciation	15·9	18·3	10·0	16·9	14·1	12·4	11·8	14·8
Net fixed assets	26·9	27·2	24·3	24·3	30·2	20·0	18·3	26·1
Stocks	31·9	31·7	32·4	32·1	31·5	29·5	30·0	27·3
Loans and advances	18·4	20·5	16·2	20·8	13·9	38·1	39·9	31·8
Cash and other	7·4	6·1	17·1	5·9	10·3			

Note: Group averages are weighted by assets/liabilities of the constituent firms.

TABLE 6.7
Selected Financial Ratios for Indian and Colombian Samples, 1968-9

Ratio	India					Colombia		
	Total	Foreign-controlled	Locally controlled	TNCs	Non-TNCs	Total	TNCs	Non-TNCs
(1) Total internal finance	53.7	58.9	41.4	56.5	48.9	44.1	41.7	53.4
(2) Total foreign finance	29.1	38.0	7.6	36.0	15.8	59.0	61.2	54.3
(3) Direct foreign inflow	13.8	17.7	4.3	17.3	7.3	36.6	36.9	35.8
(4) Direct foreign long-term inflow	13.1	16.9	3.6	16.5	6.7	19.9	17.3	29.3
(5) Total gearing	66.7	51.2	115.9	56.8	88.2	148.9	164.5	103.1
(6) Long-term gearing	22.8	13.3	53.2	19.2	28.7	29.7	27.1	36.3
(7) Foreign borrowing	7.9	10.6	4.7	11.1	3.9	43.6	45.1	37.9
(8) Bank borrowing	57.7	63.1	49.0	57.5	58.0	36.8	38.9	30.8
(9) Local financing	96.0	95.9	97.1	93.3	97.7	63.1	62.1	67.8
(10) Interest	9.4	10.1	8.4	9.0	9.8	4.3	4.0	5.5
(11) Leverage	2.2	2.0	2.9	2.1	2.7	2.8	3.0	2.2

Explanation of the ratios

(1) Equity+reserves+depreciation/total sources.
(2) Foreign equity+foreign share of reserves (i.e. total reserves × foreign equity share)+foreign share of depreciation+foreign long- and short-term loans/total sources.
(3) Foreign equity+foreign long- and short-term loans/total sources.
(4) Foreign equity+foreign long-term loans/total sources.
(5) Total long- and short-term loans/equity+reserves.*
(6) Long-term loans/equity+reserves.*
(7) Foreign long- and short-term loans/total long- and short-term loans.
(8) Bank loans/local long- and short-term loans.
(9) Local long- and short-term loans + other current liabilities/total non-internal financing (i.e. excluding sources in ratio 1).
(10) Total interest/total loans (excluding 'other current' liabilities).
(11) Ratio of net total assets to equity+reserves.*

* Equity and reserve figures for Colombia are taken directly from balance sheets and not adjusted for devaluation of the peso. Adjusted figures, in constant US dollars, are about 1·6 times higher than nominal ones for the sample as a whole.

foreign short-term borrowing in the former. These short-term loans may be a form of flexible credit financing for imports by the parent companies[25] of Colombian TNC affiliates – a presumption supported by the fact that TNCs have three times the level of short-term foreign credit used by, and less internal financing than, other foreign firms – or they may be suppliers' credits from unrelated firms; we do not know. The lower reliance of Indian firms on foreign short-term loans is a reflection of their lesser dependence on intermediate imports (see the next chapter), the main item financed by such loans; this also accounts for the Indian firms having a relatively larger proportion of local short-term financing (36·9 per cent of total sources from short-term local loans and other current liabilities, as compared to 29·8 per cent for Colombia).

The Colombian sample has higher 'gearing' (total loans in relation to net worth) and 'leverage' (total assets in relation to net worth) than the Indian.[26] This may be accounted for by two factors. First, the value of net worth as stated in balance sheets is not adjusted for devaluation of the Colombian peso, and the real dollar value of net worth, as calculated by the Central Bank, is about 1·6 times higher. Thus, real gearing has been overstated for Colombia. Second, the interest payment of Colombian firms as a percentage of their total loans seems much lower than that of Indian ones, and this may have been an inducement to higher borrowing. In fact, since the consumer price index in Colombia rose by over 13 per cent during this year, it appears that the firms were paying a *negative* real rate of some 9 per cent per annum, while in India prices rose by about 2 per cent, so that the real rate of interest was about 7 per cent. A comparison with figures published by the IMF (*International Financial Statistics*) shows that the 'commercial discount rate' in Colombia was 8 per cent, which is negative in real terms but still much higher than the sample balance-sheet figures. It may be that some items classified as 'other current liabilities' in Colombia should really be classified as 'short-term loans', but even this would not explain the entire difference. It may also be that the foreign credits provided by parent firms to Colombian subsidiaries were charged a low rate of interest; however, in the absence of detailed data on the exact amounts paid for different loans, we cannot explain the situation any better. What is worth noting is that there is no evidence that foreign subsidiaries are, despite occasional suggestions that it is profitable for them to do so,[27] using interest payments as a channel for remitting profits from Colombia. Interest charges are, if anything, being used to subsidise local affiliates, while clandestine profit remissions seem to be handled via the transfer pricing of intermediate imports.

Second, a comparison of the sample with US TNC data shows two things.

(a) The flow of funds from abroad during 1966–70 for US TNCs (defined broadly to include *all* firms with foreign investments) as a percentage of total sources, excluding profits set aside for remittance, was much lower (14 per cent) than for either the Indian (29 per cent) or the Colombian (59 per cent) samples, while borrowing from sources external to the firm was about the same for US TNCs (39 per cent) as for India (40 per cent) but much higher than for Colombia (16 per cent).[28]

(b) The leverage of US manufacturing subsidiaries in 1970 (2·4) was slightly higher than that of the Indian sample as a whole (2·2) and of foreign-controlled firms and TNCs in India (2·0), but lower than that of locally controlled Indian firms (2·9) and of Colombian firms as a whole (2·8) and TNCs in particular (3·0). The US affiliates, as well as sample firms generally, had much greater leverage than the parent US companies (1·9) and all US manufacturing companies (2·0) in that year.[29]

Third, a comparison of TNCs and non-TNCs in the samples shows that foreign financing (ratio 2) by TNCs is higher than that by non-TNCs in both countries. Analysis-of-variance tests show that this difference is significant at a 5 per cent level in India and at a 10 per cent level in Colombia. The financing pattern is a result of the fact that TNCs have higher levels of foreign shareholding and foreign borrowing than do non-TNCs, and probably reflects a greater desire on their part to retain control as well as to keep close financial links with the parent companies. Their gearing ratios vary between the two countries: in India TNCs seem to be less highly geared than non-TNCs, while in Colombia they seem to be much more so. The averages are, however, misleading, since statistical tests *fail to show the slightest significance* for the groupings in either sample. Furthermore, there is no significant difference between TNCs and others as regards bank borrowing or interest as a percentage of total loans. *Our data do not, therefore, provide any support for a general statement that TNCs gear themselves more highly than other firms or that they obtain greater access to commercial bank credit.* Whether or not TNCs are regarded as more creditworthy than other firms – and it seems very probable that they are – it appears that they tend to *conform to local patterns of financing or regulation* rather than use their superior borrowing strength to procure an extraordinary degree of external financing. We cannot, however, say whether the data for 1968–9 are typical in this respect, or, more important, whether the borrowing practices of the sample firms are governed by local convention and by government policy or are freely determined by company policy.

Fourth, the *size* of sample firms does not seem to have a significant effect on their financing patterns.[30] The F values for the size groupings are slightly better than for the TNC–non-TNC groupings, but they are not good enough to merit any generalisation. Thus, size, like transnationality, does not seem to offer firms noticeable advantages in terms of gearing, bank borrowing or interest payments.

Fifth, a comparison of local and foreign firms for the Indian sample shows that, while local firms have much higher gearing (especially in long-term loans) and leverage than foreign firms, the latter have a higher reliance on bank borrowing as a percentage of total loans. The difference between the two groups with regard to bank borrowing is not, however, statistically significant, and the *unweighted* average of bank borrowing for foreign-controlled firms is in fact somewhat lower than is that for locally controlled firms. A glance at RBI data for 330 foreign-controlled and 1072 large and medium-sized manufacturing firms shows trends in reverse of that shown by our sample. In 1968–9, the foreign-controlled group had higher total gearing (116·6 per cent) and much higher long-term gearing (40·1 per cent) than the large and medium group (100·9 and 22·2 per cent respectively), while the former's leverage (2·3) was lower than the latter's (2·5, or 2·7 if the 330 are excluded from the larger group). In terms of bank borrowing as a percentage of total loans, the 330 foreign firms had a lower ratio (34 per cent) than the 1072 firms (56 per cent).

The different tendencies shown by these ratios and the contrasting patterns observed for the two sample countries all seem to support the previous conclusion that the *origin of control or ownership does not exercise a separate influence on financial patterns.*

PROFITABILITY[31]

In this section we consider the earning, taxation and disposition of the sample firms' *declared* profits – defined as including or excluding technical payments. The reader's attention is drawn to the various reservations that the previous chapters and the next one express with regard to the usefulness of declared figures as indicators of true profitability; but here we simply take the balance-sheet figures at face value. Table 6.8 shows

Analysis of Sample Firms' Accounts

various ratios for the Indian and Colombian samples for 1968–9. We start by describing the main features of the table and then discuss the results of our attempts to explain by some statistical tests the profitability of the firms.

TABLE 6.8
Profitability of Indian and Colombian Sample Firms, 1968–9
(percentages)

Ratio	India					Colombia		
	Total	Foreign-controlled	Locally controlled	TNCs	Non-TNCs	Total	TNCs	Non-TNCs
(1)	13·5	13·6	13·3	13·5	13·6	18·3	15·4	31·3
(2)	20·2	20·4	19·7	23·3	13·9	24·1	23·5	25·7
(3)	13·0	13·8	10·5	14·0	10·6	18·2*	15·9*	24·4*
(4)	16·3	16·1	17·8	16·2	16·7	24·6*	22·7*	29·2*
(5)	35·0	38·4	26·2	45·3	19·2	49·7	48·8	51·9
(6)	47·7	46·5	52·3	49·5	41·5	41·9	46·8	30·2
(7)	47·0	43·8	60·6	42·6	60·7	37·3	34·8	41·9
(8)	9·9	9·6	11·0	9·8	10·2	11·7	10·5	13·9
(9)	4·6	5·0	3·5	4·9	3·9	7·3	5·7	14·0
(10)	5·9	6·8	3·6	6·9	4·0	6·6	5·4	11·0

Explanation of ratios

(1) Profits *before* tax + depreciation + interest/net sales (excluding resale of finished products).
(2) Net profits *before* tax/capital employed (definition (a) in the sub-section on capital–output ratios in the second section of this chapter).
(3) Net profits *after* tax/net worth (i.e. equity/reserves).
(4) Net foreign profits *after* tax + technical payments *after* tax / foreign net worth (i.e. foreign equity + foreign share of reserves).
(5) Net profits *before* tax/net fixed assets.
(6) Tax on profits/net profits *before* tax.
(7) Dividends/net profits *after* tax.
(8) Dividends/equity capital.
(9) Net profits *after* tax/sales.
(10) Net profits *after* tax/total assets.

* See Table 6.7, note on net worth.

The Colombian sample as a whole is more profitable than the Indian by every measure employed. It also distributes a smaller proportion of its after-tax profits in the form of dividends than the Indian does. Because tax rates are higher in India than in Colombia, the Colombian firms pay an effectively lower proportion of their pre-tax profits to the government than the Indian firms do. Data for US TNCs in general for 1970 show that net profits after tax as a percentage of total assets came to 5·1 per cent for the majority-owned subsidiaries, 4·5 per cent for the US parents and 3·5 per cent for all US manufacturing corporations.[32] The geographical breakdown of these data shows profitability to be 5·4 per cent in the developed and 4·0 per cent in the less-developed countries, with Colombia and India doing better than average with 6·9 and 7·8 per cent respectively. A comparison with ratio (10) of the table shows a reasonably close similarity with the sample firms, though Colombian TNCs show up somewhat worse than the US sample. In terms of effective tax rates, parent US manufacturing TNCs paid 38 per cent, and US corporations as a whole 43 per cent, in 1970, while their affiliates paid 40 per cent overall, 41 per cent in developed and 35 per cent in developing areas. These affiliates paid 37 per cent in Colombia and 57 per cent in India, so contributing more than the sample in India but less in Colombia.[33]

In the Indian sample, foreign-controlled firms are as a whole more profitable than locally controlled ones, and TNCs are more profitable than non-TNCs, in terms of after-tax returns on net worth.[34] The inclusion of technical payments in foreign profitability considerably raises the return to foreign net worth and makes foreign capital in locally controlled firms and non-TNCs more remunerative; but the weighted average figures are misleading. For instance, ratio (3) for TNCs and non-TNCs conceals the fact that the average *unweighted* profitability of the latter is higher, and the grouping is slightly significant at 15 per cent; this relationship is repeated for ratio (4), with total earnings of foreign capital in non-TNCs being significantly higher (at 10 per cent) than those of TNCs. Similarly, the apparent finding that TNCs pay less in dividends, and so reinvest more, is refuted by an analysis-of-variance test, which shows that on average they pay some 10 per cent more of after-tax profits than do non-TNCs (significant at 15 per cent). As regards the Colombian sample, non-TNCs appear to be more profitable than TNCs, but analysis-of-variance tests fail to show the slightest significance for the groupings in terms either of profitability or of pay-out ratios. Furthermore, a test for the two groups for all the six countries taken together (given the rather shaky data for the other samples) again fails to show any significant difference in their profitability.[35]

These preliminary tests imply that *profitability, like so many other indicators of performance, is not greatly influenced simply by the origin of control or transnationality of the investment.* Monopoly power, protection, managerial efficiency, financing patterns, age, and so on, also may play a part. Indeed, in view of the complex of factors that in principle may affect declared profitability (including the incentives *not* to declare actual profits), it is hardly surprising that transnationality as such fails to show a strong effect. Transnationality or foreign control certainly can be taken as a rough *index* of some factors, especially monopoly power and efficiency, but it is a very rough index and clearly not sufficient to exclude the influence of other forces.

It was impossible for us to do a full-scale investigation into the determinants of profitability.[36] However, we tested the effect of a number of variables – age, entry barriers, advertising and financing patterns – on several measures of profitability. The results are presented below.

One may expect that the *age* of firms in operation will exercise some influence on their profitability: very new firms can be expected to show losses or low profits.[37] We divided the Indian and Colombian sample firms into three age groups – less than five years old, five to ten years old, and over ten years old – but, on the basis of analysis-of-variance tests, found no significant differences in their profitability, and decided not to pursue the matter further.

We obtain similarly negative results with regard to industrial organisation. A great deal of the literature on market performance and industrial structure stresses the role of *entry barriers* and *concentration* in determining profitability.[38] We were unable to test for these factors properly, since we did not have the requisite information to enable us to calculate indices of entry barriers. We proceeded, therefore, by dividing sample firms into three groups, according to high, medium and low entry barriers, based on evidence from *developed* countries, and with regard to profitability found no significant differences between them for the Indian and Colombian samples. Our procedure was rather crude, but the results may be taken to suggest that *market barriers of a different sort may be in operation in developing countries*. Perhaps R & D and minimum-size requirements play a smaller role than protection, promotion or sequence of market entry, but we could not (except as regards advertising) test for such hypotheses empirically.

Table 6.9 sets out the more significant results of the various regressions carried out to test the effects of advertising and financial structure on profitability; a quantity of results of less statistical value are not reported. Since preliminary analysis-of-variance tests had failed to show any significant difference between the TNC and non-TNC groupings, the regressions were run on the samples as wholes and by industry groups rather than by transnationality. The main findings are as follows.

First, *promotional* expenditures (variables x_1, x_2 and x_3) seem to have a significant and positive effect on profitability in both samples, taking advertising and commissions jointly for India and separately for Colombia.[39] The impact appears to be higher in Colombia (especially for

Investment, TNCs and Developing Countries

TABLE 6.9
Selected Regression Results Explaining Profitability of Indian and Colombian Samples

	Dependent variable	Country/industry (I = India; C = Colombia)	Period	n	X_1	X_2	X_3
1.	P_1	I/various	1968–9	53			
2.	P_2	I/various	1968–9	53			
3.	P_2	I/various	1968–9	53			
4.	P_2	I/various	1968–9	45			2·16 (2·17)
5.	P_2	I/various	1968–9	45			2·33 (2·23)
6.	P_3	I/various	1968–9	45			1·51 (2·64)
7.	P_2	I/various	1968–9	53			
8.	P_1	I/transport	1968–9	19			
9.	P_1	I/electrical	1968–9	10			
10.	P_1	I/machinery	1968–9	8			
11.	P_1	I/chemical	1968–9	10			
12.	P_3	C/various	1968–9	56			
13.	P_1	C/various	1968–9	56			
14.	P_5	C/various	1966–70	53	0·84 (2·9)	0·43 (1·6)	
15.	P_5	C/pharmaceutical	1966–70	18	0·97 (1·52)	1·16 (2·50)	
16.	P_5	C/chemical	1966–70	15	−0·29 (0·6)	−0·31 (1·78)	
17.	P_5	C/metal	1966–70	10	1·01 (2·5)	0·15 (0·41)	
18.	P_1	C/pharmaceutical	1968–9	20			
19.	P_1	C/misc. excl. chemical and pharmaceutical	1968–9	20			
20.	P_1	C/misc. excl. chemical and pharmaceutical	1968–9	20			
21.	P_1	C/chemical	1968–9	16			
22.	P_1	C/chemical	1968–9	16			
23.	P_4	C/various	1966–70	53			
24.	P_4	C/various	1966–70	53			

X_4	X_5	X_6	X_7	X_8	X_9	X_{10}	X_{11}	Constant	R^2
					−0·089 (3·59)			16·74 (5·60)	0·21†
							0·210 (2·21)	5·06 (1·17)	0·09†
		+0·153 (2·05)						6·34 (1·55)	0·08†
								8·23 (2·48)	0·09†
0·27 (3·46)								0·45 (0·09)	0·24†
0·06 (1·40)								11·35 (4·14)	0·14†
	−0·09 (3·65)				0·05 (0·69)	−0·04 (0·83)		17·56 (4·89)	0·22†
0·38 (5·10)								4·44 (1·23)	0·60†
	−0·10 (4·58)				0·17 (0·67)	−0·14 (1·09)		12·67 (1·25)	0·79†
					1·78 (1·73)			−22·02 (1·09)	0·33†
							−0·08 (2·38)	18·95 (1·55)	0·41†
						−0·03 (1·89)		15·90 (7·40)	0·06*
							−0·01 (2·85)	11·95 (4·48)	0·13†
								−0·02	0·21
								−0·07	0·40
								0·01	0·26
								−0·04	0·47
			−0·33 (1·65)	0·07 (1·94)				12·82 (2·36)	0·24*
	0·07 (2·14)							14·66 (6·00)	0·20†
				0·05 (2·20)				14·70 (6·09)	0·21†
	−0·15 (1·98)							16·15 (4·26)	0·22†
				−0·08 (1·59)	0·05 (2·11)	−0·05 (0·58)		14·15 (4·10)	0·51†
	0·71 (5·92)		−0·14 (0·53)			0·04 (0·98)		0·09	0·46
	0·73 (6·43)							0·06	n.a.

TABLE 6.9 (cont'd)
Selected Regression Results Explaining Profitability of Indian and Colombian Samples

	Dependent variable	Country/industry (I = India; C = Colombia)	Period	n	X_1	X_2	X_3
25.	P_4	C/various	1966–70	53			
26	P_4	C/various	1966–70	53			
27.	P_4	C/various	1966–70	53			
28.	P_4	C/pharmaceutical	1966–70	18			
29.	P_4	C/pharmaceutical	1966–70	18			
30.	P_4	C/pharmaceutical	1966–70	18			
31.	P_4	C/pharmaceutical	1966–70	18			

Notes

Dependent variables
P_1 Net profits after tax/net worth.
P_2 Net profits before tax/net capital employed.
P_3 Gross profits before tax/sales.
P_4 Profits after tax + technical payments/'adjusted' net worth (for the Colombian sample, equity and reserves adjusted to constant US dollars for devaluation of the peso).
P_5 Net pre-tax profits + technical payments + interest/total liabilities.

Independent variables
X_1 Advertising/sales.
X_2 Commissions on sales/sales.
X_3 Advertising + commission/sales.

X_4	X_5	X_6	X_7	X_8	X_9	X_{10}	X_{11}	Constant	R^2
						0·14 (2·59)		0·11	n.a.
					0·06 (2·13)			0·11	n.a.
			0·09 (3·80)					0·08	n.a.
	0·33 (0·96)	0·20 (0·40)				0·57 (1·49)		0·10	0·81
	0·83 (8·70)							0·50	n.a.
						0·88 (7·76)		0·10	n.a.
					1·00 (6·91)			−0·04	n.a.

X_4 Bank loans/total loans.
X_5 Bank loans/net worth.
X_6 Bank loans/total liabilities.
X_7 Foreign long-term loans/net worth.
X_8 Foreign short-term loans/net worth.
X_9 Domestic short-term loans (excluding bank loans)/net worth.
X_{10} Domestic long-term loans/net worth.
X_{11} Total loans/net worth.

* Significant at the 10 per cent level in a two-tailed test.
† Significant at the 5 per cent level in a two-tailed test.
† Significant at the 2 per cent level in a two-tailed test.

Number of observations is shown in column headed n.
Figures in parentheses denote the t statistic.

The results for Colombia for the years 1966–70 are taken from Chudnovsky (1973). The levels of significance for these are not indicated; nor are the r^2 for the simple regressions.

the pharmaceutical industry) than for assorted industrial groups in India, though the t statistic shows up better in the latter.

Second, *bank borrowing* (variables x_4, x_5 and x_6) appears, in the Indian sample as a whole, to have a positive but not very large effect on profits when tried on its own (regression 3) or in conjunction with advertising (5 and 6), but a negative one when tried with other gearing ratios (7). This may have been owing to multicollinearity between the bank and other domestic borrowing variables; if so, there may be no independent causal connection between bank borrowing and profits. In Colombia, on the other hand, this variable exercises a large influence both on its own (24) and in conjunction with other borrowing (23). A similar configuration is found for the Colombian pharmaceutical industry, but the t statistic for the multiple regression (28) is insignificant and reduces the explanatory force of bank borrowing when tested together with other forms of borrowing. In the transport industry in India, bank borrowing seems to have a positive effect on profitability on its own, while in electricals it has a negative effect in conjunction with other measures of borrowing.

Third, *foreign borrowing* (x_7 and x_8) does not show up as a significant variable in any of the Indian regressions, while in Colombia as a whole foreign long-term borrowing has a faint, and statistically insignificant, negative effect (23), and short-term borrowing a faint, but significant, positive effect (27). This faint but positive effect was also found for twenty firms from the miscellaneous collection of non-chemical and pharmaceutical industries in Colombia.

Fourth, of *other domestic borrowing* (x_9 and x_{10}), short-term borrowing has a significant and negative effect in India (1) on its own, but a positive and statistically insignificant one in conjunction with other variables (7), while in Colombia it appears to have a faintly positive effect (26). Long-term borrowing shows up as statistically significant once for Colombia (26), in which case it has a small positive effect.

Finally, *total gearing* (x_{11}) has a positive effect on the profitability of the Indian sample (2) and a marginally negative one on the Colombian sample (13). This variable has a negative effect on the profitability of ten chemical firms in India (11).

In sum, therefore, *promotional expenditures appear to have a positive causal relationship with profits, while financing patterns have a more ambiguous relationship with it*. In Colombia bank borrowing appears to have a positive and independent effect, especially in pharmaceuticals, while in India overall gearing seems to be positively related to profitability but the effect of bank borrowing is unclear. Bearing in mind, first, the problems with profit data and the brief period covered by the

Analysis of Sample Firms' Accounts

tests, and, second, the fact that gearing and advertising are, in principle, only two of a multitude of influences on profitability, these results are hardly surprising. The extent of gearing will certainly affect profits: as long as the interest rate is lower than the rate of profit (including undeclared profits) and the ratio of loans to net worth is not deemed to be too high (and so too risky), it clearly pays an enterprise to increase its external borrowing. Gearing ratios can, however, explain inter-firm *variations* in profitability only to the extent that other determinants of profitability, on the demand as well as the cost side, are not significantly different; and there seems little justification for assuming this. We cannot, therefore, expect such statistical exercises to produce very strong results. In any case, since advertising and gearing ratios are not seen to differ greatly between TNCs and non-TNCs, or between foreign- and locally controlled firms, we are compelled to refrain from generalisations about their relative performances as governed by their ability to advertise or to raise external finances. Obviously, much more extensive research is needed before we can define the peculiar characteristics of such groups of enterprises.

CHAPTER 7
'Direct' Balance-of-Payments Effects

The 'direct' balance-of-payments effects of a firm (B_d), defined as those which immediately affect the foreign exchanges, may be derived thus:

$$B_d = (X + I) - (C_k + C_r + R + D)$$

where X = f.o.b. value of exports;
- I = inflows of equity capital and loans from abroad, including earnings retained out of profits, net of capital and loans repatriated;
- C_k = c.i.f. value of capital goods imported;
- C_r = c.i.f. value of raw materials and intermediate goods imported (excluding finished goods imported for resale);
- R = royalties and technical fees paid abroad after tax; and
- D = net after-tax profits and interest accruing abroad, including retained earnings.

It should be noted that, in accordance with accounting convention, we enter retained earnings simultaneously as a capital inflow and as a profit outflow, with its net balance-of-payments effect being nil. In the absence of any detailed data on the amount of salaries paid to expatriate personnel and remitted abroad, we have had to leave this item out of account. The reselling activities of sample firms,[1] especially significant for a number of Colombian firms, were excluded from all our calculations, but this raised problems inasmuch as some of the selling costs, and the profit on resales, could not be satisfactorily separated from those arising in production.

We shall start by presenting the overall direct balance-of-payments effects of the sample firms, and then proceed to review separately various components of these effects: export performance and the

TABLE 7.1
Distribution of Sample Firms by Negative Direct Balance-of-Payments Effects

Classification of firms	Total no.	Total with negative effects	(2)/(1) ×100	No. with effects from 0 to −20%	(4)/(1) ×100	No. with effects from −20% to −50%	(6)/(1) ×100	No. with effects worse than −50%	(8)/(1) ×100
	(1)	(2)	(3)	(4)	(5)	(6)	(7)	(8)	(9)
Total Sample	159	145	91	49	31	62	39	34	21
TNCs	88	82	93	22	25	36	41	24	27
Non-TNCs	71	63	89	27	38	26	37	10	14
Foreign-controlled	133	122	91	35	26	57	43	30	23
Locally controlled	26	23	88	14	54	5	19	4	15

Note: Direct balance-of-payments effects are measured as percentages of sales, both averaged over the entire sample period.

evidence on export restrictions; capital inflows and their comparison with profit outflows; extent of import-dependence of sample firms; technical payments; and, finally, profits accruing abroad and the incidence of clandestine remissions via transfer pricing.

OVERALL DIRECT BALANCE-OF-PAYMENTS EFFECTS

The overall direct effects of the samples on the balance of payments of host countries are, with one exception, negative. The average effects for the various countries, expressed as a percentage of sales for the total sample period, come to 2·7 for Kenya, $-25·5$ for Jamaica, $-11·7$ for India, $-55·0$ for Iran, $-35·3$ for Colombia and $-37·6$ for Malaysia. The Kenyan result is somewhat surprising in view of the predominantly negative effects for the sample firms in all the other countries, but can be explained by the large (and possibly, for the country as a whole, unrepresentative) exports of some of the firms which supply the East African Common Market, these five firms all having positive overall effects as a result. For the other countries, eight out of eleven firms in Jamaica, forty-eight out of fifty-three in India, fourteen out of fifteen in Malaysia and all the firms in Colombia and Iran have negative direct effects.

The nature of these effects can be seen from Table 7.1, which groups the sample firms by their transnational status, origin of control and the negativeness of the direct balance-of-payments results. While there are obvious hazards in averaging over different industries in different countries, the following observations may be advanced on the basis of our findings.

(a) The large majority of manufacturing investments in the sample countries, regardless of industry or source of control, have negative direct balance-of-payments effects. Given the nature of import-substituting industrialisation in developing countries, and the fact that few of the sample firms have been major exporters, this is entirely to be expected.

(b) On average, the TNCs in the sample have worse direct effects than the non-TNCs. This is more marked at the lower end of the scale, with 68 per cent of the TNCs having effects worse than -20 per cent of sales as compared to 51 per cent for non-TNCs.

(c) Foreign-controlled firms as a whole have worse average effects than do locally controlled firms, again with the effects being markedly

TABLE 7.2
Distribution of Sample Firms by Percentage of Sales Exported

Country, etc.	Total no.	Over 30%	15–29%	10–14%	5–9%	1–5%	Below 1%	Nil
Kenya	8	4	1	—	1	1	—	1
Jamaica	11	3	2	1	1	1	—	3
India	53	1	2	—	4	17	17	12
Iran	16	—	—	—	—	—	—	14
Colombia	56	—	3	5	6	11	11	20
Malaysia	15	—	3	1	3	—	—	6
Total	159	8 (5.0)	11 (6.9)	7 (4.4)	15 (9.4)	34 (21.4)	28 (17.6)	56 (35.2)
TNCs	88	4 (4.5)	4 (4.5)	3 (3.4)	12 (13.6)	18 (20.5)	23 (26.1)	23 (26.1)
Non-TNCs	71	4 (5.6)	7 (9.9)	4 (5.6)	3 (4.2)	16 (22.5)	5 (7.0)	33 (46.5)
Foreign-controlled	133	7 (5.3)	8 (6.0)	7 (5.3)	14 (10.5)	28 (21.1)	23 (17.3)	46 (34.6)
Locally controlled	26	1 (3.8)	3 (11.5)	—	1 (3.8)	6 (23.1)	5 (19.2)	10 (38.5)

Note: Figures in parentheses are percentages of total group. Because of rounding, these may not sum to 100.

less favourable to the former at the lower end: some 66 per cent of the former, and only 34 per cent of the latter, have effects worse than -20 per cent of sales. However, in view of the small number of firms which are locally controlled, this finding should be treated with great caution.

The overall results do not tell us anything about their causes, and we must look in greater detail into the components to gain a clearer understanding of the forces at work.

EXPORTS

Taking the average for the country samples, we find that exports accounted, over the entire sample period, for 42·9 per cent of sales in Kenya, 24·9 per cent in Jamaica, 3·2 per cent in India, 0·3 per cent in Iran, 4·3 per cent in Colombia and 8·5 per cent in Malaysia. Table 7.2 gives the distribution of sample firms by percentage of sales exported, grouping them by country and by transnationality and origin of control. It shows that over 35 per cent of the total number of firms exported nothing at all, and another 18 per cent exported under 1 per cent of sales, bringing to a total of 53 per cent the number which had negligible exports. Only twenty-six firms (16 per cent) exported over 10 per cent of their total sales, and only eight over 30 per cent (of which four were in Kenya and three in Jamaica).

The best export performances came from the Kenyan and Jamaican samples. An examination of the firms responsible shows that, for the former, the leading exporters (in such diverse fields as cement, petroleum products, soaps and detergents and shoes) aimed primarily at the neighbouring markets in the East African Common Market, while, for the latter, two firms (in food products and clothing) exported to the developed world, one of them exporting all its output, and two others (in paint) sold to the Caribbean countries. The leading export firms in India, Colombia and Malaysia were in very diverse industries and sold mainly to neighbouring markets; our sample contained no instances of firms engaged in processing components in, say, the electronics industries, for TNCs located in the developed world.

The lower part of the table indicates that TNCs performed worse than non-TNCs in terms of exporting over 10 per cent of their output (12 per cent of them did so, as opposed to 21 per cent of non-TNCs); and that the two groups were roughly equal with regard to the number of firms exporting 5 per cent or over, and the number exporting below 1 per cent, or nil. We tried to test by means of analysis of variance whether there was any significant difference in export performance between TNCs and other firms for India and Colombia, taken together as well as separately. The groupings for the individual countries turned out to be statistically insignificant, though the mean for TNCs was always lower than that for non-TNCs (the former having exports of 2·7 and 1·6 per cent for Colombia and India, the latter 4·5 and 4·1 per cent respectively). The groupings for both together, however, did show that TNCs had, as a group, significantly lower exports (2·3 per cent) than non-TNCs (4·2 per cent) at a 10 per cent level. As these two samples are the only ones with enough firms to make such calculations meaningful, this result is interesting: a very strong statement is not possible, but we can at least infer that *transnationality does not appear to have been an important aid to exporting.*

It is difficult to say much about foreign- and locally controlled firms for the whole sample, because of the small number of the latter. The only country sample for which we had sufficient observations to facilitate meaningful comparisons between the two groups was the Indian one, with thirty-three foreign- and twenty locally controlled firms. The analysis of variance showed, at a 5 per cent level, that the mean value of exports of the foreign-controlled group (1·7 per cent) *did* vary significantly from that of the locally-controlled group (5·7 per cent) for the sample period as a whole. We may therefore infer that the available evidence suggests that *foreign control does not generally seem to promote exports and may even inhibit it.*

These inferences about transnationality and origin of control are stated carefully and with qualification because the evidence does not seem strong enough to suggest that either of them actually *causes* lower exports. Nevertheless, they are interesting as a counter to arguments that TNC investment in developing countries promotes exports there (owing to the TNCs' extensive contacts abroad, their marketing skills, superior technology, product differentiation or greater know-how).[2] If anything, these inferences support the argument that foreign investors tend to inhibit exports, owing to the exigencies of their global production and marketing strategies, by means of formal or informal restrictions. We return to this in a minute, but we must note that, while export restrictions undoubtedly do exist quite extensively, the information from our samples does *not* seem to vindicate the supposition that formal restrictions are important in inhibiting exports.

The pattern of exports for the sample may be partly explained by the above factors, but clearly the policies followed by the host countries, and various factors at the individual-firm level, must also be considered. We have already remarked on the formation of common markets as an inducement to exporting. The effect of export subsidies, tariffs on imported components, export information and financing, provision of skilled manpower, and so on, may be quite significant. Thus, the Indian government offered various export incentives, in the form of cash subsidies, import-duty draw-backs, foreign-exchange licences and so on, as well as actually requiring certain industries to export a specified amount in order to receive any import entitlements at all. This caused many firms to export token amounts at a loss, in order to stay operative; their losses on this activity were amply covered by profits from domestic sales. Malaysia and Iran also offered export incentives, the former with some apparent success, the latter with very little (though this was mainly because of the newness of the investments). Colombian exports may be expected to respond to the Andean Common Market once it gets going. In general, however, the import-substitution (or exchange-rate) policies pursued by all the sample countries have clearly induced foreign capital into many industries which are not very competitive or export-oriented, and this must count as the commonest reason for low exports.

We made an attempt to test statistically whether the *size* of the firm, as an indicator of scale economies or competitive power, was significant in explaining export performance for the Indian and Colombian samples, and for individual industries within those samples.[3] The results of the regression exercises, using sales and assets as measures of size (individually and together), were largely insignificant and the signs of the correlations varied erratically, making even the few significant results appear accidental. For what they are worth, we may report that two multiple regressions, for nine machinery firms in India and sixteen chemical firms in Colombia, showed significance at the 5 per cent level and did not suffer from serial correlation. In both, exports as a percentage of sales were positively correlated with the total value of sales and negatively with the total value of assets. In both cases the regression coefficients were extremely low, and, in view of the expected relationship between exports and size, which would lead us to anticipate positive relations with both sales and assets, we must dismiss the finding as insignificant.

We also tested for differences in export performance by age of firm (up to five years, five to ten years and over ten years in operation). We found that, for all six countries taken together, and for Colombia on its own, the three age groups differed significantly with regard to export performance: the oldest firms exporting most, and youngest least, as proportions of sales.[4] For India alone, and for Kenya, Jamaica, Iran and Malaysia together, this grouping was not very significant, though the means all corresponded to the pattern just noted.

The firms' own estimates of the international price competitiveness of their output showed practically no relationship to export performance; nor did rates of profitability (taken as indirect indicators of efficiency or dynamism). We tried to see whether 'marketing entry barriers' made a significant difference, as suggested by de la Torre (1974), to TNC–non-TNC export propensities. We grouped all exporting sample firms according to whether their products faced high, medium or low marketing barriers, and used analysis of variance to test whether TNCs exported more in high-barrier industries relative to non-TNCs. The mean performances of the two groups did follow the predicted pattern, with non-TNCs doing much better in low-, slightly better in medium-, and considerably worse in high-barrier industries as compared to TNCs; however, the F values were so low that these results cannot be held to have much significance.

In general, therefore, only age appeared to be an important influence on export performance in the tests attempted. The tests were, of course, very limited in scope, and did not take into account the firm's *decision* to export, or various other factors, such as other measures of efficiency, the nature of technology used, product range, labour skills, and rates of growth.

The point about the decision to export brings us to export restrictions. There is ample evidence that export restrictive practices abound both formally and informally where foreign investment and foreign technological agreements are involved.[5] Let us start with informal restrictions. In the context of TNC operations where control is exercised from the centre, it is somewhat odd to think in terms of export 'restrictions'. The TNC generally plans its international operations on a worldwide scale and allocates markets to its various subsidiaries to conform with some objective of the firm as a whole. This necessarily involves determining exports according to such an objective rather than according to the desires or objectives of each host country; indeed, the very advantage of transnationality lies partly in the ability of the TNC to take decisions in such a way rather than to leave it to each subsidiary acting independently.[6] What are the conditions under which a developing host country would find such policies 'restrictive' towards exports?

(a) The TNC and the government may have quite different views regarding the economic viability of exporting; this certainly appears to be the case for some relatively uncompetitive industries in India. This should not count as 'restriction' on the TNC's part, since it is simply responding to objective market conditons; the government may then promote exports by offering greater subsidies or by changing market conditions, though obviously in certain circumstances this may be an inefficient way to earn foreign exchange.

(b) The TNC may limit exports for non-economic reasons, such as the minimisation of its commitment to countries that it regards as risky (though it may well invest to produce for the home market). The government may counter this by bargaining, statute, or offering guarantees.

(c) The TNC may limit exports because it has similar subsidiaries operating in neighbouring markets, and promoting one may, financially or politically, damage another. This may have limited the exports of some Colombian firms, which have affiliated plants in most other Latin American countries; it may also have affected India, Malaysia and Jamaica in the same way. Many firms indicated that market allocations were commonly made by parent companies, and the Indian government has given this official sanction by allowing certain 'permissible' export restrictions banning exports to countries where the foreign firm (or technology seller) is based or has subsidiaries or licensees. This is a very difficult restriction to overcome so long as foreign control is exercised, though in other cases the government may be able to insist on deleting it from formal contracts.

(d) The TNC may have open or tacit cartel agreements or market-sharing arrangements with other TNCs, which lead to export limitations.[7] In a way this is simply an extension of the previous case to oligopolies where, owing to stability (and sometimes threatened instability), excess capacity or other reasons, the leading firms find it expedient to divide markets among themselves.

In all such cases of informal export limitation, it clearly is not easy for a host government either to discover the nature and extent of the limitation or to deal with it in terms of promoting exports. Formal restrictions are, on the other hand, written into legal contracts and so are easy to discover. They are not, however, easy to get rid of. Many TNCs and technology sellers feel strongly about the threat to their worldwide positions posed by buyers of technology and by joint ventures, and insist upon restrictive clauses in circumstances where this threat is real. This explains why after years of effort the Indian government has not been able to have restrictive clauses excluded from technology contracts:[8]

even its acceptance of 'permissible' restrictions can be seen as a concession to TNCs' bargaining strength. The Colombian government has simply banned restrictive clauses, but it is not clear whether this has led to a reduction in foreign investment, or to their replacement by informal control (or tacit agreement with local firms), or both. Certainly any government can statutorily prohibit restrictive practices, but this does not ensure that these practices are really banished or that the country is using its bargaining power effectively.

We were told about the use of formal restrictions in most of the sample countries. Over half the Indian sample and a third of the Malaysian sample reported the existence of restrictive agreements, but it was only in Colombia that we obtained detailed evidence on their incidence. Somewhat surprisingly, this incidence was lower than we had expected, and certainly much lower than indicated by Vaitsos (1971, 1974b). Out of seventy-seven contracts entered into by forty-five sample firms up to 1970, only nine (mostly TNCs) had export restrictions, and only one stipulated complete export prohibition. Most of the restrictions (six in all) occurred in the pharmaceutical industry, and most were imposed by technology sellers other than the parent company. In terms of export performance, however, the firms with restrictions did *not* seem to suffer at all. On the contrary, of the top five exporters in the pharmaceutical sector (with exports over 5 per cent of sales), four had export restrictive clauses (limiting their markets) in their contracts; perhaps restrictions had been imposed on these firms precisely because they were capable of exporting.

While it is clearly in the interests of the host country to reduce restrictive clauses to a minimum, it is unrealistic to expect a great improvement in export performance simply from the removal of restrictions. It is quite likely that informal restrictions are more pervasive and effective than formal ones; and freedom to export is in any case only one condition out of a host of others required in exporting. This being said, however, it must be emphasised that it is a *necessary* condition, without which the industries concerned cannot even make a start, and it must be counted as one of the most important variables to be decided upon in a bargaining encounter. We shall return to policy considerations in a later chapter, but we may note that the Indian case indicates that the effects of restrictive policies grow more important the more industrialised and technologically advanced a country becomes, as do the problems of getting rid of them against the wishes of the TNCs.

CAPITAL INFLOWS AND THE COST OF SERVICING FOREIGN INVESTMENT

Net capital inflows comprise the total amount of capital (equity, long-term loans and retained earnings out of foreign profits) brought in from abroad net of repatriation; that is, excluding profits and interest remitted. Any measure of such inflows over an arbitrarily chosen period is not very meaningful, since the figures cannot by themselves indicate the total capital contribution of a firm over its life and certainly cannot be used to compare firms at different stages of their lives. Purely by way of background information, however, we shall give figures for capital inflows during the sample period for the various countries. These, expressed as a percentage of sales, are as follows: Jamaica 1·1, Kenya 12·5, India 3·3, Iran 3·4, Colombia 5·0, and Malaysia 5·3 per cent. Of the total of 147 firms with foreign equity, twenty-eight had net inflows of over 10 per cent, thirty-eight of 5·1 to 10 per cent, sixty-nine of 0·1 to 5 per cent, and twelve had negative inflows. There was no general difference between TNC and non-TNC inflows, except that eight of the twelve negatives were recorded by TNCs, mainly in Colombia.

The main point of interest about capital inflows is the *form* which the initial foreign equity investment takes. Equity can be provided not only as cash, but also as machinery and equipment and capitalised know-how. All the non-cash forms of investment, especially the last, are extremely difficult to value, and the investor may easily overstate their true value in order to raise his share *vis à vis* that of a local investor or (in Colombia) to raise his net worth, which provides the basis for calculating permissible profit remittances. As the pressure for local participation and control mounts in host countries, so does the attractiveness to the foreign firm of assigning arbitrarily higher values to its non-cash investment. The valuation of capital equipment or know-how is, of course, very difficult for the host country or the local firm to check, and reports abound in India and Colombia,[9] as well as in other developing countries, of the foreign investor inflating the value of machinery (or charging excessive prices for second-hand machinery) contributed as equity investment.

We do not possess, for the sample firms, any information on the overvaluation of non-cash investment by foreign investors. We can, however, give an indication of the form of equity investment for forty-seven of the sample firms in Colombia (the only ones for which we could obtain such information), to indicate broadly the potential scope for arbitrary valuation practices. Table 7.3 shows the percentages of cash and non-cash inflows for these firms, and reveals that 37 per cent of the

'Direct' Balance-of-Payments Effects

TABLE 7.3
Colombia: Composition of Initial Equity Investment by Forty-Seven Sample Firms, by Industry (percentages)

Form of inflow	Total	Pharma-ceuticals	Chemicals	Paper	Rubber	Electricals	Metal products	Transport
Cash	63	94	42	75	40	63	56	96
Machinery	31	5	51	2	60	36	44	3
Other	6	1	7	23	–	1	–	1
No. of firms	47	17	12	3	2	7	4	2

total inflow into the forty-seven firms (1235 million pesos) was contributed in the latter form, much lower than the comparable figure for India (81 per cent),[10] but still high enough to give the foreigner considerable leeway to overstate his contribution. There is great diversity of practice among the different industries, for no discernible reason; we should note, however, that the very large contribution under 'other' (capitalised know-how) by the paper firms occurs in the industry that is perhaps the least technologically advanced of all those represented in the sample.

Readers may like to see, for this sample, a comparison of inflows of capital and outflows of profits and interest. They must, however, be warned again about the dangers of using such comparisons to evaluate the social or balance-of-payments costs of foreign investment. (See the second section of Chapter 9 for a formally correct assessment.)

We shall use a broad definition of the cost of 'servicing' foreign investment, including in it both royalties and profits plus interest. In the absence of a detailed breakdown, we may, where royalties are paid to unrelated foreign firms, overstate the cost; but, as in most of the cases royalties are paid to the parent company and may legitimately be included under profits, the exaggeration is likely to be only slight. For the country samples as such, a comparison of net capital inflows with servicing costs gives the following results, all expressed as percentages of sales: Kenya -5.7, Jamaica -0.4, India -0.3, Iran -0.7, Colombia -6.7, and Malaysia -1.5.[11] Table 7.4 shows the distribution of the 'net financial effect' for TNCs and non-TNCs, for the entire sample period.

It appears from the table that one-third of the total number of firms with foreign equity capital have positive and two-thirds have negative

TABLE 7.4
Distribution of Firms with Foreign Capital by Net Financial Effect* as a Percentage of Sales

	Total firms	Over 10%	5% to 10%	0.1% to 5%	0 to −5%	−5% to −10%	−10% to −20%	Below −20%
Total	147	14	7	28	55	26	15	2
TNCs	88	8	5	16	26	20	13	—
Non-TNCs	59	6	2	12	29	6	2	2

* Defined as net capital inflow minus profits + interest and technical payments abroad.

effects. The distribution between TNCs and non-TNCs does not appear to be very different, except that for effects worse than −5 per cent there are proportionately more TNCs than others. On the whole the sample foreign firms do seem to be 'taking out more than they are putting in' during the period studied, and TNCs may be 'taking out' somewhat more than non-TNCs; however, this finding, which merely confirms trends observed in aggregate balance-of-payments figures, does not tell us much by itself.

IMPORT DEPENDENCE

The bulk of foreign manufacturing investment in developing countries is heavily dependent on imports. Only a few economies, such as India's in our sample, have reached a stage of industrial development capable of providing the greater part of their requirements for manufacturing industry. In others, such as Kenya, Jamaica, Iran and Malaysia, foreign investments tend simply to assemble, blend or package imported components and materials. Since the cost of imports provides the largest single charge on the host economy's foreign exchanges as far as manufacturing investment (foreign or local) is concerned, it is obviously of some value to examine how great this cost is. There are two main reasons for this.

(a) The greater the extent of reliance on imports for production, the

'Direct' Balance-of-Payments Effects 143

less is the linkage of the industry to the local economy,[12] the greater is the direct foreign-exchange cost, and the lesser, as a consequence, are the growth and spread effects of the investment.

(b) The greater the reliance on imports, the larger the scope, where foreign-controlled firms are involved, for transfer pricing, and, where locally-controlled but foreign technology-dependent firms are involved, for tying imports to high-cost sources.

There are, however, dangers inherent in taking too simple a view of import dependence. Imports–sales ratios on their own can be misleading, unless it is specified whether and to what extent the local economy is *capable* of supplying inputs into manufacturing, and what the *cost* is of providing inputs, relative to the cost of imports. Kenya, Jamaica, Iran and Malaysia have relatively simple indigenous industry and must necessarily rely on imported inputs; it would be foolish to blame investors for heavy import dependence as compared with, say, India. India, however, has pushed import substitution to great lengths and often at the cost of great inefficiency, so that low import dependence cannot always be regarded as beneficial. Foreign firms would, given a completely free hand, probably prefer to depend on imports,[13] not only for reasons of reliability, quality, cost and ease of access, but also because this gives greater scope for the use of arbitrary pricing practices. The government, on the other hand, would prefer to develop indigenous industry as far and as fast as possible, and would probably twist TNCs' arms to keep the process going. The economically 'optimum' extent of import dependence, if one can use such a static and formal concept in the context of less developed countries, would lie between the two extremes, and would be determined by correctly computed comparative costs taking into account dynamic factors and externalities. If, however, we brought in more general considerations of political–economic strategy (discussed in Part I), which may call for less reliance on imported technology, less integration into the world economy and a different pattern of distribution, consumption and social organisation domestically, the 'optimum' level of import dependence would be much lower than that dictated by conventional theory. We cannot go into such issues here, but they are mentioned in order to warn readers against paying too much attention to simple ratios and figures.

In the period studied, the average of imports of capital goods, intermediate goods and total imports, expressed as a percentage of sales, came to 14·5, 18·3 and 32·8 respectively for Kenya; 11·1, 46·6 and 57·7 for Jamaica; 2·7, 11·8 and 14·5 for India;[14] 3·7, 50·9 and 54·6 for Iran;

3·2, 29·7 and 32·9 for Colombia; and 10·4, 34·2 and 44·6 for Malaysia. Despite considerable variation around the mean, the country averages (with the exception of those for Kenya) accord well with what we would expect, given the size and level of industrial development of the country. In the case of Kenya, four firms show very low levels of imports of raw and intermediate goods, all being atypical in this respect because they belong to industries not covered in the other samples; the remaining firms correspond more to import levels in Colombia or Malaysia. The distribution of firms by total import levels is shown in Table 7.5, by country and transnationality.

TABLE 7.5
Distribution of Firms by Total Imports as a Percentage of Sales
(number of firms)

Country, etc.	Over 70%	50–70%	40–50%	30–40%	20–30%	10–20%	5–10%	1–5%	Nil
Kenya	–	–	2	2	–	2	1	1	–
Jamaica	3	2	1	3	2	–	–	–	–
India	1	2	6	2	9	20	10	3	–
Iran	4	6	1	4	1	–	–	–	–
Colombia	3	11	6	10	9	15	–	2	–
Malaysia	3	3	5	1	1	1	–	–	1
Total	14	24	21	22	22	38	11	6	1
TNCs	6	15	14	13	14	18	5	3	–
Non-TNCs	8	9	7	9	8	20	6	3	1

A number of observations may be made about the table. First, the inclusion of capital-goods imports introduces a distortion because different firms will have different propensities to invest at different stages of their lives. Second, some very new firms have exaggerated figures for imports as related to sales. Third, import propensities as related to industry are not shown here but are clearly of importance. These defects could be remedied by more detailed breakdowns of the information at hand; however, our purpose here is not to try to discover the explanation of import patterns as such, but to describe the level of import dependence and the possible scope for transfer pricing.

The general extent of import dependence is clearly very high, if one is concerned with pricing problems. In the sample period, over half the sample firms imported goods worth over 30 per cent of their sales (two-thirds if India is excluded); and, clearly, the extent to which this could affect real, as compared to stated, profits is enormous, as is discussed in the final section of this chapter. It should, however, be noted that we do not have exact figures for the contribution of *intra-firm* imports to the total. Some Colombian data show that the bulk of imports is in fact from affiliated firms, while the Reuber study of a sample of fifty-seven to sixty-four firms shows that about 45 per cent of 'total value of requirements' (including local purchases) came from parent companies and affiliates.[15] Since other *imports* seem to be marginal in the Reuber sample (under 7 per cent of requirements), we seem safe in assuming that the bulk of imports did come from affiliated firms. The Indian case may be different because of the policy of specifying the source of imports in some licences, though the incidence of this is not known. We must therefore assume that the incidence of transfer pricing is, given the level of import dependence, probably lower for the Indian firms than for the others.

There does not appear to be any significant difference between TNCs and non-TNCs, or foreign- and locally controlled firms (not shown in the table), with regard to their import propensities. There does not, therefore, seem to be any ground for arguing that these characteristics exercise an important influence on import propensities, which probably are determined more by the industry, the nature of the host economy, and government policies. The desire of TNCs to use transfer pricing, if it exists in general, does not seem to induce them to import more, on average, than other firms. This does not, as we shall see below, mean that they do not inflate the extent of import dependence on particular industries that are exceptionally profitable, but that import dependence generally does not appear to be strongly influenced by transnationality or foreign control. However, it may also be that in an exceptionally profitable industry, where world trade would tend to be heavily concentrated and monopolised, local firms are almost as liable to 'overcharging' as are foreign subsidiaries. Our data do not enable us to throw any light on this question, but other studies[16] indicate that this may be the case.

TECHNICAL PAYMENTS

We have discussed in Chapter 3 how difficult it is to evaluate the *real* 'value' of technology as expressed by the cost of royalties or lump-sum management/technical fees. Not only is the bargain often struck between two units of the same firm, or between a foreign monopolistic supplier and a relatively uninformed local buyer, but, in addition, the disparity between private and social values, between the profit that technology yields the user and the effects that it has on the economy as a whole, can be particularly wide here. On the latter issues we cannot, at this juncture, say anything specific as regards the sample firms, and so must take its social 'value' for granted. With regard to the former, however, we can certainly describe the actual costs incurred on account of payments for technology (covering royalty payments and fees for technical and related services), but we must bear in mind the following qualifications.

(a) If the technological contract is between affiliated firms, the payment may simply be a means of remitting profits and may bear little relation to the 'market value' of the technology transferred.[17]

(b) If the contract is between unrelated firms, the payment may still be rather tenuously connected to the 'value' of technology, either because the buyer is in a weak bargaining position or because, in a protected market, he can afford to collude with the seller and make excessive payments in order to steal a march over local competition, or simply because the marginal cost of bargaining is not worthwhile (this can apply equally to public-sector firms).

(c) The costs as calculated by us are related to the total value of sales and not just the sales of the product to which the contract relates. We have very little information on the actual rates agreed upon in specific contracts (except for Colombia), so that we cannot compare the technological cost to different firms on a strictly equivalent basis.

The country samples recorded the following technical payments over the period studied, all post-tax figures expressed as a percentage of sales: Kenya 1·0, Jamaica 0·8, India 0·5, Iran 1·4; Colombia 2·5 and Malaysia 1·6 per cent. As they stand, these payments appear to be relatively small. If they were, however, being used mainly as a means of remitting profits – most of the contracts were in fact with parent companies – it may be more relevant to look at them *in relation to the size of post-tax dividends remitted abroad*. For Kenya and Jamaica, where all firms except one were foreign majority-owned, technical payments came to 12 and 16 per cent of remitted profits. For India they came to 32 per cent for the sample as a whole (including local firms), 16 per cent for foreign majority-owned firms and 135 per cent for foreign minority-owned firms.[18] For Iran they came to 20 per cent for the whole sample, 420 per cent for foreign-majority and 60 per cent for foreign-minority firms. For Colombia, they came to 65 per cent for the entire sample, 57 per cent for wholly foreign firms, 88 per cent for foreign-majority (excluding wholly foreign) firms and 66 per cent for foreign-controlled firms as a whole.[19] For Malaysia, they came to 56 per cent for the entire sample, 67 per cent for wholly foreign firms, 56 per cent for foreign-majority (excluding wholly foreign) firms, and 52 per cent for foreign-controlled firms as a whole.

It is apparent from these figures that, in all the sample countries except Kenya and Jamaica, which recorded relatively high declared profits, technical payments served, for some firms, as an important vehicle for remitting profits. However, no clear firm- or country-wise pattern of remission via one or the other channel emerges from our data, signifying that different firms may have had quite different policies in this regard,[20] or that they faced different internal (for instance, the extent of intra-firm trade on which prices could be varied) or external (for example, official surveillance of royalties) constraints. In general, it seems likely that the liberal environments of Kenya and Jamaica – in terms of ownership requirements, possibilities for transfer pricing, tax concessions, and so on – reduced the TNCs' need to charge high royalties. In India the pattern clearly reflects the government's policy of permitting royalty rates to vary inversely with the extent of foreign ownership, while in Iran and Colombia (both without official regulation in the period studied) the relatively frequent use of royalties for remission of profits may reveal apprehension, on the part of some foreign investors, about pressures for local control or ownership. Unfortunately, we do not have enough information to explain the pattern of royalty charges in any detail.

Let us briefly examine the actual levels of technical payments in the sample. Table 7.6 gives their distribution by country and by different categories of firms, and shows that 18 per cent of the total number of firms (excluding one) paid over 3 per cent of total sales in this form, while 27 per cent paid no technical fees at all. Colombia and Iran contained the largest proportions of firms with high technical payments (over 5 per cent), while India had mostly low payments. It should be repeated that these figures do not show the *rates of royalty* fixed in specific contracts: because particular contracts apply to only a part of the firms' production, these rates are in most cases found to be higher than the above figures, which are deflated by total output.

There are proportionately many more TNCs than non-TNCs in the higher range of technical payments: over 25 per cent of the former pay more than 3 per cent of sales, as compared to under 9 per cent of the latter. Many of the TNCs concerned are concentrated in Colombia and Iran, where the contracts had been entered into (as in Jamaica and

Kenya) without any official regulation at all or in a period before regulation was introduced. The Iranian data show that, for all firms where technical payments exceeded 4 per cent of sales (five firms), they were also much greater than profits remitted, and the products manufactured (electric light bulbs and yeast) were either technologically very simple or were being made for much lower royalties by identical or

TABLE 7.6
Distribution of Sample Firms by Technical Payments as a Percentage of Sales

Country, etc.	Over 10%	7–10%	5–7%	3–5%	1–3%	0–1%	Nil
Kenya	–	–	–	1	2	1	4
Jamaica	–	1	–	–	2	2	6
India*	–	–	1	20	22	9	
Iran	1	–	2	3	4	1	5
Colombia	2	2	4	8	12	15	13
Malaysia	–	–	1	2	2	5	5
Total	3	3	7	15	42	46	42
(100)/	(1·9)	(1·9)	(4·4)	(9·5)	(26·6)	(29·1)	(26·6)
TNCs	2	2	7	11	22	25	19
(100)	(2·3)	(2·3)	(8·0)	(12·5)	(25·0)	(28·4)	(21·5)
Non-TNCs	1	1	–	4	20	21	23
(100)	(1·4)	(1·4)		(5·7)	(28·6)	(30·0)	(32·9)
Foreign-controlled	3	3	7	13	35	36	36
Locally controlled	–	–	–	2	7	10	6

* One firm was excluded because it was just starting production, so that royalty rates were grossly overstated in relation to sales.
* There are 158 firms in all, eighty-eight TNCs, seventy non-TNCs, 133 foreign-controlled and twenty five locally controlled.

very similar firms elsewhere (pharmaceuticals). In some cases we find that the same TNC charged very different rates of royalties for making exactly the same product in different countries: one charged nothing in Kenya and Jamaica and 4 per cent in Malaysia; another 0·2 per cent in Kenya, 8·8 per cent in Colombia and 0·7 per cent in Jamaica. In general the data confirmed our belief that the technology 'market' was indeed very haphazard and seller-dominated, and that 'prices' have little relation to the quality of the 'product' and varied rather erratically.[21]

'Direct' Balance-of-Payments Effects   149

The investigations undertaken by the Colombian Royalties Commission (*Comité de Regalías*) provided some background information on some sample firms.[22] This Commission, set up in 1967, undertook to examine each technology contract in the country and to study the value of the technology transferred (by examining its age, scarcity, quality, and so on) and the appropriateness of the charges made. In 1969 it decided to ban, to the extent possible, royalty payments to parent companies by wholly-owned subsidiaries (a practice followed for some time in India); of the 395 contracts it examined in 1967–71, it modified 334 and rejected sixty-one, saving the country some 40 per cent of the royalties paid annually.[23] We obtained information on sixty-six contracts entered into by sample firms (mostly in pharmaceuticals): sixty-three of these contracts were entered into by wholly or majority foreign-owned subsidiaries, fifty-three of them with parent companies and thirteen with other (possibly, but not necessarily, affiliated) companies. Of the sixty-six contracts, only seven were approved in their original form by the Commission (five in chemicals and one each in rubber and electricals); four of these were between wholly-owned subsidiaries and unrelated firms and so were not cancelled. Of the fifty-nine other contracts, twenty-nine were cancelled outright (all of these were between subsidiaries and parent companies, nineteen in pharmaceuticals) and thirty were considerably modified as regards the rate of royalty, duration or various restrictive clauses (eight of these were between wholly-owned, and twenty-one between majority-owned, subsidiaries and parents, sixteen in the pharmaceutical industry). The most common reason given for cancellation was that the technology was old – in one case a firm was charging 12 per cent of sales for production of a simple product the technology of which had not changed for fifty years – or easily available locally without charge. Most of the modifications reduced royalty rates, using as a benchmark rates paid for similar technology by local firms or in other Latin American countries; many obviously exorbitant charges were thus brought down to reasonable levels.

It is impossible for us to judge how rational the Commission was in assessing royalties and how tough it was in bargaining with the firms. It is likely that, in view of the complexity of the issues involved and the Commission's lack of knowledge and experience, it was too lenient in some cases and too restrictive in others, so permitting too high a cost to the economy or else deterring the inflow of technology. On the other hand, it is clear that *any* redressing of the original position could have favoured the host country and cut out many of the obvious abuses; after

150   *Investment, TNCs and Developing Countries*

this step progress was bound to be much slower and more painstaking. As the Indian experience illustrates, the problems of negotiation and regulation keep on increasing with the development of local industry, and the bargaining power of the leading TNCs which control technology can never be countered effectively. Despite all this, however, our findings do suggest that official surveillance and control yield substantial benefits and must strive to keep pace with the process of technology transfer. We shall discuss the policy implications of this later.

PROFITS AND TRANSFER PRICING

We have already (in the previous chapter) discussed profitability at some length, and here we need only show the balance-of-payments outflows on this account for the different countries, expressed, as usual, as percentages of sales. For the purposes of balance-of-payments analysis we have defined profits to include interest on foreign loans but to exclude tax and depreciation. For the country samples, the outflows came to 17·2 for Kenya, 10·7 for Jamaica, 3·1 for India, 2·7 for Iran, 8·6 for Colombia and 5·2 for Malaysia. These ratios do not reflect the return earned by the foreign investor on his net worth. The low figure for India, for instance, is mostly the result of the low percentage of foreign equity in Indian firms; the after-tax return on net worth is in fact higher in India than in Colombia.

Table 7.7 gives the distribution of firms according to the percentage of sales remitted abroad as profits and interest; only the 147 firms with foreign equity are included. The burden of such outflows generally falls in a range below 10 per cent of the value of sales, though in Kenya, Jamaica and Colombia a number of firms appear in much higher ranges. There does not seem to be a significant difference in pattern between TNCs and non-TNCs, but then, given the way in which this ratio is calculated, we should not expect to see any such difference.

We have discussed at various places in this book why declared profits are not always a good indicator of the true level of profits earned by foreign investors, and how transnational firms can use various other channels — in which 'prices' are either fixed arbitrarily by them or at least determined by their superior bargaining strength — to remit funds from one country to another.[24] These channels are, for subsidiaries or foreign-controlled firms, intra-firm imports, exports, royalties, interest payments, and fees of various kinds, and, for unrelated or locally controlled firms, various tied purchases, sales, royalties and charges. The most important ones quantitatively are traded goods and technical fees, the former being by far the leading potential vehicle for clandestine transfers. This is patently clear from the relative size of imports of sample firms as compared to their declared profits: in India, the former were 575 per cent of the latter for the whole sample, 371 per cent for the foreign-controlled companies and 341 per cent for the TNCs;[25] in Colombia, the ratios were 503 per cent for the sample as a whole and 672 per cent for the TNCs; and so on for all the sample countries. As we have already touched on technical payments above, let us now consider the use of transfer pricing on traded goods.

TABLE 7.7
Distribution of 147 Sample Firms by Post-tax Foreign Profits and Interest, as Percentages of Sales

Country, etc.	Total firms	Over 20%	15–20%	10–15%	5–10%	3–5%	0–3%	Nil or negative
Kenya	8	2	–	3	1	1	–	1
Jamaica	11	1	1	2	5	–	2	–
India	45	–	–	3	10	8	18	6
Iran	15	–	–	–	3	4	4	4
Colombia	55	6	–	5	26	9	7	2
Malaysia	13	–	–	2	3	–	5	3
Total	147	9	1	15	48	22	36	16
TNCs	88	5	–	12	31	13	19	8
Non-TNcs	59	4	–	3	17	9	17	8

There are four initial points which we should make before coming to our findings.

First, the use of 'transfer pricing' as a means of remitting profits can be judged only in relation to some standard, such as a free-market or arm's-length price, which would prevail in the absence of intra-firm or TNC-dominated trade. It is far from easy to discover such a standard:[26] for goods which are traded on open markets there are problems of discriminatory pricing in different markets, large price differences between suppliers, cartelisation, and other results of market 'imperfection'. For goods which are not openly traded, the problems of allocating overhead and research costs, joint products, risk, and so on, are even more complicated, and even the TNC concerned may have little idea of what their hypothetical free-market prices would be. All this may, of course, strengthen the firm's hand against the government's in using transfer prices deliberately, but the basic difficulties of measurement are largely unavoidable.

Second, while most of the literature has concentrated on the motives and conditions for TNCs' use of transfer pricing, the similar, and quantitatively perhaps more significant, phenomenon of price manipulation by *domestic* traders and manufacturers has been neglected.[27] This may take place independently of foreign firms or in collusion with them, but it should warn us against attaching 'blame' exclusively to TNCs. In the broader world setting, however, the preponderance of TNC-dominated trade is such that the TNCs' power to transmit funds and the sheer bulk of the sums involved must make national efforts look insignificant.

Third, on the question of 'blame' for these practices, it may be argued (implicitly from a competitive model) that profit rates between industries and countries tend to be equal and the amount of clandestine profits would not be so very large except for the host country's policy of offering protection, which enables excessive profits to be earned. The 'fault' is then largely the government's and not the firm's, which, after all, is there to make profits. This argument would be naïve, for two reasons: first, excessive profits can, and often do, arise from *international oligopoly*, with rates of profit tending to stay different in different industries. The most commonly observed case of excessive profits and use of transfer prices, in developed as well as less-developed countries, is the pharmaceutical industry: here it is its great market power, derived from sources quite unrelated to tariffs, which constitutes the source of profitability.[28] Secondly, even if protection did add to super-normal profits, rather than simply compensate for higher domestic costs or diseconomies of scale, it is often the case that the rate of protection is fixed after negotiation between TNCs and the government, or decided (in the case of import prohibition) by the market power of the TNCs. In the former instance it is easy for the TNCs to inflate their costs via transfer pricing and so demand extra protection.[29]

Fourth, given that high profits are commonly associated with TNC operations, can the government perhaps be 'blamed' for forcing TNCs to declare them elsewhere? We would not believe so. Transfer pricing may be used for a number of strategic (political, social, exchange-rate, labour-union) reasons which are not directly controllable by government policy; and, even if it were used for reasons of taxes or tariffs, which are directly controllable, it is not obvious that all less-developed countries should follow the tax policies of developed countries or of tax

'Direct' Balance-of-Payments Effects   153

havens. In general, it may be that, in order to be regarded as a safe, desirable and preferable place for TNCs to declare profits in, a developing country would need to manifest a (from its own point of view) undesirable degree of socio-political conformity to the requirements of a developed capitalist system. Certainly, of our sample countries, Colombia and India (with profit limits, price controls, high tax rates, pressures for local participation, and political hostility) offered a number of inducements to use transfer pricing. Iran (price controls, local participation, perhaps political uncertainty in the 1960s), Malaysia (long-term uncertainty, limits on royalties), and to some extent Kenya (long-term uncertainty) offered rather milder incentives, and we came across occasional references to the use of transfer pricing, without a clear picture emerging as to its extent or incidence.[30]

The only definite information we obtained in this regard was for fourteen sample firms in Colombia. The data were gathered by the Planning Office and the Import Control Office (INCOMEX) of the Government of Colombia for the period 1966–70, and pertained to prices actually charged by TNCs as compared with prices paid by local producers, paid by other Latin American countries, or ruling in world markets generally.[31] Even after making allowance for a generous margin of error, and using an average of alternative prices rather than the lowest price, irrefutable evidence was found that a number of foreign firms were charging excessive prices for their imports. The sector studied most intensively was pharmaceuticals, where individual items were found to be overpriced by up to 5000–6000 per cent.[32] The weighted average of overpricing for a wide range of products was found by the Planning Office to be 155 per cent for 1968 and by INCOMEX to be 87 per cent for 1967–70. Some rubber imports were found to have been overpriced by 40 per cent, some chemical imports by 25 per cent, and some electrical components by 54 per cent.

The data for the fourteen sample firms are shown in Table 7.8,[33] which also shows the effects on profitability of the proved amount of overpricing and of 'imputed' overpricing (if the proved overpricing applied to total imports). Overpricing is defined as $(Pa - Pw)/Pw \times 100$, where Pa stands for the price actually paid and Pw for the comparable world price. Declared profits are after tax and net of depreciation; the minus sign for firm 8 indicates that it was showing a loss.

All the firms except for nos 4 and 10 are transnational, and all are either wholly foreign-owned or foreign majority-owned. The extent of overpricing is generally higher in pharmaceutical than in other firms, and the effect on profitability is certainly more dramatic. While it is hazardous to generalise on this basis, it seems that from this and other evidence that the pharmaceutical industry is an extreme case; other industries do suffer from transfer pricing and undoubtedly particular firms are exceptionally profitable, but the difficulty of checking prices in the drug industry, given its market power and political influence, are outstanding.

TABLE 7.8
Overpricing by and Profitability of Fourteen Foreign Firms in Colombia 1966–70 (percentages)

Industries and firms	Imports investigated (1)	Proved overpricing (2)	Declared profits/ net worth (3)	Profits on proved overpricing/ net worth (4)	Profits on overpricing total imports/ net worth (imputed) (5)	(3)+(5) (6)
Pharmaceutical						
1	52·1	158·3	7·6	41·5	79·6	87·2
2	20·1	39·5	11·2	2·0	10·0	21·1
3	100·0	56·6	16·5	19·6	19·6	36·1
4	28·1	81·0	6·3	5·6	19·9	26·2
5	32·4	288·9	6·3	19·2	59·3	65·6
6	39·1	33·5	0·1	2·5	63·9	64·0
7	35·2	33·7	12·4	3·1	8·8	21·2
8	54·1	95·4	−7·4	17·9	33·1	26·1
9	48·6	83·7	42·8	111·7	229·8	272·6
10	44·2	313·8	27·5	39·6	89·6	117·1
11	30·9	138·9	5·9	9·9	32·0	37·9
Rubber						
12	60·0	40·0	8·3	6·1	10·2	18·5
Electrical						
13	22·3	24·1	8·1	0·3	1·3	9·4
14	30·4	81·1	0·7	1·8	5·9	6·6

This is not to say that host governments can afford to ignore transfer-pricing practices in other sectors. The degree of import dependence is such that even a modest amount of overall overpricing (say, 15–25 per cent) is enough to swamp the whole of declared profits. Tariffs take out part of the profits remitted in this way, of course, but in most cases they are set at low levels for intermediate and capital-goods imports. When combined with the potential use of arbitrary prices for exports,[34] interest payments and various technical fees, the danger posed to host countries is really quite formidable, and, with the growing sophistication and scope of TNC operations, it is steadily increasing.

CHAPTER 8

'Total' Balance-of-Payments and 'Social' Income Effects: Methods of Evaluation

The primary aim of our research project, to quantify the balance-of-payments effects of particular foreign investments, may not at first sight appear to raise any great theoretical difficulties. The immediate balance-of-payments effects of an investment, given by the direct impact of its operations on the host country's foreign exchanges, have all been discussed already, and have been shown to raise a number of problems regarding oligopolistic practices, regulation and bargaining – all issues of great practical importance, but not particularly complex or baffling from the viewpoint of economic theory.

The 'direct' balance-of-payments effects of a foreign investment do not, however, tell the whole story. They are deficient in two important respects: first, they do not show what would have happened had the foreign investment not occurred, in the 'alternative position';[1] and, second, they do not show the indirect effects of the investment on the balance-of-payments via domestic sales and the use of local resources. A comprehensive evaluation of the full effects must take both into account, specifying one or more alternative positions with which the actual situation is to be compared, and calculating the direct and indirect foreign-exchange effects in each of these positions. Such an evaluation does face a number of difficult (and sometimes insuperable) problems in theory as well as in practice, and some method has to be found for simplifying the issue to manageable proportions without doing too much violence to reality.

In this chapter we describe the method we used in the UNCTAD studies. We shall confine ourselves to the main analytical technique employed, leaving out others which were tried at different stages of the research but which did not yield results of enough independent interest

Balance-of-Payments and Income Effects: Evaluation 157

to merit reconsideration here. As there is a large body of literature on the sorts of evaluation techniques involved, we shall confine ourselves to a simple and brief review of the main features. The first section of the discussion describes the general approach. The second, which comprises the methodological core of the study, deals with the method of evaluating the balance-of-payments and income effects in comparison with an alternative situation where the product is imported. The final two sections deal with the evaluation of effects in comparison with alternatives where the foreign investment is totally replaced by local capital and where it is replaced to the 'most likely' extent by local capital.

THE ANALYTICAL APPROACH

The analysis was carried out on a firm-by-firm basis, comparing what had *actually* happened in the period covered with what might have happened in the *alternative situation* if that particular firm had been absent, or if foreign capital in that firm had been replaced by local capital. This approach enabled us to assume that the economic variables with which we were dealing were *marginal* in relation to the host economy as a whole, and so allowed us to take as constant such macro-economic variables as price levels, trade flows, government policies, infrastructure and institutions, habits and tastes, and so on. While a broader study, of the effects of foreign investment as a whole, would have been more interesting, this would have involved calculating large changes in important economic aggregates and would have posed an impossible task for anyone doing quantitative work. For a similar reason we ignored the *'external' effects* of individual investments, external effects being those that do not show up in the costs and receipts of the firms in question, but that do affect their social desirability.

The marginality assumption was a necessary one for our empirical work, as we had no means of quantifying even minor effects external to a firm's operations; but the limitations of this procedure should be kept firmly in view. First, while many of the sample firms, especially in India and Colombia, were relatively small in relation to the host economies, some in the other countries were not of negligible size in proportion to their manufacturing sectors, and so could not properly be considered marginal. Even in India and Colombia, some sample firms were market leaders in their respective industries and so may have had effects on price levels, industrial concentration, advertising tactics, and so on, which should, strictly, have been quantified. Second, even if the sample firms had all been fairly small, a consideration of their individual effects could not have been generalised to foreign investment as a whole – simply because the effects of the whole cannot, in such circumstances, be captured by a marginal analysis of its parts. If the reasoning in the first part of the book has any validity, it should be obvious that many of the important effects of foreign, especially transnational, investment are 'external' to individual firms and increase sharply with the total size of the foreign sector. The neglect of such factors is a major defect of our work, but it is intrinsic to all such quantitative studies; we shall return to such matters in Chapter 10.

In the context of TNC investment, there àre two possibly significant effects that we did not attempt to quantify: (a) the effect of such investment in expanding the total domestic demand for a product, and (b) its effect in displacing other domestic producers of competing products. Neglect of effect (a) involves assuming that the actual and alternative situations do not differ significantly as regards advertising and taste-creating tactics – an unsafe assumption if the entry of TNCs led to the introduction of new products or to an intensification of marketing activity. Effect (b) implies that foreign products did not compete directly with, say, traditional domestic goods, which were killed off in the process; this may not be too unrealistic for many of the sample firms, but for some in the simpler consumer industries it may be invalid. It would have been possible in principle to calculate both these effects, tracing the values of domestic and foreign resources used up or released by demand creation and substitution, but in practice the data simply did not exist for us to make meaningful estimates. The 'displacement' of domestic producers may also be interpreted more broadly, to signify the suppression of domestic entrepreneurship by TNCs' taking up the most profitable ventures, employing the most skilled or dynamic people, or simply scaring potential competitors off, by virtue of their size. This effect is not even quantifiable in principle, though one comes across it very often in the literature.

Since we were trying to estimate the effects of *foreign* investment as such, we had to specify alternative situations in which the output of an existing foreign firm would not simply be replaced by that of another. We did not investigate the national characteristics of different foreign investors, but laid down that foreign investment could be substituted for only by local investment, if at all. It may be objected that one foreign investor may be very different from another if the host government can obtain different terms from them by bargaining. This is, of course, true, and of great practical importance. It does not, however, invalidate the

Balance-of-Payments and Income Effects: Evaluation 159

use of the sort of model employed here, in which the effects of bargaining can be incorporated at any stage into any of the alternatives posited. Furthermore, the very nature of bargaining is such that it is impossible to quantify its results *a priori*, and it would have been pointless to manipulate figures merely to illustrate different outcomes.

What, then, are the alternatives to foreign investment? There may be any number of alternative situations, ranging from importing the product made by the foreign firm or doing without it altogether, to importing (or doing without) a part of it and producing the rest domestically, to producing the entire amount domestically, if necessary with purchased technology. We shall present the results of three exercises here, with the following alternatives.

Alternative I: importing the entire output of the present investment (the Little–Mirrlees procedure).

Alternative II: the entire output of the foreign investment is replaced by an identical locally owned facility ('financial replacement').

Alternative III: the 'most likely' local replacement, taking into account the technological and other advantages of the foreign investor, with the remainder being imported.

This sequence of alternative positions enables us to tackle in two stages the process of assessing the effects of foreign investment. The first stage, Alternative I, consists of a cost–benefit analysis of the investment, valuing the output at its c.i.f. price. By using a particular technique of 'social' cost–benefit analysis which also converts inputs into shadow prices given by their balance-of-payments impact, we can derive an estimate for the total foreign-exchange effect of the investment. This effect approximates very closely the net impact of the investment on 'social income', so that we can simultaneously obtain the values of balance-of-payments and income effects. It tells us, within the framework of the neoclassical model used, whether or not a particular investment, regardless of whether it is local or foreign, is socially beneficial to the host country.

The second stage, consisting of the other two alternatives, then involves adjusting the values of various inputs and outputs to discover how the 'foreignness' of an investment affects its social value. The Little–Mirrlees framework is preserved, and the foreign element is broken down into its financial and technological components to assess their separate impact. This stage must, of course, resort to very impressionistic evidence to determine what the potential for local replacement is, but in principle at least the method allows us to distinguish between two separate problems regarding foreign investments: whether or not the investment is desirable *as such*, and whether or not *foreign* investment is beneficial.

The two stages for evaluating foreign investments are derived from different sorts of economic theory and their integration is far from perfect. While social cost–benefit analysis is solidly founded in conventional neoclassical theory and its analytical tools are rigorously forged (rigorously, that is, in a particular framework), the analysis of the effects of foreign *versus* domestic investment is new, rather vague and primarily qualitative. The final results of our study must, therefore, be treated with great caution: the figures are based on a large amount of guesswork, and should not be taken to be final quantitative answers. Whether or not they are positively misleading is a moot point, a discussion of which is postponed till later.

ALTERNATIVE I: THE LITTLE–MIRRLEES PROCEDURE

This alternative consists essentially of evaluating sample firms' social costs and benefits according to the Little–Mirrlees (LM) method of project appraisal.[2] According to this method, the social value of an investment is measured in terms of free foreign exchange in the hands of the government, the shadow prices for inputs and outputs being derived from their 'border prices' or equivalents. Our application of the LM method is a simplified and crude one, in no way as sophisticated and complete as the theory demands. One of the advantages claimed for the LM method is, however, that it provides various short-cuts and simplifications in cases where the requisite information is not available (which, of course, it never is in real life). We have used short-cuts extensively, and shall describe them and our procedure in a moment.

The starting point of all methods of social cost–benefit analysis is that costs and benefits valued at market prices do not correctly measure the cost or benefit to society as a whole. The concept of 'social welfare' which underlies such analysis is derived directly from the philosophical and value premises on which most conventional economic theory rests – individual preferences as the ultimate measure of welfare, the existence of social harmony, acceptable income distribution, government neutrality, and the like[3] – which we have mentioned in Chapter 3 and shall return to briefly in Chapter 10. If we take these premises for granted for the time being, we can correct for the deviation of market from social value by applying notional 'shadow' prices to the actual ones. As mentioned above, the LM method derives shadow prices from the opportunity cost to society of inputs and outputs expressed in 'border' prices, with social values of non-tradables and labour converted to border equivalents by prescribed processes. Readers are referred to the original book, and to the other works mentioned, for a full exposition. Here we shall refer only to the ways in which our techniques differed from the standard LM method, and some of the problems we faced.

The most important ways in which we simplified our application of the LM technique are as follows.

(a) We treated consumption and savings as being equally valuable to society, and so did not distinguish between them with regard to the value of benefits accruing to the host country. Little and Mirrlees treat savings as the more valuable, and transform consumption into its savings equivalent in their estimation of the shadow wage rate; this process may be modified or reversed if income-distribution considerations call for a premium to be attached to the consumption of workers.

(b) We used a 'standard conversion factor' (SCF), an estimate of the extent to which domestic prices exceed their border equivalents, to derive the shadow price of non-tradables, rather than working out, from an input–output table, the correct (and very complicated) shadow price of each non-tradable factor.[4] The SCF in this form is simply the inverse of the 'shadow exchange rate' used in other forms of cost–benefit analysis and trade theory.

(c) We divided total personnel payments into 85 per cent for scarce labour (which would have found alternative employment in the absence of a particular project) and 15 per cent for non-scarce labour. The former was treated as a non-tradable, and its shadow price given by its SCF equivalent, while the latter was assumed to have an opportunity cost of zero, with all its income accruing as a social benefit. This avoided the controversial, but for our purposes peripheral, problem of calculating a proper shadow wage rate.

(d) We did not discount the costs and benefits of the investments back to the dates of their inception, since we had data for only a few years, relating to different stages in the lives of sample firms. Instead, we used a method of working out a current social cost of the capital employed by sample firms, bringing fixed and current inputs on to a comparable time scale. This involved assigning to each category of capital employed a 'real' cost of maintaining it intact each year,[5] and to capital as a whole an annual opportunity cost in terms of production lost elsewhere (which we took to be 10 per cent for all our countries, with sensitivity tests for 5 per cent and 20 per cent). The two costs taken together gave us the total social cost of the inputs of *local* capital employed in the sample firms. The cost of *foreign* capital, which we assumed had no local opportunity cost, was given directly by the costs of servicing it (dividends, interest and, where relevant, royalties and hidden profit remittances) in foreign exchange, with no shadow pricing being necessary. The value of capital assets was divided between local and foreign in proportion to their respective contributions to financing them each year. Thus, a capital inflow from abroad in a particular year would show up in the calculations merely as a reduction in the local cost of capital required to finance capital inputs in that year.

Given these simplifications, the net social benefit of an investment in terms of income would simply be the foreign-exchange value of its output (exports and domestic sales) minus the foreign-exchange value of tradable and non-tradable inputs, local capital costs and direct outflows abroad. The resulting net gain (or loss) in income would accrue to three factors.

(a) Non-scarce labour, whose wages would be an unequivocal gain to society.

(b) The government, whose 'fiscal effect' would be a net gain or loss, depending on whether its actual taxation and tariff gains in the actual situation exceeded or fell short of the taxes on local profits, the taxes on foreign profits,[6] and the tariffs it would have realised in the alternative situation, assuming that the final price to consumers was kept constant.[7] There are thus two components of fiscal income: the tax effect and the protection effect – the latter (very important quantitatively) being a measure of the net welfare loss or gain to the economy from the effective protection afforded to the firm. There is a simplification implicit in treating the welfare effects of protection as a fiscal effect, since it assigns the full responsibility for protective policies to the government. However, as long as we bear in mind that this is simply a convenient assumption, and that protection is in fact determined by an interaction between the government and other interested parties, there is no harm in this procedure.

(c) The local private sector and the firm itself, which would again be a net gain or loss, depending on (i) the earnings of local capitalists with the firm in question, compared to their possible earnings elsewhere, and

(ii) a residual factor for the value of changes in stocks as well as the costs of reselling goods not produced by the firm, both affecting declared profits from the firms' own production.

This method of tracking down the separate components of income effects, added as a refinement to the standard LM procedure, enabled us to identify *why* income effects turned out in particular ways and *who* gained the benefit or bore the loss. At the risk of some repetition, however, we must stress that the measurement of these effects depends crucially on the definitions of social welfare adopted, and these are themselves neither obvious nor universally acceptable.

Once we have measured income effects in terms of foreign exchange, we need yet another step in order to arrive at the final balance-of-payments effect. This involves tracing the effect of *spending* the income gain on the balance of payments, and so involves making some assumptions about spending propensities for the three components of income mentioned above. We assumed that non-scarce labour income was fully consumed and the others fully saved, so that the only difference between income and balance-of-payments effects lay in the foreign-exchange value of consuming non-scarce wages. This was generally a very small item, so we may ignore it for the remainder of the argument. The results will all be presented in terms of income effects only.

It was far from easy to derive shadow prices for tradable or non-tradable items. As far as tradables are concerned, not only did the sample firms have poor information on the relevant c.i.f. prices of their outputs or domestically purchased tradable inputs, but, in addition, the heterogeneity of large firms' products, variations in quality and models as compared to international standards, and so on, made any general estimates of the international value of outputs or inputs rather shaky. Border prices were, moreover, highly variable, depending on the source of supply and period considered; in many cases the prices were not openly quoted but depended on the outcome of a bargain. Prices on intra-firm trade of intermediate inputs were, of course, often arbitrarily decided by the foreign investor. We tried to obtain the best possible data from the firms, governments, World Bank, and other studies, but ultimately the estimates remained impressionistic and imprecise.

As for non-tradables, the values of the SCF, the opportunity cost of local capital, the rate of capital 'use', and scarce, as opposed to non-scarce, labour were based on even less firm ground. In part this was owing to our lack of time and resources, but mostly it was owing to the sort of the data available in host countries and the unquantifiable nature of many of the values required. It is very doubtful whether our estimates would have had much greater validity if we had spent far more time in the field; certainly, as we shall argue later, the dubiousness of the whole welfare foundation of social cost–benefit analysis would have rendered such an effort of questionable value.

While many gaps in information were inevitable, and simplifying assumptions necessary, the simulation model which we set up was in principle able to calculate comprehensively the 'social' effects, as defined conventionally, of foreign investments, and to trace their exact origin.[8] We adjusted for exchange-rate changes and differential rates of inflation between the sample countries and the rest of the world; we fitted in data on tax and tariff changes in relevant items from year to year and ran sensitivity tests to find out which assumptions were the most crucial ones. The results were, given the handicaps, very interesting; at the very least, they represent the first complete attempt to calculate the effects of foreign investments in a cost–benefit framework.

ALTERNATIVE II: FINANCIAL REPLACEMENT

Alternative II shows whether or not foreign capital financing (in the form of equity and loans) in an investment is *by itself* desirable for the host country, leaving all other matters (such as its value as a project or the contribution of foreign technology, management, and so on) out of consideration. It isolates the financial contribution of foreign investment, and so enables us to judge within a cost–benefit setting the value of one of the main elements of the foreign package.

Much of the discussion of the financial contribution of foreign investment in LDCs has focused on the direct capital inflows and profit outflows, and has concluded, on the basis of broad balance-of-payments data which show that foreign investment generally 'takes out of the country much more than it brings in', that it is too costly. In terms of direct foreign-exchange flows, this is correct (as we have seen above, the sample firms 'took out more than they put in' in the period studied); but in a broader context of the total impact on income or balance of payments, it may be quite misleading. The fact that profit outflows exceed capital inflows in any particular year tells us nothing about the overall effect on any macro-economic aggregate of the sum of investments which have entered the country. Furthermore, even the fact that over the life of a particular investment the profits have greatly exceeded the total capital invested says very little about the project's economic value. What is needed in both cases is an evaluation of the direct and indirect effects of the investment, and to compare this with alternatives—a far more difficult exercise than that of comparing direct balance-of-payments inflows and outflows.

If what is wanted, however, *is* just a calculation of the financial contribution of foreign capital, the correct procedure is to compare its actual cost with the cost of alternative sources of capital, taking the social value of its other costs and benefits as given. There may be two such sources: foreign borrowing and a diversion of local capital from other uses.[9] The cost of the former is the rate charged by the foreign lender, while that of the latter is the social opportunity cost of local capital (i.e. the amount of output which the capital could have produced elsewhere, valued at shadow prices). Our procedure has been to assign an opportunity cost of 10 per cent — identical to our assumption for local capital employed in the actual situation — to the capital needed to replace foreign finance, and to compare this with the servicing costs of the latter.[10] Further, a test with rates of 5 and 20 per cent enables us to work out the sensitivity of the results to the assumption made, and to compare direct investment with foreign borrowing.

Since Alternative II ignores all the non-financial attributes of foreign investment, it may not be a realistic assessment of its total impact on the host economy. Its main interest lies in that it shows the cost of one element of the total 'package', and so is valuable if the host government is trying to break down the 'package' into its components. There are, moreover, a number of industries where the nature of the foreign firm's contribution *is* mainly financial: for instance, where local firms possess the requisite technology and management. Here Alternative II can be taken to approximate its total contribution to the economy. This is particularly apt in cases where foreign investors take over existing firms and add little by way of new technology. The host economy may gain little except the injection of capital (unless we count, say, the introduction of foreign brand names as a welfare 'gain'), which it then has to service in perpetuity; Alternative II then provides a correct measure of its total contribution.

The result of this sort of exercise depends crucially on the shadow price used for calculating the cost of local capital. Since this price is bound to be little more than a rough guess, however sophisticated the model used, we must bear in mind the tentative nature of the results.

ALTERNATIVE III: MOST LIKELY LOCAL REPLACEMENT

In ideal conditions Alternative III should provide an estimate of all the financial and non-financial contributions of foreign investment, as compared with the alternative of local replacement – a true measure of 'foreignness'. Unfortunately, no such quantitative measure is feasible either in theory or in practice. What is required is essentially the comparison of an existing firm with a hypothetical one, where the latter may differ from the former in any number of ways. There are two sorts of difficulties. First, one firm may differ from another for reasons completely unconnected with its 'foreignness'. Some differences between them may be purely accidental, others may be related to their peculiar management or history, and others may be the result of external pressures: none of these can be generalised on the basis of whether the firm is local or foreign. Second, even if some differences in the behaviour, efficiency and effects of firms *were* believed to be due to 'foreignness', it would clearly be extremely hazardous to attempt to put figures on the extent to which an actual foreign firm differs from a hypothetical 'typical' local firm. The data adduced in the previous chapters give some indication of the difficulties of comparing such types, and it is unlikely that even very comprehensive figures on sample countries would have enabled us to reach a more definite opinion.

The sorts of differences which may be due to foreign (especially TNC) ownership may be divided into those which favour the foreign investor and those which favour the local replacement firm. The former are generally thought to be:

(a) managerial and organisational superiority;
(b) quicker, wider and cheaper access to technology;
(c) better knowledge of international markets;
(d) advantages in raising capital domestically and abroad;
(e) better-known brand names and more powerful marketing techniques;
(f) stronger bargaining positions relative to host governments; and
(g) a more dynamic outlook, willingness to take risks, and so on.

The local replacement firm, by contrast, may benefit from:

(a) better knowledge of local markets, culture and resources;
(b) closer working links with the government (though this may be negated by a weaker bargaining position);

Balance-of-Payments and Income Effects: Evaluation 167

(c) freedom from control by a TNC, which may otherwise restrict a subsidiary's expansion, exports and local tax payments; and
(d) a more appropriate technology and lesser dependence on imports (though these are very unlikely).

These differences are usually mentioned in the literature, but they are based on extremely impressionistic evidence and their importance varies greatly from firm to firm; we did not have enough confidence in any of them to propose precise formulas for application in Alternative III.

Consequently we decided not to spend much time playing around with various possibilities for this alternative, but to concentrate on one simple exercise to illustrate the significance of the two factors for which most developing countries look to TNCs: *technology* and *entrepreneurship*.[11] We used the device of the 'degree of local replacement' to show in one composite index the technological and entrepreneurial abilities of the host economy as compared to the foreign investor. For each sample firm we proposed a degree of replacement on this basis: the older or more easily available the technology (without direct foreign investment) and the greater the potential strength of local entrepreneurs, the higher the degree of replacement assumed; and, the more sophisticated or monopolistically controlled the technology, and the less the competition offered by local firms, the lower the degree of replacement assumed. At the one extreme, the foreign firm would be totally replaced, making Alternative III equivalent to Alternative II; at the other, there would be nil replacement and the output would be imported, making it equivalent to Alternative I. This device, crude as it is, did allow us to introduce some of the factors which we felt to be more important in determining the effects of foreign investment *in different environments*; thus, we would assume a greater degree of replacement for a foreign firm in India than for an identical one in Jamaica.

The purpose of Alternative III was very limited, and we would certainly not wish to claim that its results really captured the essential features of foreign investment in our sample. On the contrary, because of a lack of hard data on which to base better parameters, we made certain assumptions — such as constant returns to scale, or the absence of any lags in replacement — which were probably quite unrealistic. We adopted the simplest possible expedient of assuming that all inputs (valued at shadow prices) varied *pari passu* with the extent of output replaced, thus merely adjusting all the inputs and outputs proportionately within the LM framework. The net effect of a foreign firm in Alternative III would consequently be positive if its effect under

Alternative I were positive and local replacement were less than complete, or if its financial cost did not offset its other contributions. The net effect of local replacement would be positive if the Alternative I result of the foreign firm were negative and if replacement were less than complete, or if the financial advantage of the local firm outweighed the foreign firm's positive contributions on other scores.

Of all the quantitative exercises attempted in our studies, those of Alternative III were potentially the most valuable but in fact the least reliable. We shall therefore place very little emphasis on the figures produced by them, contenting ourselves with a bare iteration of the most general results. We shall return to a critique of the method later, in discussing the drawbacks of the basic conceptual framework and the value of such quantitative techniques. First, however, we review the findings of our study.

CHAPTER 9

'Total' Balance-of-Payments and 'Social' Income Effects: the Results

The findings of our studies on the 'total' balance-of-payments and 'social' income effects are presented in the order in which the alternative positions were described in the preceding chapter. The first section deals with the results of Alternative I, the Little–Mirrlees (LM) model, which forms the core of the work done to quantify the 'total' effects; the second deals with the results of Alternative II, 'financial' replacement; and the third deals with those of Alternative III, 'most likely' local replacement.

ALTERNATIVE I: THE LITTLE–MIRRLEES MODEL

In this alternative all the outputs and inputs of individual sample firms are valued at 'shadow prices' given by their balance-of-payments effects (or border prices). Since all the direct balance-of-payments transactions are already given at their shadow prices, this alternative essentially consists of our adding to the direct effects discussed in Chapter 7 the shadow-price equivalents of all the local inputs and outputs, and reducing capital transactions to a current basis. Thus,

$$Y = (X + S_d) - (C_r + R + D) - (C_t + C_{nt} + L_s + K_l)$$

where Y is the net 'social' income effect; S_d is the border value of domestic sales; X, C_r, R and D are defined as in Chapter 7; C_t is the border value of domestic current tradable inputs; C_{nt} is the derived border value of domestic current non-tradable inputs; L_s is the derived border value of scarce labour; and K_l is the current annual cost in border prices of using local capital.

The net income effect is made up of three components,

$$Y = F + P + L$$

where F stands for the income effects accruing to the governments, P for those accruing to the local private sector, and L for those accruing to non-scarce labour.

To derive the 'total' balance-of-payments effect (B_t) from the above,

$$B_t = Y - L_{con}$$

where L_{con} represents the balance-of-payments effects of consuming the whole value of L. The other income effects, F and P, are assumed to be entirely saved. Since the value of L is generally small, the difference between Y and B_t is also very small. In order to simplify the exposition, therefore, we have left B_t out and concentrated on Y; whatever is said about the one can be taken to apply more or less completely to the other.

The results for Alternative I are presented in several sub-sections, dealing respectively with the valuation of sales; local tradable and non-tradable inputs, including scarce labour; local capital costs; the final income effects; and the components of these effects.

Value of Domestic Sales

The use of the 'border price' of domestic sales as a measure of social welfare implies not only that the distribution and consumption patterns which would prevail at the shadow prices are considered optimal, but also, at a more mundane level, that a product which is physically tradable would in fact be traded if it were not domestically produced. The latter presumption is really one of consistent behaviour by the government, in the sense that, if it considers the product valuable enough to make locally, it also considers it valuable enough to import. In reality, of course, governments are often not consistent, and many LDCs often prohibit imports of various non-essentials for long periods before allowing domestic production to be undertaken. If the alternative were not to import the product but to do without it altogether, its welfare contribution could, according to the precepts of conventional welfare economics, be measured by the area under its demand curve.[1] We did try this alternative for the Colombian and Malaysian samples, but do not regard its results as interesting enough to merit repetition here.

In our version of the LM model we proceeded on the basis that all outputs were fully tradable. The assignation of shadow prices then

Balance-of-Payments and Income Effects: Results

consisted of finding the appropriate f.o.b. or c.i.f. price for the products in question,[2] and correcting for (differential rates of) inflation at home and abroad as well as for exchange-rate changes. The adjustment for inflation and devaluation was made for every year – a simple but tedious task not worth explaining at length. The estimation of border prices was, as we mentioned in the previous chapter, based on a certain amount of guesswork, since the firms and officials concerned often had only a vague idea of the international competitiveness of the relevant products. Sample firms in India seemed to be the least competitive, their output being priced approximately 33 per cent above border equivalents; firms in Iran, Colombia and Malaysia were somewhat better, with an average uncompetitiveness of 20 per cent; those in Kenya and Jamaica fared best, with about 10 per cent.

Individual firms showed considerable variation round these averages. Some 25 per cent of the total number of sample firms were in fact competitive with world prices; 23 per cent had prices ranging from 1 to 19 per cent above world prices; about 24 per cent had prices higher than 40 per cent above world prices, and the remaining 28 per cent lay between 20 and 39 per cent. There was no noticeable difference between TNCs and non-TNCs with regard to competitiveness; but then, given the quality of the data, we would not expect fine differences to show up in our estimates. In any case, there was no indication that TNCs paid any more attention, in the protected markets offered them, to attaining competitiveness than did non-TNCs.

Local Tradable and Non-Tradable Inputs

Local tradable inputs were assigned border prices in the same way as outputs, using estimates provided during the course of our field-work and by other research work in this area. The figures are, once more, subject to a (non-calculable) margin of error, since they are averaged over a diversity of industrial inputs and over many years, and information on appropriate border prices (or a whole range of border prices) is scanty.

As far as non-tradable inputs and scarce labour are concerned, we adopted the simple expedient of assigning shadow prices by using the SCF (standard conversion factor). The SCF is a general measure of the excess of domestic over world prices, which was taken to be 20 per cent for Kenya, 15 per cent for Jamaica, 25 per cent for India, 30 per cent for Iran, 20 per cent for Colombia and 10 per cent for Malaysia. These figures are based on very impressionistic evidence, but there was little to be gained by attempting a more laborious and comprehensive calculation of such magnitudes.

Local Capital Costs

The cost of employing local capital was worked out from two components: the cost of maintaining intact the total stock of local capital employed, and the value of output lost elsewhere. This method of reducing capital costs to current terms involved several assumptions about the rate at which different forms of capital (land, buildings, stocks, machinery, fittings and vehicles) were 'used up' every year, and the 'opportunity cost' of domestic capital.[3] It also involved adjusting the historic values of capital assets for inflation, and the domestic values for excess over world market prices. The actual level of these costs depended on the percentage of total capital costs financed from local as opposed to foreign sources,[4] as well as the overall capital – output ratio.

For the country samples as such, local capital costs came to about 1·5 per cent of sales for Jamaica, 3·3 per cent for Kenya, 9·0 per cent for India, 6·2 per cent for Iran, 3·4 per cent for Colombia and 6·3 per cent for Malaysia. Some twenty firms out of the total had local capital costs exceeding 20 per cent of sales, and nineteen had costs between 10 and 20 per cent; ten firms had no local capital costs at all, and the remaining 110 had costs between 0·1 and 10 per cent of sales.[5] In general, machinery, electrical and chemical (excluding pharmaceutical) firms had heavy capital costs in our samples, while pharmaceuticals and rubber had low costs, with other industries lying in the middle.

It should be noted that, despite the large number of assumptions and simplifications necessarily involved in the calculation of local capital costs, some such calculation is vital to any quantitative analysis of the welfare effects of foreign investment. Not only does the use of local capital represent a charge on a particularly sensitive resource, but, in addition, its proper valuation, though extremely difficult, is crucial to working out the net effects of foreign investment as compared with the alternative of local replacement (illustrated below).

Net Income Effect

The social income effects of the sample firms, derived after all the costs and benefits at shadow prices have been netted out, are as follows (net income effect as a percentage of sales, by country): for Kenyan firms, 12·7 per cent; Jamaican firms, 7·0 per cent; Indian firms, 1·3 per cent; Iranian firms, 5·6 per cent; Colombian firms, − 1·5 per cent; and Malaysian firms, − 4·5 per cent. Table 9·1 shows the distribution of firms by their income effects, grouped according to country and transnationality. As is to be expected, there is considerable variation around the country averages, and the country results cannot be taken to represent meaningful

Balance-of-Payments and Income Effects: Results

TABLE 9.1
Distribution of Sample Firms by Net Income Effect as a Percentage of Sales

Country. etc.	Positive				Negative			
	Over 20%	10 to 20%	5 to 10%	0·1 to 5%	0 to −5%	−5 to −10%	−10 to −20%	Under −20%
Kenya	2	2	2	–	1	–	–	1
Jamaica	2	1	2	2	1	–	3	–
India	5	7	10	7	5	4	9	6
Iran	6	4	–	1	1	1	1	2
Colombia	3	14	8	11	7	1	4	8
Malaysia	–	4	4	–	1	1	1	4
Total (159)	18	32	26	21	16	7	18	21
TNCs	10	21	10	17	8	4	8	10
Non-TNCs	8	11	16	4	8	3	10	11

Total no. of firms with positive effects: 97 (61 per cent).
Total no. of firms with negative effects: 62 (39 per cent).

groupings in terms of the performance of the respective samples. On average, TNCs perform better than non-TNCs, with 66 per cent of the former showing positive effects, as compared to 55 per cent of the latter. However, an analysis-of-variance test fails to show that the two groupings are statistically significant. Similar tests for groupings by industry, extent of foreign ownership and age in operation fail to give meaningful results, suggesting that *such external characteristics are not important in determining the final social income effect of particular investments*. In view of the methodology of calculating 'social' effects, this is hardly surprising; the assumptions which are used to work out who benefits, and by how much, are so important that they override these other characteristics.

The most important finding of these exercises, if we accept the premises of the analysis, is that *a very large proportion of manufacturing investments in the sample are undesirable from the point of view of social welfare*. The exact figures are not important, and, in view of the large number of simplifications used to calculate them, probably not very reliable. What is obvious is that, under any set of reasonable assumptions, it would probably still be the case that *one-third to one half* of the sample firms would have negative net income effects. This finding serves to confirm for foreign investments what has been observed more generally for import-substituting industrialisation policies in a number of developing countries; it has policy implications which have been discussed at length in the literature[6] and which we shall touch upon later, in the context of foreign investment.

We tried a number of sensitivity tests to see which of our assumptions were the most important in determining the final income effect of sample firms. We varied the estimates for uncompetitiveness of domestic sales and purchases and for the SCF, by 10 per cent above and below the 'most likely' assumptions used; we also tried different estimates about the opportunity cost of local capital (5 per cent and 20 per cent, the 'most likely' estimate used being 10 per cent) and the rate of 'use' of various types of capital assets, (1 per cent per annum less than the 'most likely' rate). We found that, within these ranges, the estimates for the *competitiveness of sales* and the *opportunity cost of local capital* had the largest effect on the final result (the former by about 6–7 per cent of sales, the latter by 3–4 per cent), followed by the estimates for the competitiveness of domestic raw materials and the SCF (about equal at 1–2 per cent of sales). Changes in the rate of capital 'use' had a minimal effect (less than 0·5 per cent). If our assumptions were not unduly biased in one direction or another, and there is little reason to think that they were, the general finding noted above would appear to hold within normally acceptable ranges of error.

Components of Income Effects

While groupings by industry, age, or extent of foreign ownership failed to show any significance as far as the final income effects were concerned, an examination of the components of these effects may prove more useful in understanding *why* they are what they are.

Of the three components, F, P and W, the last (wages of non-scarce labour) is an unequivocal gain to the host country of 2–4 per cent of sales, and, being derived from an arbitrary estimate of the division between scarce and non-scarce labour, does not provide any fresh information of interest. P (the income effects accruing to the domestic private sector) is a mixture of a number of different effects: the gain or loss represented by the actual earnings of local capital with the firm, as compared to its opportunity cost; the gain represented by the sum out of foreign profits set aside for depreciation; and a collection of other effects, such as changes in stocks of work-in-progress and finished goods[7] and the costs of reselling finished goods. The first component of P is fairly easy to understand in terms of standard cost–benefit analysis. The second and third are problems which arise in applying cost–benefit techniques to difficult practical circumstances where stocks vary (in quantity as well as price) from year to year and firms combine manufacturing with non-manufacturing activity.[8] We had neither the resources nor the data to try and weed out these distortionary elements in our basic information, and so lumped them under 'income effects accruing to the firm'. A rough calculation for the Colombian sample showed that, if we adjusted for stock changes in finished goods, the final income effect would improve by some 2 per cent of sales for the sample as a whole. No adjustment was possible for reselling activities, which were of importance only in the Colombian case, where thirteen firms had resales higher than 10 per cent of the value of their own production.

For the country samples, the income effect P came to -3.2 per cent of sales for India, 4·8 percent for Iran, -5.6 per cent for Colombia and -0.2 per cent for Malaysia.[9] The poor overall Ps for India and Colombia are reflected in the individual firm results: forty-one out of fifty-three firms in India, and thirty-seven out of fifty-six in Colombia, had negative income effects on this count. Bearing in mind the qualifications regarding distortions caused by stock changes and reselling, we may conclude that *local capital fared rather poorly in its employment with most of the firms in these two samples*, and would have done better in some other use. In Colombia, nearly 75 per cent of the total number of TNCs and 50 per cent of non-TNCs had negative Ps, as compared with 67 and 84 per cent in India. In general, there was no discernible difference between TNCs and non-TNCs in this respect.

The analysis of F (income or 'fiscal' effects accruing to the government) is of more analytical interest. This effect is made up of the net gains in *taxation* and the net *welfare of protection* with respect to each investment. The former consists of the tax on foreign profits, an unequivocal gain, and the tax on local profits less its opportunity cost (i.e. the tax which would have been realised in an alternative occupation); the net taxation effect is always positive, and comes to 5·9 per cent of sales for India, 2·1 per cent for Iran, 5·2 per cent for Colombia and 1·6 per cent for Malaysia. In every sample, foreign majority-owned firms make larger contributions on this score than do foreign-minority and wholly-local firms, and there is not much difference between the last two groups.

The fiscal effects of protection are conceptually very similar to the measure of 'effective protection' in the trade literature. The actual formulation we have used is different from that of standard trade theory in that (a) our denominator is the total value of sales rather than value-added at world prices; (b) we have counted scarce labour as an input rather than as a recipient of value-added (in some ways, our measure is a more comprehensive one of the total effects of offering protection, since it includes the effect that protecting material trade has on the price of non-tradables and skilled labour); and (c) a positive fiscal effect (a welfare gain) shows negative effective protection, and a negative fiscal effect (a welfare loss) positive effective protection.

For the country samples, fiscal effects of protection come to -3.5 per cent of sales for India, -2.5 per cent for Iran, -4.8 per cent for Colombia and -10.6 per cent for Malaysia. These average figures, weighted by sales, conceal the fact that the number of firms with negative effects is actually smaller than the number of those with positive ones. Table 9.2. shows that 55 per cent of the total number of firms in these four samples, 57 per cent of the TNCs and 53 per cent of the non-TNCs, have positive effects. In India and Iran, TNCs appear to do better than non-TNCs, while in Colombia the reverse seems to be true. However, in view of the rather tentative nature of the assumptions about uncompetitiveness underlying the analysis, not too much stress should be laid on these figures. They certainly do not enable us to judge whether or not TNCs were able to obtain higher *nominal* protection (on their final output) than were other firms (estimates of nominal protection being practically impossible for us to assess independently, since in most cases imports were banned).

TABLE 9.2
Number of Firms by Net Fiscal Effects of Protection

	India	Iran	Colombia	Malaysia
Total (140 firms)				
Positive (55%)	27 (51%)	11 (69%)	33 (59%)	6 (40%)
Negative (45%)	26 (49%)	5 (31%)	23 (41%)	9 (60%)
TNCs (74 firms)				
Positive (5.7%)	12 (57%)	6 (75%)	21 (55%)	3 (31%)
Negative (43%)	9 (43%)	2 (25%)	17 (45%)	4 (57%)
Non-TNCs (66 firms)				
Positive (53%)	15 (47%)	5 (63%)	12 (67%)	3 (43%)
Negative (47%)	17 (53%)	3 (37%)	6 (33%)	5 (57%)

The fiscal effect of protection is probably the single most important determinant of the variation in income effects of investments in Alternative I. It should be obvious why this is so. Since welfare is *defined* here with reference to world market prices, any deviation from these prices, assumed to be caused by protection, immediately and directly affects the final outcome. Thus, where domestic investment has been promoted behind heavy protective barriers, differences in the level of effective protection offered to firms are extremely significant in accounting for differences in the net social effect of each investment. This much is implicit in the methodology and can be held to apply *a priori* to practically any country which imposes tariffs or quotas. The point of real interest then lies in *who or what actually determines the level of protection offered*. We have for convenience assumed that the responsibility for protection lies with the government, but it must be stressed this is an assumption and not an empirical finding. The actual level of protection *depends partly on government policy, partly on the bargain struck by firms with the government, and partly on the market power of the firms themselves*. Furthermore, where an industry is monopolistic and wields market power internationally, the *measurement of protection at the national level does not give a proper measure of welfare effects* (which in theory is derived from a competitive framework). In such a case there may be a worldwide loss of welfare, owing to the TNCs' market power, and the correct policy is not simply to reduce national protection, but to attack the sources of market power. It is impossible to apportion among deliberate policy, bargaining and market power the due responsibility for protection. This is a deficiency that seriously limits the usefulness of this sort of quantitative analysis when it is directed at helping in the formulation of policy.

ALTERNATIVE II: FINANCIAL REPLACEMENT

This alternative, seeking to isolate the financial contribution of foreign investment, compares the actual cost of financing foreign capital with the social cost of providing an equal amount of local capital. Table 9.3. gives the distribution of the 147 firms with foreign capital according to their 'net financial contribution',[10] counting profits, interest and royalties as the cost of servicing foreign investment, and using the 'most likely' assumption of the opportunity cost of local capital, valued at shadow prices at 10 per cent. All the results are expressed as percentages of sales. Hidden remittances of profits via transfer pricing are not included here, but if the requisite information were available the picture for the sample would clearly be much worse.

The table shows that only 47 per cent of the sample firms made positive financial contributions if the opportunity cost of local capital was 10 per cent, and that the average performance of TNCs (43 per cent positive)

TABLE 9.3
Distribution of Firms with Foreign Capital According to
their Net Financial Contribution
(Number of firms; percentages in perentheses)

Country	Total	Positive			Negative		
		10·1% and above	5·1 to 10·0%	0·1 to 5·0%	0 to −5·0%	−5·1 to −10·0%	−10·1% and below
Kenya	8	–	2	4	1	1	–
Jamaica	11	–	–	4	1	4	2
India	45	4	4	19	18	–	–
Iran	15	3	–	4	4	4	–
Colombia	55	4	3	11	21	11	5
Malaysia	13	3	2	2	5	–	1
Total	147 (100)	14 (9·5)	11 (7·5)	44 (29·9)	50 (34·0)	20 (13·6)	8 (5·4)
TNCs	88 (100)	7 (8·0)	4 (4·5)	27 (30·7)	29 (33·0)	15 (17·0)	6 (6·8)
Non-TNCs	59 (100)	7 (11·9)	7 (11·9)	17 (28·8)	21 (35·6)	5 (8·5)	2 (3·4)

was worse than that of non-TNCs (53 per cent positive). For the country samples, the average financial contribution was 0·4 per cent of sales for Kenya, −5·4 per cent for Jamaica, nil for India, −0·5 per cent for Iran, −2·4 per cent for Colombia and 0·8 per cent for Malaysia. The final effect would be somewhat worse if we took account of the fact that most of the foreign firms which had high positive contributions were in fact making losses in the period studied, and that over a longer run, when they achieved normal profitability, their contribution would probably be negative. Furthermore, on average it would be cheaper to borrow abroad at an interest rate of 7–8 per cent to finance the foreign capital of the sample firms than to invite direct investment.

On the whole, therefore, the *purely financial contribution of foreign direct investment appears to be negligible or negative* from the sample data. Though this is not an unexpected finding – it is, after all, generally admitted that direct investment is sought for its non-financial contribution more than for its financial contribution, and that it is usually a rather expensive way to get funds as such – it must be qualified by the possibility that a rate of 10 per cent for the social opportunity cost of local capital may not be realistic. Clearly, at a higher rate the financial contribution of foreign capital would appear better. A calculation for the

Balance-of-Payments and Income Effects: Results 179

Indian and Iranian samples, however, shows that, even if we take a rate of 20 per cent, the overall financial contribution improves only by 2–3 per cent of sales, not a change which warrants a revision of the statement that the net financial contribution of foreign direct investment is generally negligible or negative.

ALTERNATIVE III: MOST LIKELY LOCAL REPLACEMENT

In the previous chapter we described the enormous difficulties involved in conducting a meaningful comparison of actual foreign investments with their 'most likely' local replacements. In view of these quantitatively insuperable problems, we resorted to a simple expedient whereby the 'degree of replacement' would measure all the technological and financial contributions of foreign investments. This was not because of any constraints on the power of the simulation model, which initially was set up to handle a complex series of replacement alternatives in which we could vary productivity, learning-by-doing, export performance, technical payments, scale factors, and so on; but because we had no real information on which to base even tentative estimates. As it ended up, Alternative III was simply an illustration, based on obvious oversimplifications, of the technological, entrepreneurial and financial capabilities of local enterprise.

We estimated for each sample firm the most likely extent of local replacement, and compared the net social income effects of these replacement firms with the Alternative I results of the actual firms. In general, the highest extent of local replacement was assumed for India, followed by Colombia, Malaysia, Jamaica, Kenya and Iran. Some 30 per cent of the total number of firms with foreign equity appeared, on reasonable assumptions, to be totally replaceable by local firms, either with existing local technology or with the purchase abroad of easily available technology. Another 50 per cent seemed to be replaceable by 20–70 per cent, the complexity and non-availability of the technology preventing the rest of their production from being replaceable. The remaining 20 per cent did not seem to be replaceable at all, again because of the nature and control of the technology. We tried to take full account of the fact that certain items of technology were owned by a few large TNCs, which may not be willing to provide them under licence to wholly local firms, and that local firms would generally pay higher royalties for technology than would firms with foreign equity.

On the basis of these admittedly crude estimates, we found that, of the

147 firms with foreign capital, fifty-five (37 per cent) had negative income effects when compared with the alternative of local replacement; the remaining ninety-two had positive net effects. The extremely tentative nature of the estimates can hardly be overstressed; and any impression of quantitative precision must be treated as spurious. We left such important factors as transfer pricing, scale economies, bargaining, efficiency and exports out of consideration in comparing the actual with the alternative situation, and so missed out what may well be the most important determinants of the net economic effects of foreign investment.

CHAPTER 10

'Social' Income Effects: Evaluating the Evaluation

INTRODUCTION

The last two chapters have described very briefly our examination of the 'social' income effects of sample firms on host economies, under a variety of assumptions. The original UNCTAD studies went into much more detail about the method and reported the results (including those of several alternative assumptions not mentioned here) at greater length. The simulation model used was ingenious and powerful. It could handle some sixty to eighty items of information for every firm for each year, transforming each into 'shadow' values according to different assumptions, allowing for different rates of tariff, taxation and inflation on each, tracking down the groups which gained or lost from the welfare evaluation of each, and simulating a number of 'alternative positions' after allowing for different rates of domestic replacement, differing efficiencies, effects of changes in scale, 'learning', and so on. In fact, only a fraction of the simulator's potential was used. The parameters required were missing, and the possibility of virtually endless simulation, in return for practically no real addition to our knowledge, was a strong deterrent.

Nevertheless, we had sophisticated techniques, some reasonable firm-level data, and an established economic method. We did, using some admittedly major simplifications, produce a quantity of results. It is now time to take stock. What have we learnt from these exercises? What more could be learnt with better data? What are the limitations of the method employed in assessing welfare effects? And what are the special problems created by applying this method to the evaluation of TNCs in host LDCs? We have already hinted at some of the advantages and drawbacks of our approach. We shall now try to draw the threads together.

WHAT WE HAVE LEARNT ABOUT 'SOCIAL' COSTS AND BENEFITS

Let us start by summarising the main findings of our analysis of the welfare effects of the sample firms and the main advantages of using social cost–benefit techniques for assessing foreign investments in LDCs. Let us also, for this section and the next, accept the conventional definition of 'economic welfare' on which the techniques of social project evaluation are based.

Since social cost–benefit analysis for LDCs is a relatively recent phenomenon, and since our UNCTAD studies represent one of the earliest attempts to apply it comprehensively to foreign investments as well as to their possible alternatives, we may claim some novelty, even originality, in adapting and developing the method in the context of the study of TNCs. (We may also claim first-hand knowledge of the difficulties and limitations of the technique in this particular context – but more of that later.) Bearing in mind the several short-cuts taken, the following are the salient results of its application.

(a) A sizable proportion of the investments studied (some 40 per cent) had negative effects on social income in the host countries.

(b) These effects were *not* related to the 'foreignness' or 'transnationality' of the sample firms – whether the firms were owned locally or by TNCs seemed to make no significant difference to their welfare effects. Nor were these effects significantly different according to industry groupings or their age in operation.

(c) The main determining factor of social income effects was the extent of effective protection granted to the firms (or negotiated by them). The results were, however, also very sensitive to the assumption made about the opportunity cost of domestic capital used.

(d) Local capital fared rather poorly in its employment with most of the firms in the Indian and Colombian samples and would probably have earned a better return elsewhere.

(e) The purely financial contribution of foreign capital was, within reasonable range of the opportunity cost for local capital, negligible or negative. It would, in other words, have been cheaper for the countries concerned – had loans, and in some cases technology, been available abroad – to borrow the money and buy out the foreign investments, or to divert local capital from other uses. However, it is unlikely either that the loans or local capital would have been forthcoming to the requisite extent or that the technology would have been available in all cases (though it may well have been in some).

(f) Though it was practically impossible to estimate with any quantitative precision the overall effect of foreign investments, as compared with their 'most likely' local replacements, it appeared, on the basis of impressionistic evidence about local capabilities and the sort of technology being employed, that about one-third of the foreign firms could be totally replaced by local ones and about one-half could be partly replaced, with the remainder being irreplaceable. However, many relevant factors (regarding managerial efficiency, scale, and so on) could not be taken into account, and this simulation must be treated with due caution.

These findings confirm what other studies, using a similar approach, have found about the effects of high rates of effective protection on industrialisation in general in LDCs (see, for instance, Little, Scitovsky and Scott, 1970), and they add to our knowledge of the effects of foreign firms in particular. Our method could have been improved in some ways, especially in the calculation of the shadow prices of non-tradables and unskilled labour (though this last item is unlikely to be very important for modern manufacturing industry), and it could have been readjusted to attach income-distribution weights to different groups (see Lal, 1975). Nevertheless, as it stands it contains all the essential features of social cost–benefit analysis and can serve as a fair example of how the technique can be applied to the evaluation of TNC investments in LDCs.

Numerous advantages are claimed for the use of social cost–benefit techniques in LDCs, and Little and Mirrlees have argued persuasively (1969, 1974) for the adoption of such techniques, in order to prevent, in future investments, some of the obvious ill effects of the haphazard, inefficient and over-protected industrialisation that has taken place in several countries. The application of these techniques to *foreign* investment projects can, similarly, ensure that projects are approved on a consistent basis by standards which reflect the real opportunity costs to society of the resources used. Furthermore, after making appropriate adjustments (as indicated in previous chapters) for the opportunity cost of obtaining and servicing foreign capital, the potential for bargaining, and possible alternatives to direct foreign investment, the method is flexible enough to yield a range of outcomes for TNC investment under different assumptions, and so enable the host government to make a clearer, more rational and more well-informed choice.

The case for the use of social cost–benefit analysis to evaluate foreign investments is strong, and we recommend its inclusion as part of a comprehensive set of tools to deal with TNCs. We must, however, stress that it can be used only *as part of a larger policy package*. Its utility is far more limited than some of its more enthusiastic proponents may claim. It does *not* provide a complete measure of social 'welfare'; it *cannot* capture all the relevant social costs and benefits of multinational investment; and so it must not be taken as a perfect substitute for a broad policy towards TNCs, which would be based upon considerations rather different from those included in the narrow quantitative confines of project appraisal.

The limitations of social cost–benefit analysis arise from two sets of factors. The first comprises those which may be traced to the lack of adequate data and the simplifications inherent in the quantification process – what may broadly be termed 'practical' limitations of project evaluation. The second comprises those which result from 'conceptual' limitations, the particular value judgements and assumptions which underlie the welfare framework. Let us consider them in turn.

PRACTICAL LIMITATIONS OF 'SOCIAL' COST–BENEFIT ANALYSIS

The difficulties in applying shadow-pricing techniques to LDCs have been amply discussed in the literature, especially in connection with the LM method,[1] and here we need mention them only briefly. First, there are the problems which arise in *evaluating any project*, regardless of whether it is local or foreign: it is difficult, when the products in question are variable in quality, outmoded in design and (to different degrees) inferior in performance when compared with internationally traded products, to assess correct 'border' prices for a range of products made by a firm behind protective barriers. It is even more difficult to predict these prices over the whole life of the investment, and techniques of risk-evaluation cannot provide a rigorous solution. It is practically impossible to assign theoretically correct shadow prices to non-tradables and skilled labour, since the requisite input–output data are never available in LDCs; even if they were, arbitrary assumptions would have to be made about the policies followed by their governments to achieve internal and external balance, which determine where the effect of using a non-tradable input falls. The very distinction between non-tradables and tradables is to some extent dependent upon the assumption made about future policy. Finally, and perhaps most significantly, the neglect of externalities, non-marginal projects, linkages, 'learning' effects and similar unquantified or unquantifiable elements in industrial investments reduces the reliability of the 'welfare' estimates produced by cost–benefit analysis.[2]

Second, there are specific problems which arise in trying to apply cost–benefit analysis *to TNCs*. A number of 'border' prices involved in TNC investments are set by the firm itself, and often have no counterpart in 'free' international markets; several other prices are decided only after a bargaining process. In these cases, it becomes very difficult to estimate a correct shadow price, because the requisite information does not exist to determine a correct 'arm's-length' price or to assess the outcome of a 'fair' bargain. The 'externalities' associated with TNC entry are particularly large (and many TNC investments are not 'marginal' in LDCs), in terms of altering the industrial structure, encouraging or suppressing local enterprise, changing government policy and institutions, and so on; yet they are difficult or impossible to quantify, and so neglected in practice. Further, the evaluation of alternative situations, which Little and Mirrlees seem to assume to be straightforward,[3] is in fact beset by so many unknowables that we could not even start to quantify them. How would an actual foreign investment differ in efficiency, export performance, government and labour relations, use of local resources, use of technology, and so on, from a hypothetical local replacement? We simply do not know. Past experience, such as it is, may not be a good guide to the future in this area, especially when 'learning' is vital to the development of domestic entrepreneurship. Indeed, our studies indicate clearly that it would be wrong to use 'transnationality' as a significant determinant of several important aspects of company performance. Thus, any quantification of the net costs and benefits of TNC investment, as compared with hypothetical alternatives, must remain largely an act of faith.

In sum, therefore, the application of social cost–benefit techniques to TNC investments in LDCs is subject to a number of important practical difficulties. While *in principle* these could be overcome if sufficient data were available, *in practice* these data are neither available nor, in many cases, ever likely to exist in a reliable form. A sensible application of cost–benefit analysis should not, in consequence, aim at producing a single figure for the present social value (or internal rate of return) for a TNC investment – any such figure is likely to be arbitrary, and perhaps highly misleading. If, on the other hand, a range of results, taking account of possible variations in the values of the important variables, is produced, it is, in most cases, likely to be so wide as to render any final decision on desirability more a matter of subjective 'feel' than one of objective, scientific analysis. Cost–benefit analysis *can* serve a useful role in supplementing the 'feel' of the decision-maker, by providing consistent and comparable sets of figures (for ranges of outcomes) for different projects. But judgement will have to be used for assessing the limits of the technique and for evaluating the non-quantified or non-quantifiable features of the project. Moreover, there are important preliminary 'total' decisions to be made (for example, as to whether to have the product at all) to which social cost–benefit analysis has nothing to contribute, and the analysis may be harmful used too mechanically, if it leads to neglect of the unquantified features in favour of the quantified ones, or if some of the qualifications are omitted (Little and Mirrlees admit this very real danger). These difficulties are aggravated by the conceptual problems to which we now turn.

CONCEPTUAL LIMITATIONS OF 'SOCIAL' COST–BENEFIT ANALYSIS[4]

The practical difficulties of methods of 'social' project evaluation are only part of the story. We have already indicated, especially in Chapter 3, that the very definition of social 'welfare' underlying the methods is open to criticism, and that the role of the government, to whom welfare prescriptions are directed, is ambiguous. Instead of repeating the arguments, let us note the main points. The correct 'social' value of products is, in the LM method, given by their 'free' world market prices, which represent to the country in question the opportunity cost of obtaining or selling these products. The relative values of these products reflect the demand patterns and preferences of the developed countries and the technological and marketing patterns of the large oligopolists which dominate production there. The value of a quantity of foodgrain in terms of, say, Dior dresses, or of simple clothing in terms of Cadillacs, bears no relation to social 'needs' in LDCs. Conventional welfare analysis claims that project analysis can use weights which correspond to 'social' priorities rather than to market prices. But, quite apart from the practical difficulties, such a procedure presupposes that, in principle, a set of values can be found that corresponds to 'society's' choices. This assumption is a more sophisticated version of the harmony doctrine or the 'communistic fiction', according to which collective choices can be analysed in the same way as individual choices. But, where clashes of interest exist, such a procedure is impossible.

Furthermore, by taking the preferences which appear on the market as autonomous and given, it cannot go into factors which shape and change preferences. In the case of the impact of TNCs on LDCs, the neglect of these factors is particularly important: not only do TNCs specialise in products and techniques which are often—though certainly not always—inappropriate in several ways to social needs in LDCs, but they also exert (if not singly certainly when they are present in large numbers), directly through marketing and indirectly through the importation of cultural patterns, a strong influence on preferences, technologies, institutions, customs and politics there. How, then, is social cost–benefit analysis of TNC projects to proceed, when a straightforward application of world prices is likely to lead to projects that further distort income distributions, produce inappropriate products and divert resources from essential needs?

The answer is to 'leave it to the government'. Conventional welfare economics does not, and cannot, provide criteria by which to evaluate how the most important economic needs of poor societies are to be met. The government must then provide these criteria, on (non-economic) political, social or moral grounds which economists cannot question. It must lay down which needs are essential, how they are to be met, and into what income-distribution patterns they should fit. Cost–benefit analysis can then be applied, after the 'objective function' of the government is known. Two problems immediately arise.[5] The first, relatively less important, is how to proceed if the government (whoever is taken to be 'the government') does not *have* the detailed, consistent and well-specified welfare function required. The second, more fundamental, is what to do if the government reflects the interests and values of just one particular social class and there is no 'national' or 'social' interest (between which there is often little differentiation). The application of social cost–benefit analysis then becomes not just difficult but in principle impossible.

If the evaluator uses his own values to define welfare and so guide the government, he is not being 'rigorous' and 'scientific' by the standards of conventional economics; if the government imposes values which are biased by class interest, then the whole exercise is pointless anyway, since the decision-maker is not providing 'objective functions' which can be used to define social welfare.

The upshot is that, if one believes, as we do, that individual preferences are not the ultimate criterion of social welfare, and that all basic problems of defining more appropriate criteria for social cost–benefit analysis cannot simply be left to be resolved by a 'neutral' government, any simple method of assigning 'shadow' prices, like using border prices, *cannot be applied without substantial modification,* especially to the evaluation of TNC projects. However, if the need for serious modification is accepted, the results of the analysis lose the objectivity, precision and generality that is their main attraction. Thus, even if none of the practical problems described in the previous section is present, the inherent ambiguity about how 'welfare' is to be defined and measured remains. Once a large dose of 'subjectivity' enters the picture, what is the use of social cost–benefit procedures?

Clearly some use does remain. If the government can be persuaded to set up comprehensive procedures and guidelines for evaluating social welfare, project evaluation can be used *when all the other valuations have been made*. Cost–benefit analysis provides, in other words, a *part of the answer*, but not the whole. However, if the government acts in the interests of a group, an elite or a class, the purpose of 'social' recommendations vanishes. Nevertheless, the next part of the book will discuss policy questions mainly on the assumption that there exists a 'national interest' and 'social welfare', and that the government is willing and able to act in accordance with it, or, at least, can be persuaded to do so. At the very end we shall return to the question of what happens if it does not, and if society is rent by divisions and there is thus no such abstraction as the 'national interest' or 'social welfare'.

The conclusion of this discussion, then, is similar to that of Part I. Social welfare is not objectively measurable, and no method of cost–benefit analysis can produce figures which quantify it. Thus cost–benefit analysis cannot by itself provide a complete policy towards TNCs: it can only be part of a much larger 'package'. Whether an appropriate 'package' is in fact adopted by a government is itself problematical, and depends on the role of political institutions in the socio-economic structure, but this is not a matter into which we can go in the present context. Even within this 'package', the usefulness of quantitative evaluations must be heavily qualified by the practical problems of lack of information on actual as well as alternative situations, and the presence of non-marginality, externalities, and several diffuse 'non-economic' effects of a large, powerful, economic presence.

Part III
Host Government Policy

CHAPTER 11
Regulation and Bargaining

INTRODUCTION

This part of the book deals with the policy issues facing host governments in LDCs. The previous discussions should have made it amply clear that TNCs raise a wide spectrum of problems for government policy. These range from the detailed work of bargaining with foreign companies and regulating and evaluating their investments to broad issues of defining national socio-economic objectives and creating the right political and institutional structures for the realisation of them.

While there are legitimate grounds for questioning whether government 'policy' in a narrow sense can cope with all these problems – partly because of the administrative weaknesses of most LDCs and the inherent difficulties of controlling TNCs even with sophisticated administrations, and partly because government policies are themselves subject to pressure and influence – it is certainly worth trying to analyse the implications of our arguments about costs and benefits of TNCs for the broad strategy that governments might adopt to ensure a suitable pattern of economic development.

In this chapter we shall discuss some of the main issues that arise in regulating, evaluating and bargaining with foreign investors. For the time being we assume that the government is willing and able to pursue the national interest in this area; in the next chapter we shall consider some of the limitations of governments in dealing with TNCs. Clearly, in an area as vast as this we cannot examine policy issues in any detail. It is hoped, however, that the generality of the discussion does not detract from the significance of studying specific policy problems at much greater length.

Before considering how to regulate TNCs, a series of questions have to be answered and decisions made by the government. The first question is whether the product or the range of products is wanted at all.

There may be several reasons why a particular government may not wish a certain type of product to be available in the domestic market. But, having decided to admit the product, the next question is whether it should be imported or produced at home. The answer to this question will depend on the outcome of shadow pricing, and social cost–benefit analysis has a contribution to make here. Having decided that the product should be produced internally, the next question is how the package consisting of capital, know-how and management, including marketing and skills, should be assembled. It may be that the components can be bought separately and then assembled, that purchases abroad may be confined to certain components (for instance, capital and experts) or that all components of the package should be mobilised domestically.

The answer to this question will depend upon the type of technology (the less novel and the less linked to other activities of the firm, the less the need for investment by the TNC). If it is then decided that direct private foreign investment by a TNC may be, in certain conditions, a better method than the other options, the question of bargaining arises.

The regulation of TNCs is considered in the following section, under three headings: the attraction of foreign investments; the control of TNCs at the macro-economic and industrial levels; and their control at the firm level. The next two sections discuss the issues of evaluation and bargaining, and in the final section a number of conclusions are drawn.

REGULATION

Attraction of Foreign Investments
The attraction of foreign direct investment to a developing economy depends upon a combination of social, political and economic factors, some of which are under the control of host governments while others are not. Those which are *not* are as follows: the determinants of foreign expansion of firms in developed countries, such as the growth of oligopoly, technological change, competitive and marketing strategies, cost pressures, and so on (see Chapter 2); the size and rate of growth of the host economy (only indirectly controlled, if at all, by host government policy); political and social (including labour) stability in the host country (again, only indirectly controlled by host governments); and the economic, social and political conditions in the home economies of the TNCs (tax regimes, insurance for and guarantees to foreign investors,[1] political relations with the LDC in question, trade-

union pressures against the 'export of jobs', the economic climate generally, and so on). There is little that host LDCs can do to influence these important determinants of TNC expansion; but there *are* several policies which could ease the inflow of TNC capital.

(a) The provision of *information* by means of agencies established in the main capital exporting countries, and the promotion of *contacts* with companies which may be interested in investing in the appropriate sectors.[2]

(b) *Fiscal incentives* may be successful in attracting some kinds of foreign capital, especially the new 'footloose' variety of sourcing investments;[3] however, their effectiveness in attracting investments of a more long-lived nature in very much in doubt.[4] The discussion in Part I should have clarified why tax concessions, the benefits of which may (in the absence of double-tax agreements) accrue to the home government in any case, do not figure as important factors in the overseas expansion of TNCs. Even so far as 'footloose' investments are concerned, it is clearly counter-productive for LDCs to compete with each other in offering greater concessions. It would be much more feasible on the part of interested countries (given that they are equally attractive on grounds of cost and risk) to co-operate on fiscal policy; as we argue below, however, the incentives for individual countries to break the rules are very great.

(c) A framework of *clear, efficiently implemented, stable policies* with respect to foreign investments can serve to attract TNCs. If supplemented by internationally or bilaterally agreed codes of conduct,[5] on auditing, taxation,[6] employment requirements,[7] arbitration, exchange controls and the like, such policies can go a long way towards establishing a favourable climate for the operation of TNCs and towards giving evidence of the host government's good intentions towards them.

(d) While the offering of *protection* can be a strong inducement to foreign investment, it is clear that the results of indiscriminate protective policies have not been very efficient. Even if we accept the need for selective protection, it is evident that tariff–quota policies have been used as effective regulatory or bargaining tools by host governments. Protection is in fact a flexible and powerful policy instrument which, as we shall argue below, can and should be used as such to obtain the best deal for the host economy.

(e) Several *other* policies can help host governments to attract foreign capital: ease of entry, flexible conditions as regards local equity participation, the provision of skilled labour and infrastructural facilities, and so on.

It may be worth reiterating, however, that it is the overall *'environment'* of a particular country, as constituted by its political, social and economic conditions, that is the overwhelmingly important factor in attracting foreign capital. Small incentives or concessions often help only in so far as they are indications of a favourable environment – otherwise they may simply cost the host government a part of tax revenue and add little by way of new foreign investment. The environment in LDCs which most attracts TNCs is one in which the host country *efficiently integrates with the international capitalist economy on terms favourable to private enterprise* – mainly by offering stable economic, social and political conditions for growth of private investment and 'free' markets; sometimes by controlling the power of labour unions; by minimum interference with the activities of the firm; and generally by not tampering too much with the pattern of income distribution which evolves naturally with industrial development.[8] In many LDCs with extreme inequalities in the distribution of wealth, power and privilege, these can be achieved only by growing inequalities and repressive regimes (as in Brazil, Iran or Indonesia); in others (such as Taiwan), with peculiar historical circumstances that destroyed feudal patterns of landholding and provided unusual amounts of skilled manpower and external aid, it may be achieved with a relatively egalitarian pattern of growth. The emerging pattern for new US manufacturing investment, with much higher rates of growth in Brazil, Indonesia, Iran, Nigeria and Mexico than in other low-wage LDCs (or even in politically troubled and trade-union dominated countries in Europe which traditionally attracted the bulk of US capital), clearly reflects the influence of these factors.[9]

Regulation at the Macro-Economic Level
It is very difficult to conduct at a general level a concise and clear discussion of appropriate government policies towards foreign investment. The government is required to formulate not just a comprehensive set of policies towards industrialisation, but an entire strategy to define and promote 'social welfare' in a broad sense, embracing cultural, political and economic aspects of national life. Any attempt at analysis or advice can easily slip into rhetoric, vagueness or impracticality. On the other hand, any effort to evade these issues, by claiming that they are irrelevant, unimportant or 'not our concern', is likely to be seriously

Regulation and Bargaining 195

misleading. The extent to which, and the terms and conditions on which, TNCs enter an LDC can have important and permanent effects on all aspects of its society, and to ignore them is *implicitly* to endorse these effects. Whether or not the host country ultimately accepts the changes that accompany integration into the TNC framework of production and trade, it should at least be aware that there are changes. As economists, therefore, we should point out where economic regulation may be needed.

We have argued in Part I of this book that the nature of TNC expansion, in the present phase of development of the capital-exporting countries, is such that it is necessarily accompanied by technological, marketing and organisational characteristics which may be unsuited to the most essential needs of the poor countries. It does, at the same time, embody the most advanced techniques of production, the most sophisticated methods of managing and selling, and the most extensive control of distribution in world markets. Much of what TNCs offer is desirable. The problem is to extricate this from features that are less so, yet are inherent in the existence and growth of TNCs.

The general regulation of foreign investments may be considered at two levels: the economy level and the industry level. At the *economy level*, the *total amount* of foreign investment – the simplest index of foreign 'presence' – may be taken to determine its social, cultural and political impact on the host economy. The greater the 'dependence' on foreign capital, the stronger the effects of TNCs are likely to be, although it may be debated how much they are due to TNCs as such rather than to the form of development more generally. In any case, what one regards as the 'right' amount of foreign influence via direct investment, and, thus, as the policy that the host government ought to pursue, is very much a question of normative and ideological assumptions. As for the economic aspects of 'general' regulation, the following major issues may be considered important.

(a) *The composition of output.* Since TNCs tend, particularly in consumer-goods industries, to specialise in highly sophisticated and differentiated products, which in LDCs may exacerbate existing inequalities in income and consumption patterns, the government may wish to ensure that TNCs enter only those industries whose output is considered socially desirable. It may, however, be objected that it is wrong to treat the symptoms (undesirable consumption patterns) rather than the disease (unequal income distribution and/or strong foreign influences on market preferences): a valid objection, and, as we shall

196   *Investment, TNCs and Developing Countries*

argue in the next chapter, one that carries particular weight in the case of TNCs. For the moment, however, let us satisfy ourselves by saying that some control may be required to save a bad situation from becoming worse.

(b) *Technology.* At the macro-economic level the importation of advanced technology by TNCs raises problems concerning employment, income distribution and technological 'dependence.' It favours the use of capital-intensive techniques and reduces the number of workers who can be employed, so worsening the problem of unemployment, while creating small labour 'aristocracies'. It inhibits local R & D, biases education and science policy, and stifles any potential for discovering more appropriate technologies. Government policy may therefore attempt to ensure that the inflow of the most advanced technology is directed towards only those sectors in which it is also the most productive, or in which there is no feasible alternative, and also to reduce the costs;[10] for other sectors it may attempt to obtain more suitable technology, either by using older techniques (though the viability of this may be dubious for much of technologically advanced industry), or by developing 'intermediate' technologies (by encouraging domestic research, by cheapening labour in relation to capital, by inducing foreign companies or governments to undertake the task, or by undertaking co-operative technological ventures with other LDCs).[11] Such measures would need to be supported by policies to ensure that appropriate technology is actually utilised. Again, doubts may be raised about the possibility (especially if no other measures for redistribution are undertaken) of developing and commercialising alternative technologies *on a wide scale* within economies that remain, to a greater or lesser extent, integrated into a worldwide capitalist structure of trade, production and consumption. But clearly there is some room for improvement, and many LDCs are in fact moving towards stimulating indigenous technology. Only time will tell whether technological 'dependence' can be loosened in any significant way.

As we mentioned in Chapter 3, it has been argued that a reform of the international patent system (as embodied in the Paris Convention) and national patent laws, even an opting-out of the observance of the rules laid down in the Convention, may be desirable for host countries wishing to ease the transfer of technology and reduce its costs. UNCTAD (1974) and Vaitsos (1973, 1976) have recommended far-reaching reforms and analysed some of the measures to be undertaken. There is little doubt that some tightening-up of administrative and legal procedures by LDCs is needed to reduce the incidence of certain abuses, and that in some sectors (especially pharmaceuticals) the national interest may be best served by not observing patent restrictions on copying patented technology and importing materials from the cheapest international sources. However, for various reasons described earlier, the role of the patent system in the *general* transfer of technology is not very significant, and it may not (for political and public-relations reasons) be worth the LDCs' while to opt out of the system altogether. Such a drastic move may create an unfavourable 'environment' for foreign investment (and reduce TNC exports) and may work against the long-term growth of domestic technology if it exhibits a potential for selling its innovations abroad. The use of more selective controls, such as automatic compulsory licensing under certain circumstances, retaining the right to import cheaply in the national interest, shortening legal processes and so on, may be equally effective while preserving the existing framework of the patent system. Moreover, governments in LDCs may interpret patent laws liberally and use them where necessary to further national goals without explicitly amending the regulations.

(c) *Marketing and consumption patterns.* This issue is closely related to the previous two. One of the main strengths of TNCs lies in their ability to promote and differentiate their products and to influence consumption patterns; this also constitutes one of their less desirable traits from the viewpoint of LDCs. It introduces costs to society (of having too many products to meet a given need, of advertising, of creating new needs, and so on) which have few accompanying benefits. The remedies are partly to confine TNC entry to sectors where they produce only the goods that society needs, and to specify the range of products that they may sell, and partly to restrict the undesirable aspects of advertising and promotion while retaining their beneficial informative qualities (see Chapter 3). In some industries of vital social importance, such as pharmaceuticals, it may be beneficial for the host government to take over the marketing and information functions entirely, in order to eliminate costs inherent in the present structure.[12] Of course, such policies would not help to solve the broader problems of 'dependent' consumption patterns, which are affected in several ways other than by TNC investment.

(d) *Local enterprise.* The issue of how TNCs affect local enterprise appears somewhat ambiguous, because it is claimed both that TNCs suppress it and that they encourage it. The two propositions are not, however, incompatible: TNCs may, if given a free hand, take over the leadership of the most dynamic technological and marketing-based industries while promoting the expansion of domestic ancillary industries. The final effect is likely to be that local enterprise in the relevant sectors is reduced to a secondary role, though a few exceptional firms (especially state-owned ones) may survive and be competitive. Thus, if the government wishes to foster domestic enterprise more widely, it could restrict the scope of foreign entry both by industry and in terms of the percentage of equity held abroad. This could be supplemented by 'divestment' arrangements (of the sort proposed in the Andean Pact) or by prohibiting the direct entry of TNCs in sectors where domestic entrepreneurship is adequate (as in India). The costs of such measures may be that particular TNCs are deterred from entering the country at all, from selling their most valuable technology, or from allowing access to their other markets.

Let us now consider some regulatory policies at the *industry level*. Once the desirable amount and pattern of TNC investment has been decided, problems similar to the ones outlined above arise at the sectoral level with regard to technological and marketing practices, industrial concentration, access to capital and infrastructure, labour relations and relationships with suppliers. Technology and marketing have been mentioned already, and need not be discussed again except to point out that local firms in an industry where TNC entry is permitted will probably adopt techniques and promotion methods similar to those of their large foreign rivals. The government may then have to decide which are to be promoted and which are not, for *both* groups of firms. A problem which might arise in such close regulation of company behaviour might be how to preserve a healthy element of competition while controlling the excesses of oligopolistic rivalry – a difficult task, and one that even the most sophisticated administrations may not be capable of fulfilling.

The problem of market structure and concentration may be dealt with by adopting the sort of regulatory legal and administrative policies used by developed countries. This again raises problems of reconciling with technological and other needs for large size the desire for competition; such issues are in practice very difficult and in theory extremely complex to resolve, as anti-trust experience in the USA and elsewhere illustrates. Many governments restrict the activities of TNCs as regards takeovers of local firms, but, clearly, it is difficult to pass a general judgement about the undesirability of *all* takeovers. Some are clearly a necessary part of the competitive market process, while others are predatory and aim to increase monopoly power.[13] The government has to find the right balance between, on the one hand, promoting domestic enterprise and fostering its growth against the enormous competitive power of TNCs, and, on the other, keeping a reasonably efficient industrial structure, which permits competition but allows for the increasing size of individual firms in response to technological and organisational progress, and is able to adapt to conditions in world markets.

TNCs are often accused of gaining privileged access to scarce capital in LDCs. This is an area in which much more evidence is needed, but, if the accusation is at all valid, the government must undertake steps to limit the local borrowing of TNCs, to induce them to accept local capital in the form of equity rather than loans, to induce financial institutions to lend more to deserving local enterprises, to create new financial infrastructure for the purpose, or to step into financial markets directly and give credit as it considers fit. Similarly, with respect to access to infrastructure and other facilities: if TNCs in fact get privileges over domestic firms, remedial action is called for to redress the balance and, perhaps, to tilt it somewhat the other way.

Labour relations have to be regulated at macro-economic and sectoral, as well as individual-firm, levels; we mention it here simply for convenience. There is clearly a large role for the government in controlling wage policies, employment conditions, trade-union activity, social-security requirements, training and so on, in the industrial sector of LDCs. TNCs may raise special problems[14] because of their superior bargaining strength and their easy access to foreign personnel, but in general the evidence that exists supports the view that they are, judged by the standards of developed countries, better employers in LDCs than local firms are, paying higher wages and providing better working conditions and more training. Readers may note that, in this narrow sense, government policy has little to do with fundamental issues of income distribution.

Governments consider relationships with local suppliers to be an important policy issue because they are concerned to encourage the use of domestic rather than imported inputs. To do so, they can specify the 'local content' of purchases of TNCs in each industry over specified periods; tax or prohibit imported components; directly promote the capabilities of suppliers; and provide profit incentives to TNCs for using domestic resources. If this policy is pushed very far, however, the cost of production may become excessive, the quality of output may fall, exporting may become unfeasible, and an inefficient industrial structure may be created. On the other hand, TNCs may, if given a completely free hand, prefer to remain dependent on imported supplies. With some combination of stick-and-carrot policies, however, governments may be quite effective in promoting the growth of domestic suppliers, even inducing TNCs to provide them with technology, skills and capital.

To sum up this section, therefore, there is an enormous and vital role for the government to play in providing the right *ambiance* for constructive and beneficial use of TNC investment in LDCs.[15] It is not an easy role. In practice its effective implementation may prove outside the capabilities of most government administrations. However, as long as it is accepted that the entry of large, powerful, high-marketing and high-technology oligopolists from developed economies can have undesirable effects upon poor host countries – and there is little doubt in our minds that this is so – there is a strong case for instituting official checks to separate the benefits from the costs. The policies envisaged stretch well beyond those usually undertaken by developed countries to regulate private enterprise. They call for extensive controls on several aspects of what, in developed capitalist countries, is regarded as the normal functioning of free markets. The problems and dangers implicit in undertaking such controls (should the government be willing to do so) should be borne in mind as well as their advantages.

Regulation at the Firm Level
In addition to the issues (labour relations, technology, product range, promotion, and so on) that have been mentioned previously and that require regulation at the firm level, there are some specific aspects of TNC operations which must be dealt with case by case on a continuing basis. These relate to the control of restrictive business practices, payments for technology and transfer pricing.

Restrictive business practices have been the subject of several exhaustive studies by UNCTAD, and readers are referred to these for detailed explanations of what these are, how they are operated, and where they are found.[16] The ones most commonly mentioned relate to restrictions on exports by the foreign subsidiary or by a local firm purchasing technology from a TNC, restrictions on sources from which imports can be purchased, and restrictions on the use and development of technology and on procedures for the arbitration of disputes. Some other restrictive practices, such as international cartels, involve several TNCs and must be tackled at the appropriate national or international level. While the ordinary laws that regulate business contain several provisions to counter the worst abuses of such practices, several of them are in fact accepted as normal commercial practice in the developed countries and left to the wishes (and bargaining strengths) of the firms concerned. It is, for instance, acceptable in many countries for a technology seller to stipulate markets in which the products of that technology may or may not be sold, how R & D benefits are to be shared, or where disputes may be settled. Many LDCs feel, rightly, that such 'normal' commercial procedures may work to their disadvantage, because the parties in the host countries are too weak, ill-informed or unsophisticated to be able to strike a fair bargain (or else are only too happy to collaborate with the wishes of the TNC in order to obtain new technology or a valuable brand name). The evidence on the monopolistic tactics of the large TNCs in developed countries illustrates how valid these fears may be, and how difficult they may be to check.

The simplest measure for host governments would be to prohibit all practices which they regard as 'restrictive'. It would, however, be naïve to think that this would solve the problem. The incidence of explicit monopolistic practices does, after all, reflect the monopolistic technological and marketing power which underlies transnational business, and the use of restrictive clauses sometimes serves as a non-price substitute for elements of a sale which cannot easily be taken into direct financial account (such as export restrictions to counter a potential threat to third markets). To prohibit them may then lead to the actual price being higher, or to implicit collusion between the buying and selling firms, or, if the government were very stringent and the TNC exceptionally monopolistic, to the transaction not being made at all. It may be considerations of this sort which have led the Indian government – in every way a strict regulator of foreign investments – to differentiate between 'permissible' and 'non-permissible' export restrictions (the former being to countries where the foreign firm has subsidiaries or selling outlets). This being said, however, there does remain considerable scope for action by LDCs in strengthening the scrutiny, registration and regulation of restrictive practices. The Mexican law on technology transfers may serve as a model of an extremely detailed, comprehensive and strong regulatory system at the national level;[17] whether it works as well as it is intended to is another matter (informal discussions with some officials lead us to believe that in practice the system is far more lax and subject to undue pressures than would appear from the letter of the law). At the international level, the 'Code of Conduct on the Transfer of Technology' proposed by UNCTAD may provide a legal–institutional framework for the elimination of undesirable practices. Again, its implementation (if the Code should reach that stage) would face similar problems of political and economic resistance from TNCs (or their home countries); the battle now raging over its coverage and legal nature illustrates the extent to which both investors and host countries feel their interests threatened.

Let us now consider the regulation of *technological payments*. Once the government has established appropriate procedures for screening out (to the extent feasible) undesirable technology, inducing adaptation to local conditions, minimising restrictive practices and deciding upon the right extent of 'unpackaging' of TNC investments, it has to tackle the problem of minimising the direct financial cost of the technology transferred. If the transfer takes place by means of a TNC setting up a wholly-owned subsidiary, the benefits to the parent company show up wholly in the profits earned; in this case, the government should (and several LDCs do) prohibit the making of separate technological payments, or tax such payments at the same effective rate as remitted profits. There is no separate issue of negotiating technological payments as such. If, however, the transfer takes place between TNCs and joint ventures or wholly local companies, the issue of bargaining and regulation does arise.

We have already indicated that the technology market is a peculiar one, and that bargaining, information and 'shopping around' can be of crucial importance in determining the prices set.[18] It is often argued that TNCs have the upper hand in bargaining over the cost of technology, because in many cases they are effective monopolists, and, even when they are not, the buyers are too weak or ill informed to play the market and strike a 'fair' deal. Moreover, the price explicitly paid for technology may not capture the true return to the seller, because of the package of other goods and services provided, and because of the potential for arbitrarily pricing these. If we leave transfer-pricing problems for the moment, we may note the need for two sets of policies to improve the host country's position.

First, it may wish to separate technology from the total foreign investment 'package' so that it does not pay for elements, such as brand names or management, that it may not need. It may also wish to limit the period for which payments are made, to ensure that the financial burden does not extend beyond the time needed to effect the transfer. The risk of this sort of policy lies in the fact that the other components needed to make new technology work in an LDC may not be present domestically, or may be excessively costly, and that a very short-term or static view of the transfer process may cut off the country from continuing changes in technology. Thus, in industries where technology is novel and developing rapidly, host governments may have to be more lenient than in industries where technology is relatively stagnant and where the marketing element is more predominant in TNC expansion. In the former case, foreign majority participation or long-term licensing contracts on liberal terms may be allowed. In the latter, technology should be bought on its own by means of short-term arrangements.

Second, in negotiating the actual rates, the government has a major role to play in helping domestic entrepreneurs: by providing information on alternatives, providing skilled negotiators, eliminating restrictive clauses, and cutting out unnecessary duplication in the purchase of technologies. The Colombian experience illustrates the potential gains: royalty payments were reduced by about 40 per cent by instituting a negotiation and surveillance process which cut out payments for outdated technology and pruned excessive rates. Some countries impose ceilings on the rates which can be charged for different types of technology. We have remarked on two drawbacks of such policies (a cumbersome or inefficient government machinery may select wrong technologies or keep out needed technologies, and domestic firms may collaborate with TNCs in circumventing official regulations) and need not elaborate on them further.

The improvement of LDCs' bargaining position on technology is one area in which international action could be of immense benefit. First, groups of LDCs could collaborate in exchanging information on technology sources and payments; the more advanced among them could provide their technology at preferential rates to the others; and they could act as a group in confronting monopolistic sellers to get the best prices.[19] Second, international organisations could act as information centres on patents, technology supplies, royalty rates, and so on. There are a number of moves afoot to do both these things, but it remains to be seen whether it is politically feasible to achieve a real shift in the balance of power. Several host governments have gone quite a long way in instituting national controls, but without more detailed study it is difficult to say how successful they have been.

Finally, there is the immensely difficult task of checking *transfer pricing*. It must be admitted at the outset that, when competitive markets have to a large extent been replaced by monopolistic markets or by transactions internal to TNCs, it is impossible to find either a theoretical solution to the problem of finding 'fair' prices or a practical means of ensuring that 'correct' prices are observed. Two sorts of difficulties are faced by LDCs, both reflecting the highly imperfect nature of present world markets: the pricing of goods and services *to independent buyers* (oligopoly pricing in a fragmented market where the buyers' information is poor) and the pricing of goods or services *to affiliates* (transfer pricing proper). While the former is generally ignored in the literature, on the assumption that world markets are competitive and buyers well informed, there are some industries where this is patently untrue. In the pharmaceutical industry, for instance, the Sri Lanka State Pharmaceuticals Corporation was able to obtain Diazepam from an Indian firm for 5000 rupees, but an identical quantity (and quality) of the drug cost 128,000 rupees when it was being imported privately from Hoffman La Roche. Similarly, for the import of pharmaceutical raw materials, simple negotiations with a TNC (Beecham) for ampicillin produced a reduction of 83 per cent.[20] The explanation of such imperfections lies in the ignorance and weak bargaining position of private buyers, and in their belief (proved unjustifiable) that only TNCs can provide products of adequate quality. The remedy, then, lies in centralised buying, better information and official regulation.

As for transfer pricing proper, the remedies are harder to come by. There are several possible ways of dealing with the problem of the pricing of commodities involved in intra-firm trade, but none of them offers a completely satisfactory solution.

First, combined tax and tariff rates could be fixed in such a way that the revenue realised would be the same whether the TNC transmits profits by declaring them or by overpricing imports (this method would not touch the problem of underpriced exports). This would limit the use of tariff policy as a flexible protective device, could lead to very high rates of duty, and could penalise local firms that do not use transfer pricing.

Second, all imports could be channelled through an official agency which would negotiate all import prices after comparing them with alternatives – the sort of remedy proposed for monopolistic pricing to independent buyers. This could prove cumbersome if spread over too many commodities, but it should be borne in mind that intra-firm trade is in fact highly concentrated in a few TNCs (see Lall, 1973), and the takeover of their imports may be quite feasible.

Third, the host government could tax TNCs on the basis of their worldwide profits, allocated to the particular country by using a formula based on the proportion of sales, capital, or some such item, accounted for by the country in question. This would be a convenient method of taxation if TNCs could be made to provide data of the sort required; however, it is to some extent inherently arbitrary and should be used only to supplement other methods of taxing TNCs with transfer-pricing potential. A special case of this is OPEC's brilliant device of levying income tax on a notional (the 'posted') price.[21]

Fourth, transfer prices could be checked and fixed directly. The US experience shows that this is a cumbersome, difficult and legally complex task, but, since many other developed countries are adopting this method (see Verlage, 1975), it is probably the best long-term national solution in relatively liberal economies. Again, the fact that ultimately only a handful of large firms would have to be really strictly monitored would reduce the apparent enormity of the task; and the savings achieved by Colombia (see Chapter 7), even by a relatively modest effort, show that it would be a worthwhile undertaking.[22]

Fifth, the promotion of local shareholding and management by host governments may lead to internal checks on transfer-pricing practices. Local managers may not, however, have the competence or the information needed to deal with the sophisticated pricing practices of TNC head-offices. They may also be persuaded to collude with the foreign partner in these practices, for such favours as the latter may offer.

Finally, the governments of all the countries in which TNCs operate could get together, ban the use of tax havens, tax the firms jointly on their global earnings and share the proceeds. While at first sight the internationalisation of fiscal policy seems a perfect reply to the internationalisation of production, we should be aware of its severe political and economic limitations. Governments may not be willing to relinquish their rights over national fiscal policy (or their right to be tax havens), and they may disagree over the right rate of taxation or over the fair division of overhead and R & D costs (LDCs may, for instance, legitimately question why they should share the cost of product development and differentiation which is primarily intended for developed countries). Furthermore, even if all tax rates were harmonised and the division of overheads agreed upon, it would be difficult to allocate the tax revenue to individual countries on the basis of their true contribution to earnings. Countries which account for the same share of sales or capital employed may, for example, account for very different shares of profits, and negotiations on such matters are likely to be contentious and divisive.

All these measures for tackling transfer pricing on commodities are subject to practical difficulties, and the best solution may lie in some combination of measures. The final outcome will depend upon the skill and bargaining abilities of the host governments, and they would be well advised to devote considerable effort to improving and extending these abilities.[23]

Transfer pricing may, of course, be practised not only on commodity trade but also on interest payments and on sales of services, brand names and technology between affiliates. These may be even more difficult to monitor effectively than commodity prices are, but it would be unwise not to make some effort to deal with all together. Certain items, such as interest payments, may be compared with rates on world markets, while others, such as technology payments, may, as noted above, be banned to parent companies or negotiated with reference to rates paid elsewhere (or by a straightforward bargaining process). However, since commodity trade is likely to be quantitatively far more important than these other channels, the greatest attention should be paid to it, and, within commodity trade, to those sectors and firms where its impact is likely to be greatest.

This concludes our discussion on the regulation of TNCs. Our analysis has been extremely condensed and somewhat selective, but it should have given a clear idea of the extent to which governments that have no objection to foreign investment in principle may have to enact policy if they wish to maximise the benefits that they hope to extract from TNC investment. The costs of undertaking such comprehensive controls, in terms of both administrative expenditure and possible inefficiency, should also be kept firmly in mind. The exact balance struck would obviously depend on the circumstances, but no government should let these issues pass, by default or through ignorance.

EVALUATION

The methods and problems of evaluating individual projects to be undertaken by TNCs (alone, or jointly with domestic partners) have been dealt with at some length in Part II, so here only a brief comment is necessary. There is clearly a need for some means of appraising investments and for ruling out inefficient ones, while comparing proposals with feasible alternatives. Project appraisal suffers, however, from several limitations, especially when applied to TNC investments. It should be used only as part of a larger policy 'package' which lays down general regulations for TNC investments and institutes an effective bargaining procedure; it must not be used on its own as the main instrument of foreign investment policy. Moreover, seemingly precise quantitative assessments of the effects of long-term investments should be treated with a great deal of caution, and attempts should be made to arrive at a plausible range of results rather than at a single value.

Appropriate qualifications have to be made when 'externalities' are expected to be particularly large. If local 'replacement' activity is to be encouraged, estimates of the capacities of domestic investors (as alternatives to TNCs) should be optimistically (but not unrealistically) made. The greatest care should be taken that cost–benefit evaluation procedures do not become simple and rigid rules which churn out decisions on foreign investment to the exclusion of other considerations.

BARGAINING

This section is divided into three parts, dealing with, first, the issues for bargaining; second, the process of bargaining; and, third, the means for strengthening the host government's bargaining position.

Issues for Bargaining

With regard to policy issues on TNCs, there may be some trade-off between issues which are kept for general regulation of the type discussed above and those which are kept for bargaining.[24] If an item is governed by regulations or laws, the advantages of generality and predictability of application must be set against a certain amount of inflexibility inherent in such procedures. If, on the other hand, an item is governed by bargaining procedures, the benefits of a case-by-case approach must be set against the possibilities of arbitrariness or weakness in bargaining and the risks of delay, bribery or intimidation. Some items (such as rates of tax on profits or other remittances, sectors and products open to TNCs, treatment of property rights, treatment of labour, and repatriation policies) must clearly be subject to general regulation, while others (for instance, tax concessions, export obligators, technology payments, protection, local content of purchases, and provision of infrastructure) should be subject to case-by-case bargaining. This leaves a number of items which may be governed by one or the other: the extent of local equity participation, use of local credit, employment of local managers, takeovers of local firms, and the like.

It is impossible to define with precision which issues particular host governments should allocate to which category, except to suggest in general terms that, the stronger the bargaining capacity of the administration, the more flexible a posture it should adopt in order to maximise its benefits. The economic environment is forever changing, and TNCs are heterogeneous. Subject to the considerations noted above, therefore, a government may benefit from keeping as large an area of discretion as it can, and expand this as it learns from experience.

The most important items on which host governments should exploit the possibility of bargaining are as follows.

(a) *Ownership and control.* The less scarce the technology that a TNC has to offer, and the larger (and more politically stable) the market, the more can a host country insist on a large domestic share in the ownership of the foreign investor. It is inadvisable to lay down rigid rules on local participation, because the relative strengths of the two parties differ from sector to sector, and often from firm to firm.[25]

(b) *Protection.* The extent of *effective* protection granted (see Chapters 8 and 9) is an important determinant of the desirability of an investment to the host country as well as of its profitability to the investor. Yet many host LDC governments leave it out of explicit account in deciding which investments are to be permitted and in bargaining with foreign investors. TNCs are in a particularly strong position to benefit from protection: when it is granted automatically, by an import ban on goods of a type produced locally, they can use their technological, marketing and managerial abilities to establish strong market positions; when it is granted by means of tariffs, they are able to hide their true costs of production by setting arbitrary transfer prices, or to use their bargaining strength to negotiate higher rates of protection. In either case, given the extent of protection on inputs, they may be able to raise the rate of protection on outputs and thus the rate of effective protection (and so their profitability). It is vital for the host government to make effective protection an explicit item of bargaining, not just initially but continuously, as the efficiency of an operation improves and the need for protection diminishes. The worst policy to follow in this respect (unfortunately, one of the commonest) is to leave tariff rates to be fixed by some authority completely unrelated to the one which deals with foreign investors: thus, in obtaining a good bargain from a TNC on other items, a fiscal or trade ministry can easily, albeit unknowingly, undo the efforts of the foreign-investment authority.

(c) *Composition of output.* Even if TNCs are allowed only into specified sectors, the range of products to be made, the frequency of model changes and so on must be negotiated in each case. The aim of policy should be to meet social needs with a minimum of product differentiation, yet allowing enough change to ensure that genuine improvements in the product are introduced.

(d) *Other items.* Several other items, such as technological payments,

Regulation and Bargaining

fiscal concessions, employment, local purchases, exports, arbitration and financing, are also open to case-by-case bargaining. They have either been discussed earlier or are obvious in their implications; so we need not analyse them separately here.

The Bargaining Process

Traditional writing in this field is not very helpful in understanding the process of bargaining. It is not uncommon in the literature on private foreign investment to assume, tacitly or explicitly, a downward-sloping marginal productivity of investment curve, relating different amounts of investment by the TNC to expected rates of return (see Figure 11.1). It then follows that any action by the host government that reduces the expected rate of return is bound to lead to reduced investment. The host government will have to balance, at the margin, more or less foreign investment (OA against OB) against less or more tax receipts or other benefits to it that reduce the attractions to the foreign investor (for instance, use of higher-cost inputs, such as local materials, or restrictions on repatriation of profits). This model, even when it is not explicitly formulated, has dominated thought and, to some extent, action in this area.

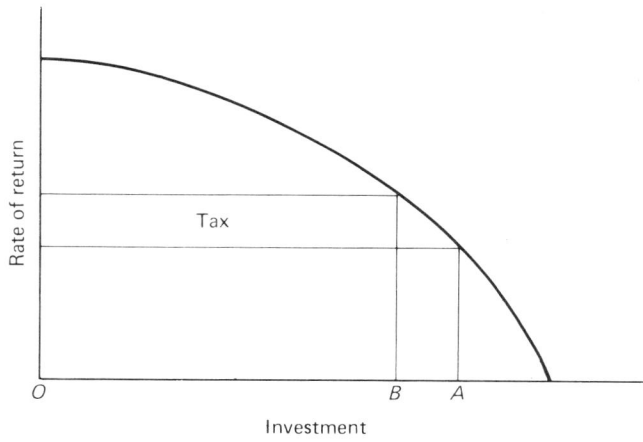

FIGURE 11.1

Reality is different. Instead of a smooth, continuous, downward-sloping marginal productivity of investment curve, there is a step-like function, as shown in Figure 11.2. The vertical sections of the steps (for instance, $ST = PQ$) are the bargaining range.[26] The lower limit of this

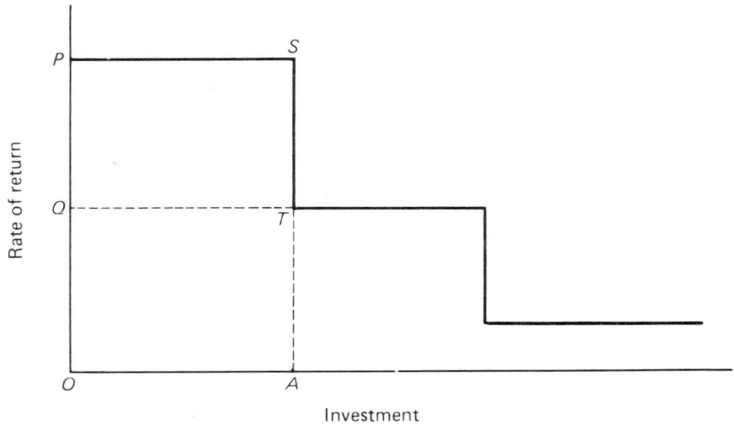

FIGURE 11.2

range is determined by the special 'advantage' enjoyed by the TNC, the upper limit by the costs to the host government of alternative access to this advantage or the cost of doing without it. The limits of the range P to Q, is the 'returns' on the investment (amount OA) that are acceptable to both the host government and the company, and under which the investment will go ahead. They are set by the maximum the company may earn before the investment becomes unacceptable to the government, and the minimum it is prepared to accept. The company will have spent money on R & D, or on advertising or other marketing costs, or it will have incurred other fixed or joint costs. Operation with investment OA in the host country will be possible at relatively low incremental costs. As long as receipts from these operations cover avoidable local costs and make some contribution towards central overheads (R & D, technology, management, advertising, administration, and so on), the operation is profitable, though clearly the firm prefers higher contributions to lower ones. Charging what the market will bear is the firm's optimum policy. Charging just above incremental costs is its least preferred policy under which the investment will go ahead.

It may be argued that this may be so *ex post*, after the expenditure at headquarters has been incurred. But if each host country squeezes

Regulation and Bargaining 211

returns to the TNC to the minimum, the source for R & D or other headquarters expenditure will dry up. Or, put another way, in deciding upon the headquarters expenditure, the firm will have expectations that the local contribution will exceed local operating costs and that it will be able to recoup its fixed expenditure by charging prices that exceed local operating costs.

While this is clearly true of the major markets in the developed countries, LDCs are normally too small a component to play an important role in this type of decision. Therefore, even *ex ante* LDC 'rates of return' play no, or only a minor, role in decisions to embark on R & D or marketing expenditures.

The upper limit of the bargaining range (P) is set by the expenditure that the host country would have to incur in order to do for itself what the TNC has been doing for its global operations (where an infrastructure of research is absent, and where the scale of operation is small, this cost may be very high), or by alternative sources of buying the 'special advantage' (either from rival TNCs or through acquiring the knowledge more cheaply, refusing to sign patent conventions, and so on), or by the cost to the country of doing without the 'special advantage' and its resulting production.

We have used the word 'returns'. It does not accurately describe what we have in mind. In view of the arbitrariness (within a range) with which the capital equipment is valued, the costs of intra-firm imported inputs and the prices of intra-firm exported outputs are fixed and fees for intra-firm services are set, nominal rates of return are of little relevance. What matters is the net ratio of benefits over costs, as seen by the TNC from the point of view of its global operations, and the ratio of benefits over costs for the host country. From the point of view of the firm, not only do the costs of capital and other inputs have to be set at their true opportunity costs to the firm, but, in addition, the operations in a particular country have to be viewed in relation to their effects on profits earned in other countries. From the point of view of the country, the whole range of economic and social objectives – not all, as we have seen, being readily quantifiable – enter into the assessment.

The concept 'returns' may well be inappropriate in an even more fundamental sense. By 'returns' we normally refer to profits earned as a ratio of capital owned, or fixed interest received as a proportion of a sum of money lent. But the sums at issue in the negotiation are a return for a package of services that includes technical knowledge, managerial services, marketing services, goodwill created by advertising, as well as returns on the services of capital. With the growing desire of countries to participate in ownership or to acquire full ownership, and the increasing tendency for TNCs to raise local capital, returns on capital owned by the foreign company have been and will increasingly be replaced by returns on other services and skills. The expression may then refer to the terms of a management contract or consultancy contract rather than equity investments, and has only a tenuous connection with any planned capital expenditure, however broadly we interpret the term 'capital'.

There will be certain elements in the bargain in which the interests of the TNC and those of the country coincide. Higher wages to local labour may increase the productivity of that labour and will, to that extent, be in the interest of both the country and the firm. The use of lower-cost local materials, the training of skilled manpower and the provision of infrastructure may also fall into this category. The exploration of these areas of non-zero-sum games is an important task both for the negotiators and for international agencies rendering technical assistance. A complication is, of course, that both sides have an interest in presenting self-interested actions as concessions to the other side, in order to gain counter-concessions on items where interests do conflict. But apart from this real complication, the separation of areas of conflicting interests, where concessions have to be met by counter-concessions, from areas in which interests coincide and progress can be made jointly, even though the division of the joint benefits may give rise to conflict, is a useful exercise.

An important corollary of the above analysis is that the TNC has an interest in shifting upwards the upper limit of the bargaining range. The higher the cost to the host country of losing the proposed investment, the better the chances of settling the bargain nearer the maximum point.

It is this tendency that in part accounts for the excessive sophistication and over-elaboration of many products and processes and their inappropriateness for LDCs. True, part of the explanation must be found in the fact that these products have been developed in high-income, high-savings, high-investment-per-worker countries, where consumer demand is sophisticated and capital per worker plentiful (see Stewart, 1974); but this is not the whole story. Companies in search of profits should not find it difficult to invent and develop cheap, mass-produced products appropriate to the lower incomes of the masses in the poor countries. But if imitation is easy and the advantage soon lost, the incentive is lacking. It is therefore in the nature of the TNC that its products and processes should be excessively sophisticated in relation to the needs of LDCs and in relation to the chances of a favourable bargain.[27]

Regulation and Bargaining

The bargaining position radically changes once capital has been sunk locally. While before the contract is signed the TNC will tend to be the stronger party, the balance will shift in favour of the host government once factors of production have been committed locally.[28] How much it does so will depend upon whether the government wishes the TNC to continue, and possibly enlarge, operations, and whether it wishes other TNCs to come in.

If the TNC has an interest in pushing up the upper limit of the bargaining range, the host country has an interest in pushing down the lower limit. Its ability to strike a good bargain will depend on three sets of factors: (a) solidarity among countries offering similar facilities, (b) fragmentation among companies eager to invest and (c) information available to the host government.[29] These sources of bargaining power are discussed below.

(a) *Solidarity*. Solidarity among sovereign nation states is difficult to achieve. The reasons for this are best illustrated by the case of a restrictive, price-raising commodity cartel, but they apply with equal force to other exercises of joint bargaining power, such as limiting tax concessions to foreign companies, denying overflying rights, refusing to sign patent conventions, or charging for military facilities. What we are concerned with here is solidarity of a type permitting joint action in negotiations with TNCs: for instance, agreement not to compete in granting tax concessions, and agreed rules on repatriation, technology, local participation, and so on. The Andean Pact and the Organisation of Petroleum Exporting States (OPEC) are examples of groupings in which rules of this type are agreed on by a number of countries.

Solidarity is difficult to achieve because, the more effective a cartel or a cartel-like agreement, the greater is the potential reward to any one member who breaks it. But the fear that someone may break the agreement will induce those who would otherwise be willing to adhere to it to prepare for the break-up. For sticking to an agreement while others abandon it makes the loyal members worse off than they would have been without it. The potential defectors cherish the *hope* of operating *outside* the agreement. But this engenders on the part of the conformers the *fear* of a situation *without* the agreement. This fear is ever-present, even if there are no actual or potential defectors, and itself leads to actions that undermine the agreement. Action outside the agreement is an ever-present hope and action without the agreement an ever-present threat.

Moreover, agreements can be renegotiated, and a partner will hope that at the next round of negotiations he will get a better deal, a larger share. The actions necessary to secure a larger share are similar to those leading to defection or breach. Again, the knowledge that some will ask for a larger share puts others on the defensive. But defence is as disruptive as attack. Cartels are the continuation of competition by other means, as Clausewitz might well have said, and only error can arise from identifying them wholly with monopolies.

The fear that the breakdown of the cartel (for instance, an agreement not to give tax concessions to TNCs) will make everyone worse off is not a sufficient deterrent to prevent the breakdown; for any one member believes, in most cases rightly, that the threat of breakdown comes from the other members. However, the defensive response of one member has the same effect as aggressive undermining by another. It explains why, in spite of the obvious rational interest of the group, successful, lasting agreements of this type are so rare, whether in the field of commodity cartels or agreements to follow common policies towards foreign companies, or in that of trade boycotts or sanctions.

The problem is that of the 'Prisoner's Dilemma'. Peter and Paul are arrested and put in separate cells, and not permitted to communicate. The Prosecution knows that they have committed a crime, but has not enough evidence for a conviction in a court. If neither confesses, they get a minor punishment on a trumped-up charge, say one year. If Peter confesses and Paul does not, Paul gets the maximum penalty, say ten years, and Peter only a light one, say three months, for turning Queen's evidence. Similarly, the other way round. If both confess, they get some remission, say eight years. Though it is clearly in their interest that neither should confess, neither can rely on the other's not confessing, and the result of (individual) rational actions on the part of both is that both confess.

It is, of course, this type of situation which has provided the justification for collective coercion wholly in the interest of individual preferences.[30] Only a penalty as great as that imposed by the disastrous, though fully rational, option will ensure that they are not driven to the 'stupid' result. Co-ordinated rationality must be enforced in order to avoid the results of unco-ordinated rationality.

An *n*-person analogy to the Prisoner's Dilemma, relevant in the present context, is price competition among sellers, where profits are eroded as a result of each trying to snatch a gain and rents are transferred to buyers as consumers' surplus. Competition results in the erosion of monopoly profits and therefore benefits the buyers of the product. The desirable outcome depends, *inter alia*, on producers and consumers forming part of the same community, and income distribution being optimal. Clearly, neither of these conditions is met in the relations among countries or between poor producers and rich consumers, and co-ordinated action can therefore improve the allocation and distribution of resources by conserving monopoly rents as poor producers' surpluses instead of passing them on to rich consumers.

A cartel has, of course, greater co-ordination than the separated, non-communicating prisoners have. But the penalties for defection are normally too weak to ensure adherence. Those emphasising solidarity, joint actions, common fronts, which give rise to situations in which choices of the Prisoner's Dilemma type have to be made, should, therefore, pay attention to instituting *a system of rewards and penalties that shifts the incentives so as to make the unstable optimum solution stable.*

In order to raise the stability of agreements with respect to the treatment of TNCs there must exist not only rewards for adherence and penalties against defection, but also a sense of a fair distribution of the gains, among and within countries. This may require compensatory payments from **large** to small gainers. The reconciliation of the pressures of producers on the country's negotiating position and the pressures of countries on the agreements reached in the cartel will be possible only if each party believes it has more to lose from breaking than from keeping the agreement.

The fair distribution of gains is further complicated by differences of view on what constitutes 'fairness'. There may be conflicts between fairness and bargaining power, and bargaining power may change over time. Here, a sense of solidarity derived from sources other than the agreement (for instance, ethnic, religious, ideological or linguistic unity) may be a help in achieving acceptance of a system of sharing, by inducing those with greater power to make sacrifices for those with less.

Further complications arise from differences over the time distribution of gains. Some partners may prefer short-term gains at the expense of longer-term ones; others the reverse. Different partners may have different preferences for independently given time distribution of gains. In addition, the time distribution of gains may itself be partly determined by the actions of the agreement. Tougher action now may discourage investment later below what it would have been had present action been less tough. Successful agreements will have to find methods of reconciling such interest conflicts among partners to the agreement.

(b) *Competition among TNCs*. The second factor determining the bargaining power of the host country is the extent to which the TNC in question is competing with others eager to invest. The host country's position will be weaker if either the TNC has a world monopoly or the foreign companies collude for joint negotiations. Where the host country promises the firm a monopoly in the home market, or special facilities, the competition among foreign firms for the investment permit will tend to be fiercer; but, even where several foreign companies are permitted to share in the market, competition for entry may exist. If, on the other hand, the host government provides an environment in which only normal, competitive profits can be expected to be earned, there is a strong incentive for foreign oligopolies to collude and reach market-sharing agreements on their operations.

(c) *Information*. Solidarity among protagonists and division among antagonists is not enough for the success of the cartel. For effective bargaining power, knowledge and information are also needed. In the case of negotiations with transnational enterprises, it is important to know about accounting methods, transfer pricing, over-invoicing of imported inputs and under-invoicing of exported outputs, and to have realistic figures for management fees, royalties and interest charged against the local subsidiary and to the credit of a company located in a tax haven or in the parent country.

Several commentators have argued the case for an international agency to render assistance to low-income countries in gathering this type of information and supporting them in their negotiations. Bilateral technical assistance is bound to be suspect where companies are concerned that reside in the country giving the assistance; so this is *par excellence* an area for multilateral technical assistance or for joint agencies run for and by LDCs. The Andean Group, comprising Peru, Bolivia, Chile, Ecuador, Colombia and Venezuela, have agreed to lower tariff barriers, co-ordinate industrial development, and adopt common policies towards foreign companies, as well as to collect and pool relevant information from all members. Similarly, OPEC is an organisation that, in addition to raising the price of oil, collects information and has numerous other functions aimed at co-ordinating the policies of different countries.

Strengthening the Host Government's Position
Having considered ways in which LDC host governments could strengthen their bargaining position by acting in concert, let us now

briefly note some ways in which individual governments may improve their position.[31]

(a) *Learning*. The process of negotiation, bargaining and regulation will itself help the government to learn the requisite skills over time. However, in order to cope with a highly sophisticated and skilled opponent, the government must devote to the task of bargaining an equally well-trained and well-informed, and also honest, body of nationals, drawn from several sectors and disciplines. There may be a trade-off between the need to build up an experienced and mature organisation and the danger of laxness or corruption, arising from continuous exposure to a tempting adversary.

(b) *Centralisation*. In many LDCs, different items for negotiation are decided upon by different ministries or departments, which do not see the issue as a whole and often act in contradictory ways. The TNC, on the other hand, acts as one coherent unit with a fairly clear idea of what its objectives are. The result often is that the TNC is able to secure advantages which it would not be able to secure if all the official functions, or, at least, the responsibility for important decisions concerning them, were centralised in one powerful body.

(c) *Information*. As we have argued above, there is a vital need for information on particular TNCs as well as on alternative sources of technology, finance or management. LDCs must build up their own stock of knowledge, draw on each other's experience, seek help from consultants and sympathetic groups in developed countries, and secure assistance from the various international organisations (UNCTAD, the United Nations Industrial Development Organisation (UNIDO) the World Health Organisation (WHO), the International Labour Office (ILO), the Food and Agriculture Organisation (FAO), the UN Commission on Transnational Corporations, and several regional organisations) that are competent to offer advice on different aspects of TNC operations and give technical assistance. Ultimately, of course, the results of all such efforts will depend largely upon the host government's own ability to act intelligently and firmly in a game played with an uncompromising and sophisticated rival. In the next chapter we shall consider some limitations on this ability.

CONCLUSION

The nature of TNC expansion in the context of poor host countries raises a large variety of problems which governments can, and should, try to tackle by undertaking appropriate measures. These measures range from the regulation and control of foreign investments at the broadest level to the evaluation of particular investments and bargaining with individual TNCs. Every measure offers a potential benefit to the host country, but may also have a potential cost – if maladministered, it may inhibit desirable inflows, encourage distortions in the economy and negate the purpose for which it was instituted. The choice of policies must be made on the basis of practical and rational criteria; but what is vital is that a *choice* be made, and that the issues should not (as they are at present in many countries, and as many proponents of TNCs would advocate) be settled by default, either because governments are unaware of their existence, or because they believe that neutral and efficient market forces operate so as to maximise their benefits from foreign investment, with no special need for regulation on their part.

The main argument of this chapter has been that some of the influences that TNCs may have on developing countries are favourable to development, while others are damaging. The net effects may be positive or negative, but what matters from the point of view of policy is the gross effects. *If it is accepted that these effects can be separated*, it follows that it is neither necessary nor desirable to take either a completely *laissez-faire* or an extreme communist view. The skill in framing a policy and in negotiating a contract with transnational companies is to maximise the surplus of beneficial over detrimental effects that is still acceptable to the TNC. The key to policy, then, is selectivity, not ideology.

CHAPTER 12

The Implementation of Policy

INTRODUCTION

In the previous chapter we assumed that host governments in LDCs were willing and able to formulate and implement comprehensive policies towards TNCs. It is now time to drop this assumption and to be more realistic.

While the role that governments of poor countries have to play in the area of foreign private investment is of tremendous importance, and while most governments do undertake a wide range of policies to deal with several aspects of such investment, there are two sorts of problems that arise in the implementation of desirable policies. The first arises from the possibility that governments may not be willing to pursue the 'national interest' as we might define it, but may wish to promote the well-being of particular (and usually small) sections of the population. The second arises from the possibility that, even if governments do want to promote the national interest, they are unable to do so, either because of their administrative weakness and incompetence, or because of interference and socio-political 'constraints'. Since motives are normally mixed, it is possible to have cases in which the two are mixed in various proportions.

It can hardly be doubted that both possibilities are very real. Many policies secure, in effect if not in proclamation, the betterment of particular interest. Many policies are badly administered, or in their implementation are thwarted by various forces generated by internal and external factors. We cannot examine these matters in any detail here, but it would be useful to spend some time on them so as to be fully aware of the limitations of the role of economic recommendations (and, so, of economists) in the real world.

LIMITATIONS ON WILLINGNESS

Let us return briefly to a theme introduced in Chapter 3, on the role of the state in economic analysis. Conventional economics proceeds on the assumption that the state is a neutral and final arbiter of the national interest. Thus, whatever the definition of national objectives adopted by the government in power, that definition is a valid one, which we as economists should accept as ethically correct for our analysis. In part this assumption follows logically from the fundamental 'vision' of conventional economics (that there are no intrinsic conflicts of interest, particularly on the basis of class, in society), and in part it is necessary because economists could hardly make general policy prescriptions without it.

It has been increasingly felt, especially in the field of development studies, where lines between economics and other social sciences are not so rigidly drawn, that such an assumption is often unwarranted and misleading. In a recent book on the political economy of Kenya, Colin Leys argues that conventional development theories in politics as well as in economics have revealed

> a marked disinclination to distinguish clearly between the different interests at stake in the countries of the third world, let alone to make the antagonisms between them the central focus of enquiry. Their focus has rather been on 'nations', and even more on the 'leadership' of 'nations', seen as confronting various obstacles to 'development' – 'development' being treated as an ultimately universal good. This perspective presupposes that the 'leadership' is more or less representative, or at least more or less benevolent; or, failing this, it presupposes that there is no 'serious' alternative to the existing 'leadership', or at any rate none with which it is the business of 'development theory' to be concerned. And since it does not start out from an analysis of the way in which different 'patterns of development' embody the dominance of different combinations of class interest, in practice it tends to take as given the interests which the 'leadership' represents, and more or less thoroughly reflects these interests in the concepts it uses, the questions it asks and the answers it offers.[1]

If there is any truth in a view of the state which sees its actions as determined not by enlightened considerations of national interest, but by pressures of different groups dominated by a combination of socio-economic elites (if one adopts a mildly radical or structuralist point of view) or by the balance of class forces of the capitalist system (if one is a Marxist),[2] then we need to take a completely different view from the conventional one on the relevance of much economic analysis and the usefulness of the sort of policy recommendations advanced in the last chapter. Some of the main implications of the alternative view (assuming the continued existence of predominantly capitalist system in host LDCs) are as follows.

(a) Policies implemented by the government (in this instance on foreign investment and industrialisation) may correspond to the interests of *particular sections of the dominant classes* rather than to those of the majority of the population. This is not to assert that the state will be a mere 'executive arm of the bourgeoisie', but to say that it will respond to shifting balances of power within a heterogeneous elite: thus, freedom of policy manoeuvre will tend to be far more limited than is conventionally assumed, and in certain areas, such as income distribution, may be very narrowly proscribed indeed.[3] In these circumstances, it may be pointless to conduct analysis in terms of the assumption that the 'right' policies will be undertaken, or to recommend policies which go against the existing political–economic reality.

Let us illustrate this with an example which may be taken as symptomatic of much of the discussion on policy measures. We argued in the previous chapter that, since TNCs tend to specialise in sophisticated and differentiated products which cater to the consumption of elites in LDCs, host governments should, in formulating foreign investment policies, attempt to direct TNC investment to sectors whose output is considered socially desirable, and to restrict severely the TNCs' marketing efforts. This would seem to provide a second-best solution (the first-best, of drastic income redistribution and changing 'dependent' consumption patterns, being generally unfeasible in the present situation) to the problem of meeting 'basic needs' within the existing socio-political–economic structure.

But how far is it sensible to think that such solutions will (ignoring practical problems) be implemented? Not, we believe, very far. If 'undesirable' consumption patterns are a reflection of the distribution of power, income and wealth in the present capitalist structure (and TNCs are the 'highest forms' of capitalist production), it is probably impossible over a long period to regulate the symptoms without curing the disease. Some cosmetic exercises may well be undertaken to restrain 'undesirable' consumption, but, without a major change in the structure itself, it is probably naive of economists to recommend that foreign investment in LDCs be geared to an equitable and 'sensible' consumption programme. The likelihood is that, cosmetics aside, policies will in effect continue to cater to elite demands, and will give a much larger role to TNCs than we have recommended.

Policy clearly is not determined in any direct or simple way by the interests of a dominant group. There are conflicts between different groups and classes, and concessions are occasionally made in order to buy consent from intermediate groups. The influence of ideological conditioning may be very important, and the perception of 'welfare' and its implementation may vary over time. Thus, policy may vacillate between giving relative freedom to market forces and trying to amend their worse effects. In the context of TNCs, policy may vacillate between providing liberal conditions for their entry and strengthening national control over the economy. This is, however, a long way from a situation where the sort of far-reaching recommendations that we made in the previous chapter (whatever their merits) can be implemented within the given structure of a large number of LDCs.

(b) The interaction of forces which determine policy are not purely internal, but may be *strongly influenced or conditioned by external forces*. The international capitalist system, in its various manifestations (TNCs themselves, aid, trade and military relationships, political pressures, and so on), can exercise a powerful influence on the behaviour of governments – directly by inducing them to adopt particular policies, and indirectly by shaping the outcome of internal social –political–economic conflicts. The evidence on this is, in our opinion, so extensive – ranging from specific instances of bribery, intimidation and political interference to the more general recent experience of LDCs – that it is unnecessary to argue the point at length. Let us, however, be clear about what we are saying. We are *not* saying that every LDC is forced against its will to adopt policies favourable to TNCs. We *are* saying that policies are subject to the interplay of internal and external political–economic forces, and that in most LDCs today the constellation of forces favouring capitalist growth is very powerful.[4]

(c) If the above reasoning is valid, it follows that *the 'right' policies will not be adopted unless they happen to conform to the underlying forces operating in particular LDCs*. If they do not so conform, we can hope to achieve very little unless the very act of stating what is 'right' can induce a change in the underlying structure. Of course, some of the policies prescribed previously may be implemented by host LDCs *within* the given structure: bargaining can be made more efficient, taxes realised more fully, restrictive business practices controlled better, and projects more rationally evaluated. These policies do not pose significant challenges to domestic elites or to TNCs. Those that do, such as the strict control of TNC entry, tight selection of technology, ruling out of 'unnecessary' products, and so on, will not be implemented by host governments unless the political environment is suitable. They can be meaningfully undertaken only as part of a larger effort to redistribute wealth and promote 'independent' economic development, and there are not many LDCs today which are actively pursuing such a strategy.

In sum, therefore, although we have followed the normal economic practice of making recommendations for policy in a sort of political vacuum, it is important that we have a clear understanding of the world in which these policies are supposed to be formulated. Each government has, according to the social forces which it embodies, a different conception of the 'welfare' which it is maximising, and each is subject to different political and economic pressures in devising and carrying out policies. Here and in Chapter 3, we have only touched upon these issues, but they may be central to an analysis of the role of TNCs in developing host countries.

LIMITATIONS ON ABILITY

While the conventional development literature has not paid very great attention to the factors that shape the formulation of policy, it has spent considerable time in analysing the weakness of the administrative machinery of LDC governments. We need not, therefore, devote much space to these problems.

The implementation of policies as complex and extensive as those recommended above requires great skill, dedication, efficiency and honesty. Bureaucracies in many developing countries are not renowned for these qualities. In a narrow sense, they may lack the training, motivation, experience or integrity to implement such complex programmes. In a broader sense, they may be representatives of sectional and class interests which benefit from positions of power that depend upon *not* implementing those programmes.[5]

Furthermore, there are, in dealing with large powerful TNCs, ample opportunities for persuasion or bribery. The recent evidence on the activities of US TNCs confirms that bribery is the normal *modus operandi* in many countries – not just for foreign firms but for anyone engaging in business enterprise. The greater the number of regulations imposed upon business, the greater are the dangers of inefficiency and corruption. Whether the remedy lies in reducing the number of regulations – and so giving rise to ills of a different kind – or in improving (not an easy task) the efficiency and honesty of the administration, is not for us to say. Perhaps the real answer lies in changing the social context in which these administrations operate, but this is not a matter for deliberate 'policy' on the part of existing governments.

What is clear is that most host governments are evincing a greater desire to control TNCs and to improve their own bargaining position relative to them. The international climate for TNCs has changed greatly in recent years. Some trade unions in developed countries have gone 'multinational' to cope with TNCs, with some modest success.[6] A new international organisation (the UN Commission on Transnational Corporations) has been established to deal exclusively with the policy problems created by the TNC phenomenon; others, such as UNCTAD, UNIDO, FAO, ILO, WHO, the Economic Commission for Latin America (ECLA), the Economic Commission for Asia and the Far East (ECAFE) and the Economic Commission for Africa (ECA), work on particular aspects of TNCs. The TNCs themselves have shown a willingness to collaborate with some of the demands of developing countries. They have also established centres to improve their public image and to promote 'social responsibility'.[7] Whether all this adds up to a fundamental change in the effects of TNCs on LDCs is doubtful: our view of the forces behind the growth of transnational enterprise suggests that, in terms of benefiting the majority of the world's poor, the difference will not be very great. Unless there is a drastic change in the *internal* structures of the poor countries themselves, the undesirable effects we have analysed in this book will continue to be felt as these countries become more clearly integrated into the international structure of production and trade.

Notes

CHAPTER 1

1. See Lall and Elek (1971), Lall (1972), Lall and Mayhew (1973) and Streeten and Lall (1973).
2. UN(1973), Table 5. It is suggested that these figures understate the share of European direct investment. Stobaugh is reported by Howe (1976) to estimate that by 1970 non-US TNCs were selling some 25 per cent more abroad than US TNCs.
3. UN (1973), Tables 12 and 29. The largest recipients of foreign manufacturing investment (over $200 million each) were Argentina, Brazil, India, Mexico, and the Philippines.
4. Reuber (1973), Appendix A.
5. UN (1973), Table 13. For a description of country differences in sectoral allocation of investment, see ibid., pp. 11–12.
6. More recent data (*Survey of Current Business*, 1975) show that, of the total of US direct investment abroad (including equity and loans) in manufacturing at the end of 1974, estimated at $50·9 thousand million, developed countries accounted for 82 per cent and LDCs for 18 per cent, with Latin America taking 82 per cent of the latter. The 'skill-intensive' industries (chemicals, machinery of all kinds and transport equipment) increased their share from 60 per cent of total manufacturing investment in 1970 to 62 per cent in 1974.
7. US Tariff Commission (1973), p. 409.
8. For a recent study of the relationship between the expansion of US foreign investment and the domestic market power of the firms concerned, see Horst (1975).
9. See UN (1973), Annex II, for twenty-one definitions which have been used in recent literature. We have chosen to follow the recent United Nations convention of calling such firms 'transnational corporations'.
10. See Vernon (1971).
11. US Tariff Commission (1973), p. 81. When launching on the actual analysis, however, this study 'reduces the definitional problem' by covering 'all U.S. firms engaging in foreign direct investment in production facilities' (p. 83). The UN study covers 'all enterprises which control assets – Factories, mines, sales offices and the like – in two or more countries' (p. 5), and so is even broader. Despite its strictures on the differences between TNCs and other foreign investors, therefore, it does not distinguish between them very clearly; its data deal with practically *all* foreign investments, while its analysis concentrates on the *largest* firms.
12. Parker (1974), p. 149.

13. Of the 'real' multinationals (MPE2), 210 (60 per cent) are from the US, forty-seven (13 per cent) from the UK, twenty-five (7 per cent) from West Germany, sixteen (5 per cent) from France, ten (3 per cent) from Japan and the rest from other developed countries. See Parker (1974), Table 8.4.
14. The term 'transnational' is not used in these contexts, because management specialists are not interested in the political–economic connotations of different labels attached to TNCs, and because they generally have an interest in promoting a more congenial (see following note) image of these companies.
15. It has been argued – and the UN has accepted the argument and reversed its earlier practice – that the term 'multinational' is inappropriate for describing these large corporations, since it suggests that the firms concerned have no national or regional bias in their operations, recruitment, ownership, loyalties or profit declaration. The term 'transnational' is considered more apt, especially with reference to LDCs, because it conveys a clearer picture of (private) firms from one area operating in others – with the potential, discussed in Chapter 3, of many kinds of conflict of interest between the practices and loyalties of the firms and the welfare of the host countries.
16. For some recent data on the significance of TNCs, see Buckley and Casson (1976).
17. UN (1973), p. 7. See also Vernon (1971), for a discussion of the importance of the 187 US TNCs used in the Harvard studies.
18. Hymer and Rowthorn (1970).
19. UN (1973), p. 8 (emphasis added). The report is referring here to large firms with sales of over $100 million rather than to all foreign investors. See also Rowthorn (1971), Chapter 6.
20. The 100 largest firms in UK manufacturing industry accounted for 20 per cent of net output in 1948 and about 50 per cent in 1970; the 100 largest industrial and commercial companies accounted for 47 per cent of total net assets in 1948 and 64 per cent in 1968. The average five-firm concentration ratio (i.e. the percentage of total industry sales accounted for by the leading five firms) in the UK increased from 52 per cent in 1935 to 69 per cent in 1968. In the USA, the 100 largest companies increased their share of manufacturing assets from 40 to 50 per cent during 1947–66. For more detail, see George and Silberston (1975) and Aaronovitch and Sawyer (1975) on the UK, and Blair (1972) and Blumberg (1975) on the USA. For data on Japan, see Caves and Uekusa (1976).
21. UN (1973), p. 13. See also Weisskopf (1974).
22. UN (1973), Table 1.
23. This is cogently argued by Kindleberger (1974).
24. Foreign direct manufacturing investment in the US came to $10,300 million by the end of 1974, over 20 per cent of total US manufacturing investment abroad. While we have no data on their import and export propensities, clearly their inclusion would significantly raise the proportion of US trade under the direct control of TNCs as a whole. See *Survey of Current Business* (1975).
25. Calculated from Bradshaw (1969).
26. Calculated from UK Government, Department of Industry (1974), Tables 55 and 57.

27. Reported in the *Financial Times* (1974b).
28. See UN (1973), p. 21; Helleiner (1975b); Cohen (1975); and Nayyar (1975). It may be noted that these sources give rather different estimates for several countries.
29. This ignores exports channelled through transnational buying companies, which are quite significant in exports from South East Asia.
30. US Tariff Commission (1973), pp. 8–9 (emphasis added).
31. With the exceptions of defence industries (where, for obvious reasons, transnational production is restricted), aircraft (where strategic factors as well as the overwhelming importance of economies of scale similarly limit international production, though R & D is *highly* concentrated) and the electronic subsector of electrical machinery (where the relative novelty of the technology and its rapid diffusion has led, at least at present, to a *low* level of concentration combined with widespread international production). See US Tariff Commission (1973), Chapter 6 and other references cited below, as well as National Science Foundation (various dates) for details of industrial R & D spending in the USA.
32. For a simple but concise treatment see Freeman (1974) and Aaronovitch and Sawyer (1975), Chapter 9, and for a recent survey of the literature see Kamien and Schwartz (1975). Parker (1974) and Mansfield (1974) discuss the role of TNCs in the production and international diffusion of technology.
33. Although there has been a tendency in recent years for TNCs to spread their R & D facilities in different countries (for reasons of cost and availability of personnel, as well as closeness to growing large markets), the economies of scale and need for communication inherent in research have meant that the bulk of research, especially 'basic' research, is still done 'at home'. A recent survey of 500 US TNCs shows that only 10 per cent (about $1100–1200 million in 1971–2) of company-financed R & D was carried out abroad, and of this 10 per cent only 3 per cent was carried out in LDCs (mostly in Brazil and Argentina). See Conference Board (1976).
34. US Tariff Commission (1973), p. 78.
35. UN (1974), p. 26.

CHAPTER 2

1. For recent reviews see Stevens (1974), Hufbauer (1973), Buckley and Casson (1976), Horst (1975) and Dunning (1973), and for a bibliographical guide see Chapters 2–4 of Lall (1975a). For Marxist approaches and surveys, see Amin (1974), Baran (1957), Barratt Brown (1974), Murray (1972), Palloix (1973), Poulantzas (1975) and various papers in Owen and Sutcliffe (1972).
2. See Corden (1974a, b) and Johnson (1972). Chapter 4 below gives a few more references on the 'pure' theory of direct investment.
3. See Horst (1974c) and Stevens (1974).
4. Oligopolistic theories of foreign investment were first advanced in general terms by Hymer (1960), and subsequently by Kindleberger (1969), Caves (1971), Hirsch (1976), Knickerbocker (1973), and Vernon (1966, 1971).

Penrose (1959, 1968) and Marris (1964) contributed to the understanding of the motivation and internal structures of large firms, while Bain's classic work (1956) on barriers to competition was followed by important contributions by Scherer (1970), Shubik (1959), Mansfield (1974), and several others. For recent work and references see Aaronovitch and Sawyer (1975), Blair (1972), Blumberg (1975) and Buckley and Casson (1976).

5. For the importance of mergers and takeovers for the growth of firms in the UK, see Singh (1971).
6. For a review of evidence on the determinants of US expansion in Canada by merger, see Baumann (1975).
7. For a theory of international conglomerate acquisitions, based on theories of capital asset pricing, see Adler and Dumas (1975). The main factors which distinguish international from national capital markets are taken to be segmentation of private portfolio investments and the existence of exchange risk.
8. Aliber (1970), pp. 28–30.
9. For some evidence from the UK mechanical engineering industry that foreign affiliates may be more skilled in choosing good location sites than local firms are, see Ingham (1976).
10. See Negandhi and Prasad (1975) for a comparative study of the managerial practices and efficiency of US TNCs and local firms in LDCs that finds that some of the latter are just as efficient as the former. While the method of measurement (using 'indices' of managerial efficiency) should be treated with some caution, the results should at least warn us against taking the superiority of TNCs in this respect too much for granted.
11. This is not to say that TNCs do not also flourish in many 'medium' or 'low' technology industries, drawing their market power from other sources. On the importance of technology see the US Tariff Commission (1973), Chapter 6; Vernon (1971); Severn and Laurence (1974); Pavitt (1971); Freeman (1974); and Parker (1974). For a more general analysis, see Johnson (1975).
12. See UNCTAD (1974) and UN (1964). We shall return to patents in LDCs later.
13. National Science Foundation (1975). A survey by the Conference Board (1976) shows that the proportion of *applied* R & D expenditure by US TNCs is even greater for subsidiaries than for parents.
14. The US Tariff Commission (1973), pp. 552–4, assigns 65 per cent of total US R & D to 'development'. The proportion would be much higher if its estimate for 'basic' research (15 per cent) was brought down to National Science Foundation levels. For data on other countries, see OECD (1970a).
15. Though many Marxists may also assign technical progress the functions of increasing capitalist control over the production process (by automation), of promoting the dominance of monopoly capital (by encouraging concentration) and of increasing capital's repression of labour (by imposing greater discipline and perhaps more alienation).
16. See Freeman (1974), Chapter 8, for an interesting discussion of various types of innovation strategy.
17. Ibid., pp. 259–66.
18. There is no precise Marxist equivalent of 'technology' of this type, but clearly its function lies more in the realm of *realising* surplus value than in

that of increasing it.
19. Freeman (1974), p. 267. For more on the meaning of product differentiation, see Grubel and Lloyd (1975).
20. On pharmaceuticals see Lall (1974b, 1975b).
21. The role played by patents changes similarly. See Parker (1974) and Freeman (1974). The implications of patents for LDCs are touched on later.
22. A good example is the recent work by Johnson (1975). The welfare implications of this aspect of TNC growth are sometimes further confused by including *marketing* with technology (broadly defined) as 'knowledge'—with all its (implicitly) desirable attributes—and using 'knowledge' to explain such growth. See, for instance, Buckley and Casson (1976).
23. In this context, the importance of such 'scouting' activities is illustrated by the US Tariff Commission (1973), which remarks that 'except for a few unusual years during and following World War II, the Europeans have led in the output of scientific discoveries and basic research. American companies' prowess has lain in quickly converting such results into commercially successful products and processes' (p. 553). The division of R & D work between small firms which 'innovate' initially and large firms which 'develop' innovations is also noted in the case of the hovercraft by P. S. Johnson (1975; see especially p. 313), and in general by Mansfield in *Business Week* (1976b).
24. See Vernon (1971) and, for a study of IBM, Brock (1975).
25. See *Financial Times* (1974a, c).
26. See Vernon (1974b), Pickering (1974), and references mentioned there, as well as various UNCTAD reports entitled *Restrictive Business Practices*. For a popular description of the various illegal and semi-legal practices undertaken by IBM to retain monopolistic control of its technology, see Malik (1975).
27. This is noted for the energy field in the USA by Rosenberg (1976).
28. Though the large firms are not always the most successful innovators. See Freeman (1974) and Kamien and Schwartz (1975, 1976).
29. See, for instance, Vernon (1971), Parker (1974), Baumann (1975), Horst (1975), Aaronovitch and Sawyer (1975), Dunning (1973, 1974) and Severn and Laurence (1974).
30. As well as some technologically 'new' industries where the market structure has not yet stablised on oligopolistic lines (electronics, for example).
31. For the recent contributions to the enormous literature on this subject, see Comanor and Wilson (1974) and Cowling et al. (1975), on the USA and the UK respectively. See also Galbraith (1967), for a more controversial general discussion.
32. Even low-technology industries have large numbers of TNCs. See Parker (1974) for a general description, and Horst (1974a) for an analysis of the role of advertising, product differentiation and brand promotion in the US food industry.
33. The role of marketing in the success of firms is crucial even in a high-technology industry like pharmaceuticals. See Lall (1975b).
34. Caves (1974) notes this as a possible advantage of TNCs in the US–Canadian case.
35. Kindleberger (1969), pp. 19–23.

36. See Grubel and Lloyd (1975), Chapter 1, for explanation and references.
37. For an interesting discussion, see Blair (1972), Chapter 5. However, see Pickering (1974), Chapter 2, for a brief review of the evidence that plant-level economies may be important.
38. This is illustrated for India in a recent study by Kochanek (1974), who analyses the open and hidden pressures exerted, sometimes successfully and at other times not, and the emergence of business (local and foreign) as the 'best organized pressure group in the country'. See also Kidron (1965). On more general issues see Streeten (1971), dos Santos (1970), Frank (1969, 1972) and Sunkel (1969–70, 1973).
39. This assumes that the 'Law of Proportionate Effect' or Gibrat's Law, which postulates that the growth of firms is a purely chance phenomenon, is not applicable to the growth of TNCs. For references and a recent empirical examination of the law with respect to the UK, see Singh and Whittington (1975).
40. See Horst (1975) for evidence that the external growth of US TNCs has strengthened their *domestic* market power and raised *domestic* profits. Parker (1974), reporting on a study of 411 subsidiaries of foreign companies in the UK, finds that they grew faster than their respective domestic counterparts, showing a relative 'commercial independence' of their host environment (pp. 198–205). See also Wolf (1975) and Severn and Laurence (1974).
41. Cohen (1975) lays a great deal of stress on risk-spreading as a motive for foreign investment, but it is more likely that this is a consequential and cumulative benefit of international expansion than that it is an initial cause. (See Jacquemin and Saez (1976) for a recent study of the relationship between size and stability of profits.) TNCs are *able* to spread risks more widely only because they possess certain other advantages; these advantages are not created *in order to* spread risks. In fact, after a detailed econometric exercise, Cohen concludes that, while the data show that TNCs enjoy more stability in profits and sales, 'This result does not, of course, allow one to conclude that US firms invested in foreign countries in order to reduce their risks. Reducing risk (or increasing sales or profits) may be the unintended result of corporate action taken for other reasons' (p. 54). We are not even sure that it is fair to class risk-reduction in the same category of motivation as growth or profit, but the moral as regards the former is clear. For a survey of such theories, based on a 'portfolio theory' of investment behaviour, see Stevens (1974); a brief critique is provided in Buckley and Casson (1976).
42. 'High' and 'low' technology industries are defined with reference to the proportion of R & D expenditures in total costs (see, for instance, Parker (1974) and the US Tariff Commission (1973), Chapter 6; *within* each industry, transnational firms may generally be assumed to use the most advanced techniques available.
43. For orthodox expositions of this view, see Kindleberger (1969), Chapter 6, and Corden (1974a); for a Marxist interpretation, see Murray (1972).
44. On developed areas see Adam (1972), and on LDCs see Watanabe (1972), Helleiner (1973), Finger (1975a) and Sharpston (1975).
45. A detailed survey of the electronics industry is provided in UNCTAD (1975). Two interesting points noted in this report are that, with a rise in

wage costs in the 'older' centres, such as Hong Kong and Singapore, TNCs have moved to cheaper areas, in South East Asia, Central America and the Caribbean (p. 16); and that East European firms are also entering into subcontracting arrangements with LDCs in this industry (p. 2.).
46. For a concise and simple exposition see Vernon (1974b).
47. See Hirsch (1976).
48. See the excellent study by Knickerbocker (1973), based on the investment behaviour of 187 large US TNCs, which clearly demonstrates the importance of such reaction as a defensive and not, except obliquely, as a profit-maximising measure. See also Vernon (1974b), for a discussion of three different types of oligopolies—'innovative', 'mature' and 'senescent'—and the different pressures these generate for the firms concerned.
49. Knickerbocker (1973), p. 195.
50. See, for instance, Barratt Brown (1974), Magdoff (1972) and Hymer and Rowthorn (1970).
51. Hymer and Rowthorn (1970), pp. 81–2. Newfarmer and Mueller (1975) present evidence on the effect of US TNCs in increasing concentration in Mexico and Brazil, both relatively 'open' countries where this hypothesis can be verified. See also Subrahmanian (1972) on India, and Willmore (1976) on Central America.
52. Hirsch (1967) and Vernon (1966). For subsequent work on this model, see Finger (1975b), Grubel and Lloyd (1975), Wells (1972) and Hirsch (1975, 1976). The relationship between trade patterns and technological change was analysed earlier by Posner (1961) and developed by Hufbauer (1965). For a synthesis of product-cycle and technology–trade analyses, see Johnson (1972) and Grubel and Lloyd (1972); for a simple exposition, see Buckley and Casson (1976). Klein (1973) provides an interesting attempt to merge 'learning' and product-cycle into a new comparative advantage theory.
53. Since military R & D is very important in the USA, clearly the pressures to locate manufacturing plants for military innovations in the home country are greater, both for security and for testing.
54. For an interesting application of the product-cycle theory to innovations in petrochemicals, a somewhat untypical industry (with great economies of scale, relatively insignificant labour costs, lumpiness in investment requirements), see Stobaugh (1971).
55. Vernon (1971), p. 109. For a more recent exposition which takes newer developments into account, see Vernon (1974b) and Grubel and Lloyd (1975).
56. See Baranson (1970), Baumann (1975), McManus (1972), Parker (1974), Stopford and Wells (1972) and Vernon (1971).
57. This assumes that the TNC, once it sells a licence, does nothing further to profit from its other advantages. However, it is worth noting that full or majority ownership is not essential for the full exploitation of the package: an appropriate combination of management contracts, fees, technology agreements and interest charges can give it nearly the same advantages as ownership and control, even with minority or nil participation. Nationalisation of foreign firms has, for this reason, often failed to gain the host country a greater share in foreign profits.

58. The discussion has been confined to the economics of *modern* international manufacturing investment; it is conspicuously incapable of explaining older forms of investment which were governed by the advantages of direct political and/or economic domination (for instance, early British investment in India and public utility investments by US firms in Latin America; see Bimberg and Resnick, 1975) or by cultural, family and political ties (for instance, the movement of capital accompanying migration from Europe to the 'new' white-settler countries). On the importance of the latter to the growth of the USA, Canada, Australasia, and so on, see Bagchi (1972); such investment was not, of course, available to the non-white colonies, which, on the contrary, probably provided the bulk of the resources which were channelled to these areas. Nor does the discussion apply to investment determined by the location of natural resources (plantations or mines) where the rights were granted under colonial or semi-colonial rule. In some types of resource-based investments, however, TNCs do have advantages in the form of technology, capital, or market control, or simply the ability to spread exploration risks where finding the resource is a problem.
59. For recent summaries, see Dunning (1973), Stevens (1974) and Reuber (1973).
60. Here we are referring not to market or exchange-rate instability, with which TNCs are well-equipped to cope, but only to instability which could threaten their very existence or mode of operation. This description of firm behaviour simplifies a complex process of decision-making in large organisations (see Aharoni, 1966), but does not seem to do violence to the general evidence on TNC behaviour.
61. See Stevens (1974) and Dunning (1973).
62. Dunning (1973), p. 304.
63. See the detailed discussion of such incentives in Reuber (1973), pp. 120–32.
64. Stopford and Wells (1972), p. 11.
65. See, for instance, Stopford and Wells (1972), Vernon (1971), Rumelt (1974), Brooke and Remmers (1970), Hymer (1972) and, at a more popular level, Barnet and Müller (1974).
66. See Stopford and Wells (1972) for a detailed study of the evolution of 170 US TNCs.
67. And given also the development of quick, efficient and widespread means of international communication and travel, on the significance of which see Kindleberger (1969).
68. '... in mature enterprises a seasoned financial corps comes into place, trained within the system of the enterprise and stationed at various key points in the field and at headquarters. This corps has generally been made up of men attuned to the signals and conditioned to the rules of thumb that the system has devised ... fortified by internal manuals. ... Enough conditioning, it is assumed, will breed the necessary conformity while allowing for local initiative and local adaptation' (Vernon, 1971, p. 134). On the use of various devices such as 'corporate acculturation' and 'systems transfer', see Weichmann (1974), and, on TNCs as transmittors of 'business culture' from home countries to host countries, see Sauvant (1976).
69. See Robbins and Stobaugh (1974).
70. US Tariff Commission (1973), pp. 420–1. Evidence from our sample of

firms in India and Colombia indicates, however, that foreign investors may tend to follow financing practices of the host country, and that TNCs may not gear themselves more highly than other firms. See below, Chapter 6.
71. See also Singh (1971) and Aaronovitch and Sawyer (1975), on the theory of takeovers.
72. Vernon (1974) p. 19. For evidence on Mexico and Brazil, see Newfarmer and Mueller (1975).
73. 'A system with twenty-five units (a parent and twenty-four subsidiaries) and ten different types of links between each pair of units would have 3,000 intercompany financial links. The number of alternative solutions for the entire system would run into the millions' (Robbins and Stobaugh, 1974, p. 17). See also Brooke and Remmers (1970).
74. *Financial Times* (1976).
75. International concern about such practices has reached such a level that the United Nations has been asked to look into the matter and propose remedies. See UN Economic and Social Council (1976).
76. Robbins and Stobaugh (1973), p. 171.
77. UN (1973), p. 12. On attitudes of foreign investors, see Reuber (1973), pp. 224–5, and Tomlinson (1970).
78. Vernon (1974), p. 19. The source of the data is the Harvard Multinational Enterprise Databank.
79. TNCs with high-technology or high-marketing specialisations resent joint ventures most, as do firms which are in the process of 'rationalising' production; see Franko (1971) and Stopford and Wells (1972) for detailed discussions. Similarly, the possibility of maximising post-tax rents through transfer pricing is seen by the US Tariff Commission (1973, p. 134) as 'a principal reason why multinational companies prefer 100 percent ownership of foreign subsidiaries'.
80. As noted above, even a minority position with appropriate management and technology contracts, and the use of transfer pricing, may give a TNC sufficient control over buying, selling and production to yield high rents. If the alternative to a joint venture is not investing at all and losing a market, the TNC may in any case be prepared to accept a lower (but still positive) rate of return on its 'package'. On some advantages of joint ventures, based on a sample of British investments in India and Pakistan, see Tomlinson (1970).
81. This is more likely to occur in LDCs in a mature oligopoly with technological stability, where co-operation in a particular venture in a new area will not cause one TNC to give up any special asset to another, and will not impinge on its established market position in its own area of dominance.
82. For a brief review of this sort of co-operation, which occurs mainly (for manufacturing industry) in developed countries, see Tharp (1976).
83. See Franko (1973) for a recent description of international staffing policies of TNCs. Franko finds that high local staffing occurs in *subsidiaries* after a certain stage of transnational expansion, but it is *never* significant at the headquarters. Thus, he concludes, 'The continued dominance of home-country managers at headquarters further leads one to suspect that a multinational management mix may be an unrealistic target.' Hymer (1972) analyses the broader consequences of this phenomenon.

84. See Behrman (1970), Gilpin (1976), Ball (1968), Johnson (1975), Vernon (1971), and Stephenson (1972) for good discussions.
85. For different Marxist interpretations of the relationships between capitalists and state power, see Poulantzas (1973a, b; 1975; 1976), Miliband (1969), and the recent survey by Gold et al. (1975). For others, see Galbraith (1967), Blumberg (1975), Gilpin (1976), Barnet and Müller (1974) and Streeten (1971).
86. On the functions and role of the capitalist state *vis á vis* international firms, see Poulantzas (1975) and Murray (1971).
87. Bergsten (1974) argues that the US government may have to intervene on behalf of its TNCs to protect them against pressures exerted by other governments. A similar argument about clashes between different 'imperialist' blocs is advanced by several Marxists; for a review and convincing refutation, see Poulantzas (1975).

CHAPTER 3

1. On different attitudes to TNCs, see Streeten (1971), Lall (1974a) and Kindleberger (1975).
2. One of the best discussions of this is still an early work, published in German in 1932, by Myrdal, translated into English in 1953. See also Streeten's contribution in this book, as well as Dobb (1973), Robinson (1962), Nath (1973), Rowley and Peacock (1975) and, for a simplified treatment, Stilwell (1975).
3. See Streeten (1973).
4. See Foster-Carter (1976) and Lall (1976b).
5. The 'alternative situation' is a hypothetical situation where foreign investment (marginal or non-marginal) is assumed absent, against which its costs and benefits in the actual case can be gauged. For the alternative assumed in our case studies, see Chapter 8.
6. See Foster-Carter (1976) for a discussion of the conflicts resulting from a Kuhnian 'paradigm change' in the field of development economics.
7. For a fuller discussion, see Lall (1976b).
8. See Myrdal (1953) who calls it the 'communistic fiction', and analyses the precise meaning of interest harmony. See also Rowthorn (1974) and Stewart (1975).
9. See Robinson (1962), Rowley and Peacock (1975) and Stilwell (1975).
10. Some economists may object to the fulfilment of utility from material consumption as the basic value judgement underlying welfare economics, and may, like Rowley and Peacock (1975), propose other value judgements. These are now rather rare birds, but we should note that their criticisms of 'mainstream' welfare economics do not usually stretch to questioning the harmony-of-interest premise. For other difficulties in deriving social welfare from individual welfare in the neoclassical framework, see Stilwell (1975).
11. See, for instance, Adelman and Morris (1973) and Chenery et al. (1974). On theoretical problems raised by distribution, see previous references as well as Sen (1973) and Stewart and Streeten (1976).
12. Good examples of this sort of approach are Kindleberger (1969), Reuber (1973) and Lal (1975).
13. For a philosophical critique see Hollis and Nell (1975). For an explicitly

'radical' attack on these liberal–individualistic premises, see Gintis (1972).
14. See Foster-Carter (1976).
15. For US evidence, see Horst (1975) and research by Vaupel mentioned in Dunning (1973).
16. As long as the rate of profit is higher than the rate of interest. See Chapter 6 for more information on gearing.
17. However, this in turn raises the problem about how to distinguish between short- and long-term borrowing when short-term loans are 'rolled over' from year to year. Most governments allow TNCs free access to commercial bank 'short-term' borrowing for purposes of inventory financing; such loans can easily be rolled over and extended to long-term uses, but the net contribution is bound to be fairly marginal.
18. This is noted for India by Carlsen and Neerso (1973) and for Colombia by Vaitsos (1974b).
19. See Brooke and Remmers (1970), Stopford and Wells (1972), Vernon (1971) and Barnett and Müller (1974).
20. There is, however, some evidence from Asia and Latin America that certain kinds of local firms are just as efficient as US TNC subsidiaries. See Negandhi and Prasad (1975).
21. Though the actual nationality of the particular people involved is less significant than the division of authority and status among the constituent units of the TNC (i.e. its *structure*).
22. Hymer (1972), pp. 126, 129.
23. For a colourful account, see Barnet and Müller (1974).
24. This is the burden of the argument of the *dependencia* school as well as of that of the neo-Marxists (though not of the palaeo-Marxists). For references and critiques, see Philip O'Brien (1975) and Lall (1975c).
25. See Lall (1973), Vaitsos (1974b), US Tariff Commission (1973), Hanson (1975), Robbins and Stobaugh (1974) and Brooke and Remmers (1970). Some indirect evidence on export pricing is produced by Müller and Morgenstern (1974) for Latin America, but their case is not conclusively established, because of the lack of direct price data.
26. Estimates by Lall (1973) indicate that roughly one-fourth to one-third of total manufactured trade among *developed* countries was intra-firm by 1970, with its share of total trade growing over time. Its share in LDCs' trade of manufactures as a whole was smaller; but, for Mexico and Brazil, two countries relatively well integrated into the TNC framework, had reached 80 per cent of total exports of foreign affiliates by 1972 (see Newfarmer and Mueller, 1975).
27. On different attitudes and internal constraints to transfer-price manipulations, see Shulman (1969) and Verlage (1975). On the use of 'optimal' financial policies, see Robbins and Stobaugh (1974).
28. See UN (1974), the main text and the 'Technical Papers' on taxation.
29. See Fleck and Mahfouz (1974).
30. On the theoretical aspects, see Horst (1971); on the implications for LDCs, see Lall (1973) and Vaitsos (1974b); on financial strategy, see Robbins and Stobaugh (1974); on taxation, see Musgrave (1974); and, on managerial and legal aspects, see Verlage (1975).
31. For instance, the 1971 Indian Government study shows that, around

1969–70, each 'examiner' in the port of Bombay had to handle over 26,000 shipping bills, and each 'appraiser' nearly 8000 original valuations and 66,000 rechecks of shipping bills annually. This study notes several difficulties in the adequate control of import–export prices and points out how these lead to a loss of foreign exchange.
32. See Verlage (1975) for a discussion of how several governments of developed countries attempt to deal with these problems.
33. See Keegan (1969) and Verlage (1975).
34. But less rigorously; as the US Tariff Commission (1973, p. 133) remarks with some sarcasm, 'Perhaps surprisingly, European government and EC officials remain rather calm over the issue of the MNC's tax behaviour.... The chief strategy of tax minimisation by multinational companies is manipulation of transfer prices.'
35. Some African countries, such as Kenya and Tanzania (and some others, but precise information is not to hand) employ a Swiss firm, the General Superintendence Company, to check prices and shipments on trade, but it is not clear how effective this is as a means of controlling transfer pricing on firm-specific products.
36. If, on the other hand, the realisation of taxes via the assignation of transfer prices becomes a point of inter-government conflict, it might well be the TNCs that suffer from effective overall taxes that are higher than nominal ones. This may, in turn, provoke retaliatory state action of the type discussed by Bergsten (1974).
37. See, among many others, Hirschman (1969) and the *dependencia* writers mentioned above. This argument may, of course, be extended to other sources of TNC superiority, such as technology or marketing, but, for ease of exposition, we shall deal with it here.
38. For instance, it is widely accepted that hedging and speculative action by US TNCs so exacerbated pressures on the dollar in the early 1970s that a devaluation became necessary. This may, however, have been a 'good thing' in so far as it forced the authorities to adopt a more sensible, if less popular, economic policy.
39. While there is good reason for thinking that oligopolistic competition among private firms in LDCs would, in the long run, take the same form as seen in developed countries, it is likely that the entry of TNCs significantly speeds up the process of oligopolisation in developing host countries. For evidence from Mexico and Brazil, see Newfarmer and Mueller (1975), and on Central America see Willmore (1976).
40. For examples of the four approaches, see Servan-Schreiber (1968), Levitt (1970), Newfarmer and Mueller (1975) and Frank (1969), respectively.
41. See the document on this subject submitted by the UNCTAD secretariat to UNCTAD IV in Nairobi (UNCTAD, 1976).
42. For general discussions, see references mentioned in the discussion of technology in the previous chapters. On the implications of transfer of technology for LDCs, see Streeten (1972), Stewart (1974), Helleiner (1975a), Morawetz (1974), Pavitt (1972), Vaitsos (various dates), Reuber (1973), Griffin (1974), Chudson and Wells (1974) and the numerous references given there.
43. A number of proponents of free capital flows continue to regard technology

as a neutral factor (for example, Johnson, 1970 and 1975, and Kindleberger, 1969). Their analysis is based upon a logical application of the neoclassical welfare paradigm outlined above in which value judgements about 'appropriateness' are not allowed; see Lall (1976b).
44. For an analysis of the interaction of technological and marketing factors in securing market power in the US computer industry, see Brock (1975).
45. See Horst (1974a).
46. See Streeten (1972), Vaitsos (1974b) and Johnson (1970).
47. Streeten (1972), p. 227.
48. See Wilkins (1974), Stopford and Wells (1972) and Helleiner (1975a).
49. A TNC which against its preference accepts a minority position may well transmit technology of older vintage than it would to a wholly-owned subsidiary.
50. Given a relatively free hand, however, even a TNC in a low-technology but high-marketing sector may prefer wholly-owned subsidiaries if it is in the process of reorganisation or rationalisation of its product lines (see Franko, 1971). In the context of LDCs, where most countries now demand local participation (usually over 50 per cent) as a precondition for TNC entry, these considerations become irrelevant: it is only the TNC in a strong bargaining position, offering high technology or (increasingly) export markets, that can demand high equity participation. See Chapter 2 above.
51. See the section on transfer pricing above.
52. See various studies by UNCTAD under the titles *An International Code of Conduct on Transfer of Technology* and *Restrictive Business Practices*; Vaitsos (1974b); Peter O'Brien (1975); and the discussion on exports in chapter 7 below.
53. See Penrose (1973), UN (1964), UNCTAD (1974), Vaitsos (1973, 1976), Grundmann (1976) and Greer (1973) and references there.
54. This may be especially significant for TNC investments in export-oriented industries, which seem to require a more congenial environment than do import-substituting industries. There are some indications, from Latin American evidence, that strong patent protection encourages export performance by pharmaceutical TNCs. See Mundowski and Sell (1976).
55. See Lall (1976a) and Taylor and Silberston (1973).
56. Vaitsos (1976) presents an analysis of the main reforms needed and the difficulties in achieving them.
57. We cannot cover this subject in depth here, but see Helleiner (1975a), Morawetz (1974), and Stewart (1974) for fuller discussions and references.
58. See Helleiner(1975a), Agarwal (1976), Wells (1973), White (1976), Pack (1976), Bhalla (1975), Courtney and Leipziger (1975), Reuber (1973), Vaitsos (1974a), Willmore (1976), Morawetz (1974), Mason, (1973), Stewart (1974), Morley and Smith (1974) and Stobaugh (1974), as well as some indirect evidence adduced in Chapter 6.
59. See Chapter 6.
60. See Helleiner (1975a), Streeten (1972) and UNCTAD (1976).
61. This greater adaptability arises from the possibility that 'It may be easier and cheaper to alter the number of shifts or the machine speed in an automated plant, in response to fluctuations in demand, than to hire and

train, or lay off employees in a labour-intensive one' (Helleiner, 1975a, p. 169).
62. See Cooper (1974) and Sunkel (1971).
63. For an interesting example of how technological 'dependence' may afflict even public enterprises, see Aurora and Morehouse (1972), who cite the case of a public-sector firm in India that refused to use domestic in preference to imported (from Eastern Europe rather than a TNC) technology for producing small tractors. For other examples of biases against local technology in India, see Kidron (1965); and, for a discussion of how the Chinese have managed to promote local technology, see Ishikawa (1976).
64. See Reuber (1973) and, on pharmaceuticals, Lall (1975b).
65. For instance, a number of capital-goods industries and export industries that complete with those of advanced countries.
66. See Helleiner (1973, 1975b), Sharpston (1975), UNCTAD (1975), US Tariff Commission (1970) and Finger (1975a).
67. As Streeten (1973) has argued about sourcing investments, 'Specialisation between countries is not by commodities according to factor endowments, but by factors of production: the poor countries specialising in low-skilled labour, leaving the rewards for capital, management and know-how to the foreign owners of these scarce but internationally mobile factors. The situation is equivalent to one in which *labour itself* rather than the *product of labour* is exported' (pp. 5–6).
68. See Nayyar (1975).
69. See Newfarmer and Mueller (1975) and König (1975).
70. Helleiner (1975b).
71. See, for instance, Barnet and Müller (1974), Ledogar (1975) on food and drugs, Lall (1975b) on drugs, Langdon (1974) on soap, and *The New Internationalist* (1975) on baby foods.
72. This may account for the fact that, for our sample firms (Chapter 6), no significant difference between the advertising expenditures of TNCs and those of non-TNCs was found in Colombia. It should be noted, of course, that advertising expenses on their own are only a part of what is broadly defined as 'marketing': various other types of promotion and product differentiation are part of the cost of production and are impossible to assess separately.
73. On this aspect of marketing see, for instance, Lonsdale (1966).
74. Such as footwear, clothing or sports goods; see Helleiner (1973, 1975b) and Sharpston (1975). This is more the province of large buying companies than of transnational manufacturers proper (see Hone, 1974).
75. Such as some processed food products, televisions, automobiles, cameras and tobacco. See de la Torre (1974) for a study of some Latin American countries, and Frankena (1973) on India.
76. See Ledogar (1975).
77. See Nayyar (1975).
78. See Cohen (1975) and Chapter 7 below.
79. See Chapter 7 below.
80. For a 'liberal' critique see Rowley and Peacock (1975). Kindleberger (1969), Reuber (1973) and Lal (1975) may be taken as examples of this school in the area of foreign investment in LDCs.

81. Behrman (1974) and Goodsell (1974) provide good illustrations.
82. Streeten (1971), or Bell's chapter on the 'The Political Framework' in Chenery et al. (1974).
83. See Poulantzas (various dates), Murray (1971), Alavi (1972) and the survey by Gold et al. (1975), as well as various *dependencia* writers, such as dos Santos (1970).

CHAPTER 4

1. However, doubts have occasionally been expressed about the *division* of benefits. From the point of view of the recipient, see the classic article by Singer (1950); and, from that of the investing country, see Balogh and Streeten (1960).
2. MacDougall (1960).
3. See the summary in Corden (1974a), and the exposition in Batra (1973), Chapter 13.
4. More realistic theories of trade, based on the oligopolistic features of TNCs, have been referred to in Chapter 2.
5. As with Bos et al. (1974).
6. The controversy was started by Keith Griffin and involved several economists, such as Weisskopf, Papanek, Reuber and others. For Griffin's position, see his 1971 paper; and, for a critical survey of the debate, see Stoneman (1975).
7. Stoneman (1975).
8. See Little (1972) and Little and Mirrlees (1974).
9. Other applications to foreign investments are Lal (1975) and several in Little and Scott (forthcoming).
10. See the symposium on the Little–Mirrlees method in *BOUIES* (1972).
11. On this point see Vaitsos (1975).
12. See Stewart (1975) and Lall (1976b).

CHAPTER 5

1. For published information on Colombia see DANE (1971), UNCTAD (1971a), and Vaitsos (1971; 1974a, b).
2. See, in particular, Kidron (1965), Indian Government (1971), NCAER (1971), RBI (1968, 1974), Subrahmanian (1972) and UNCTAD (1971b). The *Reserve Bank of India Bulletin* periodically carries surveys of the extent of foreign investment in India and detailed balance sheets and profit-and-loss accounts of foreign firms in various sectors in the country, while the Indian Investment Centre publishes guides to investing in India (see IIC, 1974).
3. On Jamaica, Girvan (1971) provides a little information on manufacturing investment but concentrates on bauxite. Nowshirvani and Bildner (1971), and CAPFI (1969) review the available evidence for Iran, and ILO (1972) and Leys (1975) that for Kenya. Stikker (1971) has a useful summary of the recent data and policies in Malaysia, though he confines himself to 'Pioneer

Companies', on which the Federal Industrial Development Authority regularly publishes data. Edwards (1975) discusses foreign investment as part of a more general analysis of industrialisation in West Malaysia.

4. These impressions are supported by similar evidence in Edwards (1975) for Malaysia; Nowshirvani and Bildner (1971) for Iran; and ILO (1972), Carlsen (1973) and Leys (1975) for Kenya.
5. We have taken a 25 per cent foreign equity shareholding as the minimum for foreign control of firms; this is arbitrary, since foreign control could be effectively exercised with a much smaller shareholding, or, if the local shares were highly concentrated in ownership, could be blocked even if the foreign holding were larger. In the absence of better information, however, this division has been used for some of the calculations discussed below.
6. See Furnish (1972) for a detailed review of the Andean Pact's regulations, and Vaitsos (1974a) for an analysis of the Pact's policies and the reactions of foreign investors and governments to them.
7. Leys (1975), pp. 128–35. The net effect on the manufacturing sector appears, however, to be very small.
8. See UNCTAD (1974) for a review of the issues and legislation of various countries.

CHAPTER 6

1. For some sample data on LDCs, see Reuber (1973), and, for aggregated figures from annual accounts of foreign investors in India, see *RBI Bulletin* (various dates), which seems to provide the most detailed information currently available on the operations of foreign investors in a developing country. Some data on Argentina are provided by Katz (1974), on Mexico by Wionczek et al. (1974), and on Central America by Willmore (1976). For US data, see the US Tariff Commission (1973) and various issues of the US Department of Commerce's *Survey of Current Business*. Vaupel and Curhan (1969, 1973), provide detailed figures on a selected sample of TNCs, but not of a type which would permit a firm-by-firm analysis of financing or performance; see Vernon (1971) for a discussion of some of the main findings on US TNCs, based on this evidence. For data on a sample of British firms in developing countries, see Reddaway et al. (1967–8).
2. For a recent survey of the theoretical issues, see Sen (1975), Chapter 5.
3. See J. Bates, 'Alternative Measures of the Size of Firms', in Hart (1965).
4. The average sales of 298 US TNCs (surveyed by the US Department of Commerce) to unaffiliated buyers within the USA came to $970 million in 1970, while their consolidated total sales came to $1400 million. These TNCs include some companies outside the manufacturing sector. Calculated from Lupo (1973).
5. Knickerbocker (1973) and Brash (1970).
6. For an interesting analysis of the relationship between the size and foreign investment and profitability of US firms, see Wolf (1975). In an earlier study, Horst (1972) found that 'once interindustry differences are washed out, the only influence of any separate significance [in explaining the foreign investment of US firms] is firm size' (p. 262).

7. Data published by the Reserve Bank of India on 330 foreign-controlled manufacturing firms and 1072 large and medium public limited manufacturing companies show that the average size of total assets came to $6·0 million and $5·6 million respectively in 1968–9, while net fixed assets came to $2·5 million and $2·4 million respectively (*RBI Bulletin*, Sep 1972 and Mar 1973). The Indian sample firms in general were larger than these firms, and sample TNCs were considerably larger.
8. Parry (1974).
9. We are not convinced by Parry's argument that the TNCs' larger size denotes higher 'revealed technological efficiency'. Relative size is determined by a number of forces, technological and others, which govern a firm's market power, and cannot be traced to technology alone, unless, of course, 'technology' is *defined* to include all sources of growth and market power.
10. For a discussion of these measures and their application to selected foreign and local firms in India, see Balasubramanyam (1973) and RBI (1974). For a more general discussion, see Bhalla (1975), Chapter 1.
11. Only two sample firms, both foreign pharmaceutical subsidiaries in India, had R & D expenditures of 2–3 per cent of sales; all the others (some twenty-two firms in India and Colombia) had R & D expenditures of well under 1 per cent of sales. See RBI (1974, pp. 1075–6) for a brief discussion of R & D activities of foreign and local firms in India, and Frankena (1973–4) for an analysis of how the Indian Government's trade and licensing policies have led to a reduction in the rate of technology transfer and indigenous innovation.
12. See Helleiner (1974), Stewart (1974), Stobaugh (1974) and the survey by Morawetz (1974).
13. On the problem of adaptation by TNCs, see Courtney and Leipziger (1975) and Morley and Smith (1974) and the references therein. Neither study finds evidence of adaptation to *factor endowments* in developing countries, but Morley and Smith find that US TNCs in Brazil adapted technology to the requirements of a *lower scale* of operations. Reuber (1973, pp. 194–7), in his sample of seventy-eight firms, also finds little evidence of adaptation to labour costs. See Morawetz (1974, p. 523) for other references to evidence on both sides of the question of whether adaptation by TNCs takes place.
14. Though investment in 'human capital' is counted as a return to labour rather than to capital.
15. Two particular characteristics of the industrial samples must be noted: first, Colombian 'other chemical' firms are much more capital-intensive than Indian ones because their products are much more 'basic', being concentrated on industrial chemicals rather than paint and cosmetics (as with the Indian sample); second, one of the two Colombian transport firms is very new and has large stocks of imported finished goods for resale, accounting for the combination of the low fixed-asset and fairly high total-asset ratios.
16. The 330 foreign-controlled and 1072 large and medium companies surveyed by the Reserve Bank of India (RBI, 1974) hold stocks of 29 and 31 per cent, and other current assets of 24 and 22 per cent of sales, respectively. Thus, Indian firms in general seem inclined to hold lower current assets as a proportion of sales than do Colombian ones.

17. Data for the 330 foreign and 1072 large and medium firms (RBI, 1974) show that the four ratios given in the table are, in the same order, 56·5, 87·3, 92·5 and 39·1 for the 330 firms, and 44·2, 72·8, 92·1 and 39·2 for the 1072 firms. Similar findings are reported for a sample of Central American foreign and local firms by Willmore (1976); while Agarwal (1976) finds that foreign firms in a number of industries in India use more capital per employee than do local firms.
18. The 330 foreign-controlled firms have percentages of PPs to total and fixed assets of 13·7 and 32·4, while the 1072 large and medium companies have percentages of 15·2 and 35·6 respectively.
19. This finding is the opposite of Agarwal's (1976), but the method employed by Agarwal, using 'productive capital stock' per employee for industrial averages, is different from ours and may account for the discrepancy.
20. A similar exercise for foreign- and locally controlled firms also fails to give any significant results.
21. Balasubramanyam (1973) finds, for a sample of eighty-five firms in four industrial sectors in India, that local firms with foreign technology were more capital-intensive than other local firms and foreign firms. In view of the fact that his data cover six years and his groupings appear to be statistically significant, more faith may be put in his findings than in ours. As with our results, however, there are grave problems with regard to interpretation and the validity of the assumptions underlying the theory of factor prices and intensity. See Chapter 1 of Bhalla (1975).
22. Value-added figures are distorted by transfer-pricing profits, but we do not attempt to adjust for such distortions here.
23. See Lall (1974b, 1975b).
24. For a flow-of-funds account for US TNCs abroad (for 1966–70), see US Tariff Commission (1973), p. 420.
25. See Robbins and Stobaugh (1974), pp. 50–8, on the advantages to TNCs of using credit rather than equity as a means of financing subsidiaries.
26. Vaitsos (1974, p. 84), finds that leverage for foreign subsidiaries in Colombia in 1968 (3·5) was much higher than for local firms (1·8). Our sample data confirms the figures for foreign firms, with leverage for TNCs (3·3) being higher than for non-TNCs (2·6); we have practically no information on wholly local firms.
27. Ibid.
28. These US data are calculated from the US Tariff Commission (1973), p. 420. We assume here, perhaps wrongly, that all foreign borrowing by sample firms is from parent companies.
29. These data pertain to 298 large US TNCs and their 5237 majority-owned affiliates. See Leftwich (1974).
30. A detailed econometric analysis of 200 British firms does, however, find a positive relationship between size and bank and trade credit in periods of credit stringency. See Davis and Yeomans (1974).
31. See also the section entitled 'Profits and Transfer Pricing', Chapter 7 below.
32. Leftwich (1974).
33. Ibid.
34. The 330 foreign-controlled and 1072 medium and large firms surveyed by the RBI show lower profitability than do the foreign- and locally

controlled firms in our sample. For instance, their rates of after-tax profit on total assets are 3·8 and 2·6 per cent, as compared to 6·8 and 3·6 per cent for the sample. As for tax payments, the share of their profits that the 330 and the 1072 firms pay to the government is 56·6 and 51·5 per cent respectively, as compared to 46·5 and 52·3 per cent for the sample groups.
35. See Wolf (1975) and Horst (1975) for recent empirical evidence that US TNCs are more profitable than other US firms; and Willmore (1976) for evidence that there is *no* significant difference between foreign and local firms in Central America.
36. A member of the UNCTAD project did, however, analyse the profitability of the Colombian sample in more detail in a Ph.D. thesis, later published in Spanish (Chudnovsky, 1973, 1974). Some of his results are mentioned below.
37. On some evidence for this for US TNCs, see Leftwich (1974).
38. The classic work on this is Bain (1956). A large number of papers have appeared on the subject, especially in the *Journal of Industrial Economics*; for a recent study, see Orr (1974).
39. For some evidence on the relationship between advertising and the growth and profitability of the US food-processing industry, see Horst (1974a); and, on advertising and market power generally, see the interesting work by Comanor and Wilson (1974).

CHAPTER 7

1. 'Reselling' refers to goods not manufactured or processed by the sample firm, but simply sold on behalf of the parent company.
2. For studies which show that TNCs perform better than local firms in *developed* countries, see Dunning (1969) and Hirsch (1973); for *less-developed* countries, see de la Torre (1974) on Colombia, Mexico and Nicaragua. See also Cohen (1975) for a study of the export performance of forty-six TNCs and local firms in Singapore, South Korea and Taiwan. He finds that TNCs do better in South Korea, equally well in Taiwan, and worse in Singapore, as compared with their local counterparts.
3. See Hirsch and Adar (1974) for a theoretical explanation of why exports should be positively related to size in imperfect markets with uncertainty. This article also describes in brief the results of a study by Hirsch of several hundred firms in Denmark, Holland and Israel, in which he finds that larger firms (according to size of sales) do export significantly more than smaller ones.
4. This supports the 'life-cycle' hypothesis advanced, with reference to the performance of TNC subsidiaries, by Prachowny and Richardson (1975), who argue that subsidiaries tend to export more with age: however, since our data pertain to *all sorts* of firms, we may conclude that this pattern is general to manufacturing industry.
5. UNCTAD (1971b) gives figures for India showing that 50 per cent of the total number of agreements effective up to 1969 had restrictive clauses, of which 88 per cent related to export restrictions. The largest proportion of restrictive clauses figured in agreements with firms with foreign minority

capital participation, followed by wholly local firms and foreign subsidiaries. Clauses banning exports completely were relatively rare, accounting for only 6 per cent of total export restrictive clauses; the commonest clause allowed exports only to specified countries. Vaitsos (1974b) suggests that export restrictive clauses, especially those prohibiting exports, are far more common in the Andean Pact countries (86 and 81 per cent of total number of contracts), and that local firms had a much higher incidence of restrictive clauses than foreign subsidiaries did (92 and 79 per cent). See also various UNCTAD documents entitled *Restrictive Business Practices* for information on cartels, restrictive clauses, and so on, in several countries.

6. It is argued by de la Torre (1974, p. 142) that TNCs' control over affiliates' export policy is much stricter for firms relying on product differentiation and extensive utilization of marketing inputs as a basis for their competitive strategy' than for TNCs which produce relatively easily marketable products. Since high-marketing-barrier' industries are often also those using advanced technology and retaining high equity participation, it may be best to regard tight export control as a concomitant of TNCs' *market power in general*, high market power both endowing greater bargaining strength and requiring careful preservation and exploitation through worldwide production and selling strategy.

7. An UNCTAD *Restrictive Business Practices* study on the UK, the USA and Japan (UN, 1973, TD/B/390) cites evidence on the existence of such arrangements in a variety of industries in these countries and their application to developing areas.

8. It has, however, been able to reduce the incidence of export restrictions from 51 per cent of the contracts approved in 1964–6 to 41 per cent in 1967–9 (see UNCTAD, 1971b, p. 8). More recent data provided by the *RBI Bulletin* (June 1974, pp. 1071–2) show that, of the 1050 agreements outstanding for the manufacturing sector in March 1970, 548 (52 per cent) had export restrictive clauses, the incidence varying from 39 per cent for foreign subsidiaries to 53 per cent for wholly local firms and 56 per cent for foreign-minority firms. These 548 agreements contained 956 restrictive clauses, of which eighty were applicable to subsidiaries, 457 to foreign-minority and 419 to wholly local firms. Some 43 per cent of the clauses were of the 'permissible' type; 7 per cent prohibited exports to other than permissible countries; 21 per cent required the foreigners' permission to export; 2 per cent banned exports outright; 6 per cent prohibited the use of trademarks for export; and the remaining 21 per cent had restrictions of various other types.

9. See, for instance, Kidron (1965, pp. 300–1), on India, and Vaitsos (1974, pp 51–2), on Colombia. Unfortunately, the evidence remains scattered and scanty—as is in the nature of the case—but there is little reason to doubt that the danger is a very real one.

10. Out of the inflow of equity capital into foreign-controlled companies (excluding branches) in India between 1964–5 and 1967–8, 81 per cent (484 million rupees) was in non-cash forms. Although the proportion of non-cash to total equity was declining steadily over these four years, from 90 per cent to 82, 74 and 70 per cent, even the last figure is very high and raises grave misapprehensions about this policy. See *RBI Bulletin*, March 1971, p. 358, Table 3.3.

11. If technical payments are excluded from the cost of servicing, the results are: Kenya −4·7, Jamaica 0·4, India 0·2, Iran 0·7, Colombia −4·2 and Malaysia 0·1. Of the total number of 147 firms with foreign capital, eighty-nine (60 per cent) had negative effects.
12. The term 'linkage' is used broadly to denote direct as well as indirect, and static as well as dynamic, effects – for instance, raising domestic investment, innovation, entrepreneurial activity, labour skills, and the like.
13. On some reasons for import dependence, taking into account local economic conditions, see Reuber (1973), p. 163.
14. The value of total imports (excluding those financed by foreign equity or loan capital) for India as a whole came to 17·4 per cent of output in 1960–4 and declined to 9·8 per cent in 1974–70. In the latter period, the figure for subsidiaries was 8·4 per cent (our sample 11·3), for foreign-minority firms 11·0 per cent (our sample 25·0), and for wholly local firms 10·1 (our sample 10·0). See *RBI Bulletin*, June 1974, Table 38.
15. 'Parent-company suppliers' provided about 5–6 per cent of total requirements in 1970–2, while the parents directly supplied 37–43 per cent. See Reuber (1973), p. 153, Table 5.10.
16. Such as Vaitsos (1974b) and Kidron (1965). Carlsen and Neerso (1973) argue that overcharging for imports often takes place in India with the consent and participation of local industrialists.
17. TNCs may use this method in cases where declared and remitted profits are taxed at a higher rate than technical payments (as in India, Iran and Colombia), when it is deemed politically more expedient to use such payments rather than show higher profit, when there is a ceiling imposed on profit remittances (as in Colombia), and when it is cheaper to use this channel rather than to raise transfer prices (which bear tariffs). All this assumes that technical payments are not strictly controlled: of the sample countries, Jamaica, Kenya and Iran are the most lenient, India the strictest, and Colombia and Malaysia have been lenient in the past but have tightened controls recently.
18. Recent figures for the six-year period 1964–5 to 1969–70 for India show that technical payments for the private sector as a whole came to 46 per cent of dividends for all firms, 23 per cent for foreign-majority, and 75 per cent for foreign-minority, firms. (Calculated from *RBI Bulletin*, June 1974, Table 33.)
19. Vaitsos (1974, p. 86) calculates that the ratio for the pharmaceutical industry in Colombia was 400 per cent, for rubber 53 per cent, and for chemicals 25 per cent; our sample gives figures of 256, 129 and 32 per cent respectively.
20. See Robbins and Stobaugh (1974).
21. See Indian Government (1969, vol III, pp. 64–78) for details on seventy selected products where different foreign firms were charging greatly varying rates for identical or very similar technology.
22. For a general description see Vaitsos (1971, 1974b).
23. These modifications took effect after 1970 and are not shown in the sample data.
24. See Lall (1973), Robbins and Stobaugh (1973) and Vaitsos (1974b).
25. Aggregate data for India show that imports exceeded dividends plus interest

by 611 per cent for foreign subsidiaries and by 705 per cent for foreign-minority firms in the six years preceding 1969–70. See *RBI Bulletin*, June 1974.
26. For a discussion of these problems in theory and practice (based on the laws and experience of some developed countries), see Verlage (1975).
27. See, however, Bhagwati (1969, 1974) and Indian Government (1971). The latter study reveals the use of an amazing variety of devices by which Indian and foreign businessmen procure foreign exchange for sale on the black market or remittance abroad.
28. See Lall (1975b). For the Colombian examples given below, we should note that the pharmaceutical firms were required to sell at 'world-market' prices and received no protection.
29. Crawford (1974) also remarks on the possibility of a method of transfer pricing, extremely difficult to detect, whereby two or more TNCs *collude in trade among themselves* to declare profits in a preferred area by appropriate pricing.
30. An unpublished doctoral thesis by Salehkhou (1974) on the pharmaceutical industry in Iran confirms that overpricing of intermediate imports by drug TNCs is extensively practised. Of the seventy-two cases investigated, four charged less than comparable world prices, seventeen overcharged by 0–100 per cent, twenty-seven by 100–500 per cent, four by 1000–1400 per cent and one by over 10,000 per cent. The data pertain to the period 1968–72; for details of the products and companies concerned, see Table A, Appendix III of the thesis.
31. For a description of the method see Vaitsos (1974b).
32. This is not as surprising as it first sounds; the firm concerned, Hoffman La Roche (Switzerland) was found (by the British Monopolies Commission) to be overcharging by about the same amount in such a highly competitive and well administered country as the UK. For a discussion, see Lall (1974b), and, for data on the Andean Pact, see Vaitsos (1973, 1974b); on Argentina, Katz (1974); and, on Iran, Salehkhou (1974).
33. Taken from Lall (1973), p. 187.
34. On export pricing some indirect evidence is produced for Latin America by Müller and Morgenstern (1974); the Indian Government (1971) reports on export-price manipulation by local and foreign firms.

CHAPTER 8

1. For the pioneering work on 'alternative positions' in the context of the balance-of-payments effect of foreign investment, see Reddaway et. al. (1967–8) and Hufbauer and Adler (1968). Both studies are, however, aimed at assessing the impact on the capital-exporting rather than the host country.
2. See Little and Mirrlees (1968) and (1974). For an application of LM methods to selected foreign investments see, Lal (1975); and, for various evaluations of the method, see the symposium in *BOUIES* (1972). A theoretically similar, but perhaps not as easily applicable, method of project

evaluation is proposed by UNIDO (1972). For a clear and concise exposition, see Sen (1975).
3. See Dasgupta and Pearce (1972) for a recent survey of the theory of cost–benefit analysis, and Nath (1973) for a concise and lucid exposition of the present state of welfare economics. See Lall (1976b) for a discussion of the welfare paradigm in neo-classical economics and its relevance to LDCs.
4. Non-tradables in this context would only be such inputs as power, construction, water, transport, and so on. All outputs, being manufactured, were assumed to be tradable, as were all inputs which could be imported.
5. We assumed that the 'real'cost per annum would be on a straight-line basis over the lives of each item of capital, at the following rates: land and current stocks, zero; buildings 3 per cent; furniture and fittings 5 per cent; plant and machinery 10 per cent; and vehicles 12 per cent. Though similar to the accountant's concept of depreciation, this cost is worked out on the basis of replacing capital 'used up' in production rather than the cost of the initial purchase written off each year, and the capital is valued in shadow rather than market prices.
6. Taxes on foreign profits would be zero in the alternative situation, since by assumption there would be no foreign capital employed, while taxes on local profits would be positive on the assumption that local capital would earn its opportunity cost in some other employment.
7. The assumption that final prices are unchanged enables us to assume that buyers do not experience a change in welfare between the actual and alternative situations. All welfare changes owing to differences between domestic and international prices can then be attributed to the government, which is assumed to manipulate tariffs so as to keep domestic prices constant.
8. For a full description of the method and simulation model, see Lall and Elek (1971), appendix to Chapter 1; and Lall and Mayhew (1973).
9. This assumes that foreign aid is already fully utilised and extra aid is not available to replace foreign direct investment, and that local capital has an alternative employment and is not lying idle because the foreign investor has used up all profitable opportunities.
10. We have not simply compared the actual return earned on foreign net worth with a national return of 10 per cent, but have compared it with the foreign portion of existing assets *valued at shadow prices* and *allowing for inflation*. The foreign portion is worked out as the percentage of total long- and short-term finance provided from abroad.
11. The capital contribution of the foreign firm is already taken into account by attaching a price to the local capital used by the hypothetical replacement firm.

CHAPTER 9

1. See UNIDO (1972) for a fuller discussion.
2. Many firms were exporting despite having domestic prices above world market prices; in such cases we added the f.o.b. value of exports to the equivalent c.i.f. value of domestic sales.

3. For details, see Chapter 7, second section.
4. See Chapter 6 for a description of financing patterns.
5. Data on local financing are very sketchy for Kenya, Jamaica, Iran and Malaysia, and it is very likely that our estimates *understate* the true cost of local capital and so *overstate* the final income gains in these samples.
6. For the findings of studies in several developing countries, and the policy implications, see Little, Scitovsky and Scott (1970); and, for the results of applications of the LM method to foreign investments, see Little and Scott (1975), with ten case studies from various developing countries, and Lal (1975), with case studies from India and Kenya.
7. Stock changes in raw materials were properly accounted for, the calculations being conducted in terms of the actual consumption of materials.
8. For a detailed discussion of the problems raised, see Lall and Mayhew (1973), especially pp. 24–5 and 128–31.
9. The components of income effects were not calculated for the Kenyan and Jamaican firms, as this refinement was added at a later stage in our research.
10. Not to be confused with the 'net financial effect' discussed in the third section of Chapter 7, where we compared the inflows of foreign capital with the cost of servicing it in the sample period.

CHAPTER 10

1. See *BOUIES* (1972) and especially Stewart and Streeten (1972). The UNIDO *Guidelines* (1972) go into these problems in some detail, but their proposed solutions are so complex as to make their method inoperable (without recourse to drastic simplifications).
2. For a discussion of these in the context of evaluating the transfer of foreign technology, see UNCTAD (1972).
3. 'It is clear that all such alternatives should, if possible, be examined, and that with the highest PSV [present social value] form the subject of the final examination. This is in principle no different from any project whether foreign or domestic' (Little and Mirrlees, 1974, p. 121). The 'possibility' of practical examination is not discussed.
4. See Lall (1976b) and Stewart (1975).
5. Some of these are discussed in Sen (1972).

CHAPTER 11

1. For surveys of schemes in developed countries for protecting foreign investments, see OECD (1970b) and Delupis (1973).
2. UNIDO (1973) has a critical evaluation of investment-promotion centres.
3. See König (1975a) and Sharpston (1975). Certain tax incentives may turn a country into a 'tax haven' and so attract non-manufacturing investment. See Shoup (1974).
4. See Reuber (1973).
5. Several versions of codes of conduct for TNCs are currently being prepared

or propagated by UNCTAD, the OECD, the International Chamber of Commerce and the UN Commission on Transnational Corporations.
6. On international tax policies for TNCs, see Musgrave (1974) and Shoup (1974).
7. The ILO has undertaken several studies on this subject. An early statement is given in ILO (1973).
8. Some East European countries have, in a curious manner, managed to reproduce these conditions of stability and profitable operation in a planned socialist framework, and have recently shown some success in attracting TNCs to low-wage areas on increasingly lenient terms.
9. See Howe (1975) and figures given in the *IMF Survey* of 20 May 1975.
10. This is partly a problem of firm-level bargaining, but partly a problem of reforming the institutional structure of technology transfer, especially the patent system. See the brief discussion of this below.
11. For a discussion of various measures to reduce technological 'dependence' see UNCTAD (1976). On science and education policies, see Cooper (1974) and Sunkel (1971); and, on 'intermediate' technology, see Stewart (1974) and Pack (1976). Ishikawa (1975) has an illuminating discussion of an 'alternative' route to technological development—that of China, with respect to the agricultural machinery and implements industry.
12. In Sri Lanka, for instance, the State Pharmaceuticals Corporation, set up in 1972, has successfully undertaken the direct import and distribution of finished intermediate drugs. It has cut the number of pharmaceuticals sold by over 50 per cent and reduced the cost of the fifty-five most important items by 37 per cent; domestic promotional costs have also been drastically cut. (Information kindly provided by the Chairman of the Corporation.)
13. On the theory of takeovers and its application to the UK, see Singh (1971).
14. See ILO (1973).
15. In our description of economic policy, we have not mentioned measures to control 'corrupt practices' of TNCs, but see the UN Economic and Social Council (1976) for a review of possible regulations of such practices.
16. See the documents issued by UNCTAD under the title *Restrictive Business Practices*, as well as case studies under the title *Major Issues in Transfer of Technology to Developing Countries*.
17. For a brief description, see Wionczek (1973).
18. See Streeten (1972, 1975a).
19. This was proposed for the pharmaceutical industry by Lall (1975b). A scheme based on this proposal, for establishing COPPTECs (Co-operative Pharmaceutical Production and Technology Centres), was formally endorsed by the Summit Meeting of Non-Aligned Nations held in Colombo in August 1976.
20. Data kindly provided by the Chairman of the Corporation.
21. For a clear and concise exposition of the working of the OPEC pricing system, see Mabro (1975–6).
22. If it were also true that certain industries, especially high technology ones, were far more susceptible to transfer pricing than others, this would reduce even further the effective areas to be watched. On the sort of data needed to monitor transfer pricing, see Green (1975).

23. Some of these issues with respect to taxation of TNCs are discussed by Shoup (1974) and Musgrave (1974).
24. For a discussion of these problems, see the report of the Canadian Government (1972).
25. See above, Chapter 2, fourth section, for a discussion of the considerations involved.
26. The scales of Figures 11.1 and 11.2 are not necessarily the same.
27. For a longer discussion, see Chapters 2 and 3.
28. Similarly, in an oligopolistic industry, once one TNC has entered a country, other TNCs wishing to follow suit will be in a weaker bargaining position. See Knickerbocker (1973).
29. Parts of the arguments of this section are taken from Streeten (1975b).
30. J. S. Mill saw clearly the need for state intervention 'not to overrule the judgement of individuals respecting their own interest, but to give effect to that judgement; they being unable to give effect to it except by concert, which concert again cannot be effectual unless it receives validity and sanction from the law.' He illustrates this by workers' restriction of their working hours. See Mill (1902), p. 581 (Book V, Chapter XI, section 12).
31. See, Vaitsos (1975) for a useful discussion. The supplement to UNCTAD (1976) also has detailed, practical recommendations on how the regulation of foreign investments (with special reference to the transfer of technology) and foreign licensing may be improved.

CHAPTER 12

1. Leys (1975), p. x.
2. For references, see notes to Chapter 3.
3. See Bell, 'The Political Framework', in Chenery et al. (1974). For analyses of the state in LDCs, see Alavi (1972), Leys (1975), Weisskopf (1973) and various *dependencia* writers mentioned in Chapter 3.
4. For a subtle theoretical analysis of such interactions in the context of developed countries, see Poulantzas (1975); and, for the 'functions' of the state as regards TNCs, see Murray (1970). For a discussion of the influence of US TNCs on US policy in a more conventional (i.e. not based on class analysis) framework, see Gilpin (1976) and Helleiner (1975c). For some examples relating to LDCs, see, among others, Turner (1973). The recent weakening of the Andean Pact's original intent on foreign investment policies, with Chile and Bolivia (followed at a distance by the others, with the exception of Venezuela) taking a very 'liberal' stance with respect to TNCs, provides an excellent illustration of the strength of internal and external forces favouring 'the system'. See *Business Week* (1976).
5. See, for instance, Stinchcombe (1974), for a study of the sociology of administration with reference to Latin America.
6. See an excellent paper on this subject by Wedderburn (1973), who examines the inherent advantage that present labour legislation gives to employers opposed to unions in the process of international expansion.
7. One such centre is the European Centre for Study and Information on Multinational Corporations (in Brussels).

References

Aaronovitch, S., and Sawyer, M. C. (1975), *Big Business: Theoretical and Empirical Aspects of Concentration and Mergers in the United Kingdom* (New York: Holmes and Meier).

Adam, G. (1972), 'Some Implications and Concomitants of Worldwide Sourcing', *Acta Oeconomica*, pp. 309–23.

Adelman, I., and Morris, C. T. (1973), *Economic Growth and Social Equity in Developing Countries* (Stanford, NJ: Stanford University Press).

Adler, M., and Dumas, B. (1975), 'Optimal International Acquisitions', *Journal of Finance*, Mar, pp. 1–19.

Agarwal, J. P. (1976), 'Factor Proportions in Foreign and Domestic Firms in Indian Manufacturing', *Economic Journal*, pp. 589–94.

Aharoni, Y. (1966), *The Foreign Investment Decision Process* (Boston: Harvard Graduate School of Business Administration).

Alavi, H. (1972), 'The State in Post-Colonial Societies: Pakistan and Bangladesh', *New Left Review*, no. 74, pp. 59–81.

Aliber, R. Z. (1970), 'A Theory of Direct Foreign Investment', in C. P. Kindleberger (ed.), *The International Corporation* (Cambridge, Mass.: MIT Press).

Amin, S. (1974), *Accumulation on a World Scale* (New York: Monthly Review Press).

Aurora, G. S., and Morehouse, W. (1972), 'Dilemma of Technological Choice: The Case of the Small Tractor', *Economic and Political Weekly* pp. 1633–44.

Bacha, E. L. (1974), 'Foreign Capital Inflow and the Output Growth Rate of the Recipient Country', *Journal of Development Studies*, pp. 374–81.

Bagchi, A. (1972), 'Some International Foundations of Capitalist Growth and Underdevelopment', *Economic and Political Weekly*, pp. 1559–70.

Bagchi, A. (1973), 'Foreign Capital and Economic Development in India: A Schematic View', in K. Gough and H. P. Sharma (eds) *Imperialism and Revolution in South Asia* (New York: Monthly Review Press).

Bain, J. (1956), *Barriers to New Competition* (Cambridge, Mass.: Harvard University Press).
Balasubramanyam, V. N. (1973), *International Transfer of Technology to India* (New York: Praeger).
Baldwin, R. E. (1970), 'International Trade in Inputs and Outputs', *American Economic Review*, pp. 430–4.
Ball, G. W. (1968), 'Cosmocorp: The Importance of Being Stateless', *Atlantic Community Quarterly*, Summer, pp. 163–70.
Balogh, T., and Streeten, P. P. (1960), 'Domestic versus Foreign Investment', *Bulletin of the Oxford University Institute of Statistics*, pp. 213–24. Reprinted in P. P. Streeten, *Economic Integration* (Sijthoff: Gravenhage).
Baran, P. A. (1957), *The Political Economy of Growth* (New York: Monthly Review Press).
Baran, P. A., and Sweezy, P. (1966), *Monopoly Capitalism* (New York: Monthly Review Press).
Baranson, J. (1970), 'Technology Transfer through the International Firm', *American Economic Review*, pp. 435–40.
Barnet, R. J., and Müller, R. (1974), *Global Reach: The Power of the Multinational Corporations* (New York: Simon and Schuster).
Barratt Brown, M. (1974), *The Economics of Imperialism* (Harmondsworth, Middx: Penguin).
Batra, R. (1973), *Studies in the Pure Theory of International Trade* (London: Macmillan).
Baumann, H. G. (1975), 'Merger Theory, Property Rights and the Pattern of US Investment in Canada', *Weltwirtschaftliches Archiv*, pp. 676–98.
Behrman, J. (1970), *National Interests and the Multinational Enterprise* (Englewood Cliffs, NJ: Prentice-Hall).
Behrman, J. (1974), 'Actors and Factors and Policy Decisions on Foreign Direct Investment', *World Development*, Aug, pp. 1–14.
Bergsten, F. (1974), 'Coming Investment Wars?', *Foreign Affairs*, Oct, pp. 135–52.
Bhagwati, J. (1969), 'Fiscal Policies, the Faking of Foreign Exchange Declarations and the Balance of Payments', in his *Trade, Tariffs and Growth* (London: Weidenfeld and Nicolson).
Bhagwati, J. (ed.) (1974), *Illegal Transactions and International Trade: Theory and Measurement* (Amsterdam: North-Holland).
Bhalla, A. S. (ed.) (1975), *Technology and Employment in Industry* (Geneva: International Labour Office).
Birnberg, T. A., and Resnick, S. A. (1975), *Colonial Development: An*

Econometric Study (New Haven, Conn.: Yale University Press).

Blair, J. M. (1972), *Economic Concentration: Structure, Behaviour and Public Policy* (New York: Harcourt, Brace, Jovanovich).

Blumberg, P. I. (1975), *The Megacorporation in American Society* (Englewood Cliffs, NJ: Prentice-Hall).

Bos, H. C., with Sanders, M., and Secchi, C. (1974), *Private Foreign Investment in Developing Countries: A Quantitative Study of the Evaluation of Macro-Economic Effects* (Dordrecht: Reidel).

BOUIES: see under, *Bulletin of the Oxford University Institute of Economics and Statistics*.

Bradshaw, M. T. (1969), 'US Exports to Foreign Affiliates of US Firms', *Survey of Current Business*, May, pp. 34–51.

Brash, D. T. (1970), 'Australia as Host to the International Corporation', in C. P. Kindleberger (ed.), *The International Corporation* (Cambridge, Mass.: MIT Press).

Brems, H., (1970), 'A growth Model of International Direct Investment', *American Economic Review*, pp. 320–331.

Brock, G. W. (1975), *The US Computer Industry: A Study of Market Power* (Cambridge, Mass.: Ballinger).

Brooke, M. Z., and Remmers, H. L. (1970), *The Strategy of Multinational Enterprise* (London: Longman).

Buckley, P. J., and Casson, M. (1976), *The Future of the Multinational Enterprise* (London: Macmillan).

Bulletin of the Oxford University Institute of Economics and Statistics (1972), 'Symposium on the Little–Mirrlees Manual of Industrial Project Analysis in Developing Countries', Feb.

Business Week (1976a), 'The Breakdown of US Innovation', 16 Feb, pp. 56–68.

Business Week (1976b), 'The Silent Crisis in R & D', 8 Mar, pp. 90–2.

Business Week (1976c), 'Reversal of Policy: Latin America Opens the Door to Foreign Investment Again', 9 Aug, pp. 34–50.

Canadian Government (1972), *Foreign Direct Investment in Canada* ('The Gray Report') (Ottawa).

CAPFI (1969), *Investors' Guide to Iran* (Teheran: Centre for the Attraction and Protection of Foreign Investments).

Carlsen, J. (1973), 'Danish Foreign Investment in Kenya' (Copenhagen: Institute for Development Research), mimeo.

Carlsen, J. and Neerso, P. (1973), 'Transfer of Technology to India' (Copenhagen: Institute for Development Research), mimeo.

Caves, R. E. (1971), 'International Corporations: The Industrial Economics of Foreign Investment', *Economica*, pp. 1–27.

Caves, R. E. (1974), 'The Causes of Direct Investment: Foreign Firms' Share in Canadian and UK Manufacturing Industries', *Review of Economics and Statistics*, Aug, pp. 279–93.

Caves, R. E., and Uekusa, M. (1976), 'Industrial Organisation', in H. Patrick and H. Rosovsky (eds), *Asia's New Giant: How the Japanese Economy Works* (Washington, DC: The Brookings Institution).

Chenery, H., Ahluwalia, M. S., Bell, C. L. G., Duloy, J. H., and Jolly, R. (1974), *Redistribution with Growth* (London: Oxford University Press).

Chipman, J. (1971), 'International Trade with Capital Mobility: A Substitution Theorem', in J. Bhagwati et al., *Trade, Balance of Payments and Growth* (Amsterdam: North-Holland).

Chudson, W. A., and Wells, L. T. (1974), *The Acquisition of Technology from Multinational Corporations by Developing Countries* (New York: United Nations, ST/ECA/12).

Chudnovsky, D. (1973), 'Foreign Manufacturing Firms' Behaviour in Colombia: A Study of the Influence of Technology, Advertising and Financing upon Profitability, 1966–70', D. Phil. thesis, St. Antony's College, Oxford. Published in Spanish as *Empresas Multinacionales y Ganancias Monopolicas* (Buenos Aires: Siglo XXI, 1974).

CIS (1975), *Unilever's World* (London: Counter Information Services).

Cohen, B. (1975), *Multinational Firms and Asian Exports* (New Haven Conn.: Yale University Press).

Comanor, W. S., and Wilson, T. A. (1974), *Advertising and Market Power* (Cambridge, Mass.: Harvard University Press).

Conference Board (1976), *Overseas Research and Development by United States Multinationals, 1966–1975* (New York).

Cooper, C. (1974), 'Science Policy and Technological Change in Underdeveloped Economies', *World Development*, Mar, pp. 55–64.

Corden, W. M. (1974a), 'The Theory of International Trade', in J. H. Dunning (ed.), *Economic Analysis and the Multinational Enterprise* (London: Allen and Unwin).

Corden, W. M. (1974b), *Trade Policy and Economic Welfare* (London: Oxford University Press).

Courtney, W. H., and Leipziger, D. M. (1975), 'Multinational Corporations in Less-Developed Countries: The Choice of Technology', *Oxford Bulletin of Economics and Statistics*, Nov, pp. 297–304.

Cowling, K., Cable, J., Kelly, M., and McGuiness, T. (1975), *Advertising and Economic Behaviour* (London: Macmillan).

Crawford, M. (1974), 'Transfer Pricing in International Business',

Multinational Business, no. pp. 1–12.
DANE (1971), *Boletín Mensual de Estadística*, no. 239 (Bogotá: Departamento Administrativo Nacional de Estadística).
Dasgupta, A. K., and Pearce, D. W. (1972), *Cost–Benefit Analysis: Theory and Practice* (London: Macmillan).
Davis, E. W., and Yeomans, K. A. (1974), *Company Finance and the Capital Market: A Study of the Effects of Firm Size* (London: Cambridge University Press).
de la Torre, J. (1974), 'Foreign Investment and Export Dependency', *Economic Development and Cultural Change*, Oct, pp. 133–50.
Delupis, I. (1973), *Finance and Protection of Investment in Developing Countries* (Epping: Gower Press).
Dobb, M. (1973), *Theories of Value and Distribution since Adam Smith: Ideology and Economic Theory* (London: Cambridge University Press).
dos Santos, T. (1970), 'The Structure of Dependence', *American Economic Review*, pp. 231–6.
Dunning, J. H. (1969), *The Role of American Investment in the British Economy* (London: Political and Economic Planning).
Dunning, J. H. (ed.) (1971), *The Multinational Enterprise* (London: Allen and Unwin).
Dunning, J. H. (ed.) (1972), *International Investment* (Harmondsworth, Middx: Penguin).
Dunning, J. H. (1973), 'The Determinants of International Production', *Oxford Economic Papers*, pp. 289–336.
Dunning, J. H. (1974) 'The Distinctive Nature of the Multinational Enterprise', in Dunning (ed.), *Economic Analysis and the Multinational Enterprise* (London: Allen and Unwin).
Economist Intelligence Unit (1973), 'IBM under World-Wide Antitrust Onslaught', *Multinational Business*, no. 4, pp. 42–5.
Edwards, C. (1975), 'The Effects of Measures to Promote Industrialisation in West Malaysia since 1960', Ph.D. thesis, School of Development Studies, University of East Anglia.
EIU: see under Economist Intelligence Unit.
Financial Times (1974a), 'IBM Confronted by Major Anti-Trust Challenge', 7 Nov.
Financial Times (1974b), 'Swedish Report on Multinationals', 8 Nov.
Financial Times (1974c), 'Xerox Ordered to Share Patents with its Rivals', 16 Nov.
Financial Times (1974d), 'Anti-Trust versus the "Technological Lock-in"', 20 Nov.

Financial Times (1976) 'The Cash Trail Leading Back to America's Boardrooms', 12 Feb.

Finger, J. M. (1975a), 'Tariff Provisions for Offshore Assembly and the Exports of Developing Countries', *Economic Journal*, pp. 365–511.

Finger, J. M. (1975b), 'A New View of the Product Cycle Theory', *Weltwirtschaftliches Archiv*, pp. 79–99.

Fleck, F. H., and Mahfouz, R. (1974), 'The Multinational Corporation: Tax Avoidance and Profit Manipulation via Subsidiaries and Tax Havens', *Schweizerische Zeitschrift für Volkwirtschaft und Statistik*, June, pp. 145–60.

Foster-Carter, A. (1976), 'From Rostow to Gunder Frank: Conflicting Paradigms in the Analysis of Underdevelopment', *World Development*, Mar, pp. 167–80.

Frank, A. G. (1969), *Capitalism and Underdevelopment in Latin America* (New York: Monthly Review Press).

Frank, A. G. (1972), *Lumpenbourgeoisie and Lumpendevelopment: Dependence, Class and Politics in Latin America* (New York: Monthly Review Press).

Frankena, M. (1973), 'Marketing Characteristics and Prices of Exports of Engineering Goods from India', *Oxford Economic Papers*, pp. 123–32.

Frankena, M. (1973–4), 'The Industrial and Trade Control Regime and Product Designs in India', *Economic Development and Cultural Change*, pp. 249–64.

Franko, L. G. (1971), *Joint Venture Survival in Multinational Corporations* (New York: Praeger).

Franko, L. G. (1973), 'Who Manages Multinational Enterprises?', *Columbia Journal of World Business*, Summer, pp. 30–42.

Freeman, C. (1974), *The Economics of Industrial Innovation* (Harmondsworth, Middx: Penguin).

Furnish, D. B., (1972), 'The Andean Common Markets' Common Regime for Foreign Investments', *Vanderbilt Journal of Transnational Law*, Spring, pp. 313–39.

Furtado, C., (1973), 'Underdevelopment and Dependence: The Fundamental Connections', paper presented to Faculty Seminar, Centre for Latin American Studies, Cambridge (mimeo.)

Galbraith, J. K. (1967), *The New Industrial State* (London: Hamish Hamilton).

George, K. D., and Silberston, Z. A. (1975), 'The Causes and Effects of Mergers', *Scottish Journal of Political Economy*, June, pp. 179–93.

Giddens, A. (1973), *The Class Structure of the Advanced Societies*

(London: Hutchinson).
Gilpin, R. (1976), *US Power and the Multinational Corporation* (London: Macmillan).
Gintis, H. (1972), 'A Radical Analysis of Welfare Economics and Individual Development' *Quarterly Journal of Economics*, pp. 572–99.
Girvan, N. (1971), *Foreign Capital and Economic Underdevelopment in Jamaica* (Kingston, Jamaica: University of West Indies).
Gold, D., Lo, C. Y. H., and Wright, E. O. (1975), 'Recent Developments in Marxist Theories of the Capitalist State', *Monthly Review*, Oct, pp. 29–43, and Nov, pp. 36–51.
Goodsell, C. T. (1974), *American Corporations and Peruvian Politics* (Cambridge, Mass.: Harvard University Press).
Green, R. H. (1975), 'Statistics on the Multinational Corporations as a Means to Exercise Sovereignty', *IDS Bulletin*, Oct, pp. 11–15.
Greer, D. F. (1973), 'The Case Against Patent Systems in Less-Developed Countries', *Journal of International Law and Economics*, pp. 223–66.
Griffin, K. B. (1971), 'The Role of Foreign Capital', in Griffin (ed.), *Financing Development in Latin America* (London: Macmillan).
Griffin, K. B. (1974), 'The International Transmission of Inequality', *World Development*, Apr, pp. 3–16.
Grubel, H. G., and Lloyd, P. J. (1975), *Intra-Industry Trade: The Theory and Measurement of International Trade in Differentiated Products* (London: Macmillan).
Grundmann, H. E. (1976), 'Foreign Patent Monopolies in Developing Countries: An Empirical Analysis', *Journal of Development Studies*, Jan, pp. 186–96.
Hanson, J. S. (1975), 'Transfer Pricing in the Multinational Corporation: A Critical Appraisal', *World Development*, Nov–Dec, pp. 857–66.
Hart, P. E. (1965), *Studies in Profit, Business Saving and Investment in the United Kingdom, 1920–1962* (London: Allen and Unwin).
Helleiner, G. K. (1973), 'Manufactured Exports from Less Developed Countries and Multinational Firms', *Economic Journal*, Mar, pp. 21–47.
Helleiner, G. K. (1975a), 'The Role of Multinational Corporations in the Less Developed Countries' Trade In Technology', *World Development*, Apr, pp. 161–89.
Helleiner, G. K. (1975b), 'Transnational Enterprises, Manufactured Exports and Employment in Less Developed Countries', paper

prepared for the World Employment Conference (Geneva: International Labour Office), mimeo.
Helleiner, G. K. (1975c), 'Transnational Enterprises and the New Political Economy of US Trade Policy', paper presented to the IDS Conference on New Approaches to Trade (Institute of Development Studies, University of Sussex), mimeo.
Hirsch, S. (1967), *Location of Industry and International Competitiveness* (London: Oxford University Press).
Hirsch, S. (1973), 'Multinationals: How Different Are They?', in G. Bertin (ed.), *The Growth of the Large Multinational Corporation* (Paris: Centre National de la Recherche Scientifique).
Hirsch, S. (1975), 'The Product Cycle Model of International Trade – A Multi-Country Cross-Section Analysis', *Oxford Bulletin of Economics and Statistics*, Nov, pp. 305–17.
Hirsch, S. (1976), 'An International Trade and Investment Theory of the Firm', *Oxford Economic Papers*, July, pp. 41–6.
Hirsch, S., and Adar, Z. (1974), 'Firm Size and Export Performance', *World Development*, July, pp. 41–6.
Hollis, M., and Nell, E. (1975), *Rational Economic Man: A Philosophical Critique of Neo-Classical Economics* (London: Cambridge University Press).
Hone, A. (1974), 'Multinational Corporations and Multinational Buying Groups: Their Impact on the Growth of Asia's Export of Manufactures', *World Development*, Feb, pp. 145–50.
Horst, T. (1971), 'The Theory of the Multinational Firm: Optimal Behaviour under Different Tariff and Tax Rates', *Journal of Political Economy*, pp. 1059–72.
Horst, T. (1972), 'Firm and Industry Determinants of the Decision to Invest Abroad: An Empirical Study', *Review of Economics and Statistics*, Aug, pp. 258–66.
Horst, T. (1974a), *At Home Abroad: A Study of the Domestic and Foreign Operations of the American Food-Processing Industry* (Cambridge, Mass.: Ballinger).
Horst, T. (1974b), 'American Exports and Foreign Direct Investment', Harvard University Institute of Economic Research, Discussion Paper no. 362 (mimeo).
Horst, T. (1974c), 'Theory of the Firm', in J. H. Dunning (ed.), *Economic Analysis and the Multinational Enterprise* (London: Allen and Unwin).
Horst, T. (1975), 'American Investments Abroad and Domestic Market Power' (Washington, DC: Brookings Institution), mimeo.

Howe, R. (1975), 'US Investment in Europe: The Glow Wears Off', *Vision*, Jan, pp. 47–9.

Howe, R. (1976), 'Uncle Sam Outfaced by Europe's Global Giants', *Vision*, May, pp. 57–60.

Hufbauer, G. C. (1965), *Synthetic Materials and the Theory of International Trade* (London: Duckworth).

Hufbauer, G. C. (1973), 'The Multinational Corporation and Direct Investment', (Princeton: International Finance Section). Later published in P. B. Kenen (ed.), *International Trade and Finance* (London: Cambridge University Press, 1975).

Hufbauer, G. C., and Adler, F. M. (1968), *US Manufacturing Investment and the Balance of Payments* (Washington, DC: US Treasury Department).

Hymer, S. (1960), 'The International Operations of National Firms: A Study of Direct Investment', Ph.D. thesis, MIT, Cambridge, Mass. To be published by the MIT Press.

Hymer, S. (1970), 'The Efficiency (Contradictions) of Multinational Corporations', *American Economic Review*, pp. 441–8.

Hymer, S. (1972a), 'The Multinational Corporation and the Law of Uneven Development', in J. Bhagwati (ed.), *Economics and the World Order* (New York: Macmillan).

Hymer, S. (1972b), 'The Internationalization of Capital', *Journal of Economic Issues*, Mar, pp. 91–111.

Hymer, S., and Rowthorn, R. (1970), 'Multinational Corporations and International Oligopoly: The Non-American Challenge', in Kindleberger (ed.), *The International Corporation* (Cambridge, Mass.: MIT Press).

IBRD (1973), World Bank Atlas (Washington, DC: International Bank for Reconstruction and Development).

IIC (1974), *Industrial Licensing and Foreign Collaboration: Policies and Procedures* (New Delhi: Indian Investment Centre).

ILO (1972), *Employment, Incomes and Equality: A Strategy for Increasing Productive Employment in Kenya* (Geneva: International Labour Office).

ILO (1973), *Multinational Enterprises and Social Policy* (Geneva: International Labour Office).

Indian Government (1969), *Report of the Industrial Licensing Policy Inquiry Committee* (New Delhi: Department of Industrial Development).

Indian Government (1971), *Report of the Study Team on Leakage of Foreign Exchange through Invoice Manipulation* (New Delhi).

Ingham, K.P.D. (1976), 'Foreign Ownership and the Regional Problem: Company Performance in the Mechanical Engineering Industry', *Oxford Economic Papers*, pp. 133–48.

Ishikawa, S., 'The Chinese Method of Technological Development', *The Developing Economies*, Dec, pp. 430–58.

Jacquemin, A., and Saez, W. (1976), 'A Comparison of the Performance of the Largest European and Japanese Firms', *Oxford Economic Papers*, July, pp. 271–83.

Johnson, H. G. (1970), 'The Efficiency and Welfare Implications of the International Corporation', in C. P. Kindleberger (ed.), *The International Corporation* (Cambridge, Mass.: MIT Press).

Johnson, H. G. (1972), *Comparative Cost and Commercial Policy for a Developing World Economy*, Wicksell Lecture (Stockholm: Almquist and Wiksell).

Johnson, H. G. (1975), *Technology and Economic Interdependence* (London: Macmillan).

Johnson, P. S. (1975), *The Economics of Invention and Innovation* (London: Martin Robertson).

Kamien, M. I., and Schwartz, N. L. (1975), 'Market Structure and Innovation: A Survey', *Journal of Economic Literature*, Mar, pp. 1–37.

Kamien, M. I., and Schwartz, N. L. (1976), 'The Degree of Rivalry for Maximum Innovative Activity', *Quarterly Journal of Economics*, pp. 245–60.

Katz, J. (1974), *Oligopolio, Empresarios Nacionales y Corporaciones Multinacionales* (Buenos Aires: Siglo XXI).

Keegan, W. J. (1969), 'Multinational Pricing: How Far is Arm's Length?', *Columbia Journal of World Business*, May–June, pp. 57–66.

Kidron, M. (1965), *Foreign Investments in India* (London: Oxford University Press).

Kindleberger, C. P. (1969), *American Business Abroad: Six Lectures on Direct Investment* (New Haven: Yale University Press).

Kindleberger, C. P. (ed.) (1970), *The International Corporation* (Cambridge, Mass.; MIT Press).

Kindleberger, C. P. (1974), 'Size of Firm and Size of Nation', in J. H. Dunning (ed.), *Economic Analysis and the Multinational Enterprise* (London: Allen and Unwin).

Kindleberger, C. P. (1975), 'The Multinational Corporation in a World of Militant Developing Countries', in G. W. Ball (ed.), *Global Companies* (Englewood cliffs, NJ: Prentice-Hall).

Klein, R. W. (1973), 'A Dynamic Theory of Comparative Advantage',

American Economic Review, pp. 173–84.

Knickerbocker, F. T. (1973), *Oligopolistic Reaction and Multinational Enterprise* (Boston: Harvard University Graduate School of Business Administration).

König, W. (1975a) 'International Subcontracting Involving LDCs', *Intereconomics*, no. 2, pp. 53–6.

König, W. (1975b), 'Towards an Evaluation of International Subcontracting Activities in Developing Countries' (Washington, DC: UN ECLA (Economic Commission for Latin America)), mimeo.

Kochanek, S. A. (1974), *Business and Politics in India* (Berkeley, Calif.: University of California Press).

Lal, D. (1975), *Appraising Foreign Investment in Developing Countries* (London: Heinemann).

Lall, S. (1972), *Balance-of-Payments Effects of Private Foreign Investment in Manufacturing: Summary of Case Studies of India, Iran, Jamaica and Kenya* (Geneva: UNCTAD, TD/134/Supp. 1).

Lall, S. (1973), 'Transfer Pricing by Multinational Manufacturing Firms', *Oxford Bulletin of Economics and Statistics*, pp. 173–95.

Lall, S. (1974a), 'Less Developed Countries and Private Foreign Direct Investment: A Review Article', *World Development*, Apr, pp. 43–8.

Lall, S. (1974b), 'The International Pharmaceutical Industry and Less-Developed Countries, with Special Reference to India', *Oxford Bulletin of Economics and Statistics*, pp. 143–72.

Lall, S. (1975a), *Foreign Private Manufacturing Investment and Multinational Corporations: An Annotated Bibliography* (New York: Praeger).

Lall, S. (1975b), in collaboration with the UNCTAD Secretariat, *Major Issues in Transfer of Technology to Developing Countries: A Case Study of the Pharmaceutical Industry* (Geneva: UNCTAD, TD/B/C.6/4).

Lall, S. (1975c), 'Is "Dependence" a Useful Concept in Analysing Underdevelopment?' *World Development*, Nov–Dec, pp. 799–810.

Lall, S. (1976a), 'The Patent System and the Transfer of Technology to Less-Developed Countries', *Journal of World Trade Law*, Jan–Feb, pp. 1–16.

Lall, S. (1976b), 'Conflicts of Concepts: Welfare Economics and Development', *World Development*, Mar, pp. 181–95.

Lall, S. and Elek, A. (1971), *Balance-of-Payments and Income Effects of Private Foreign Investment in Manufacturing: Case Studies of India and Iran* (Geneva: UNCTAD, TD/B/C.3(V)/Misc.1).

Lall, S. and Mayhew, K. (1973), *Balance-of Payments and Income Effects of Private Foreign Investment in Manufacturing: Case Studies* of Colombia and Malaysia (Geneva: UNCTAD, TD/B/C.3 (VI)/Misc. 1).

Langdon, S. (1974). 'Multinational Corporations, Taste Transfer and Underdevelopment: A Case Study of Kenya' (Institute of Development Studies, University of Sussex), mimeo.

Ledogar, R. J. (1975), *Hungry for Profit: US Food and Drug Multinationals in Latin America* (New York: IDOC/North America).

Leftwich, R. B. (1974), 'U.S. Multinational Companies: Profitability, Financial Leverage, and Effective Tax Rates', *Survey of Current Business*, May, pp. 27–36.

Levitt, K. (1970), *Silent Surrender* (Toronto: Macmillan).

Leys, C. (1975), *Underdevelopment in Kenya* (London: Heinemann).

Little, I. M. D. (1972), 'On Measuring the Value of Private Direct Overseas Investment', in G. Ranis (ed.), *Gap Between Rich and Poor Nations* (London: Macmillan).

Little, I. M. D., and Mirrlees, J. A. (1969), *Manual of Industrial Project Evaluation in Developing Countries* (Paris: OECD).

Little, I. M. D. and Mirrlees, J. A. (1974), *Project Appraisal and Planning for Developing Countries* (London: Heinemann).

Little, I. M. D., Scitovsky, T., and Scott, M. F. (1970), *Industry and Trade in some Developing Countries: A Comparative Study* (London: Oxford University Press).

Little, I. M. D., and Scott, M. F. (eds) (forthcoming), *Using Shadow Prices: Case Studies in Foreign Investment Appraisal* (London: Heinemann).

Lonsdale, J. E. (1966), *Selling to Industry* (London: Business Publications).

Lupo, L. A. (1973), 'Worldwide Sales by US Multinational Corporations', *Survey of Current Business*, May, pp. 27–36.

Mabro, R. (1975–6), 'OPEC after the Oil Revolution', *Millennium*, Winter, pp. 191–9.

MacDougall, G. D. A. (1960), 'The Benefits and Costs of Private Investment from Abroad: A Theoretical Approach', *Economic Record*, pp. 13–35. Reprinted in J. H. Dunning (ed.), *International Investment* (Harmondsworth, Middx: Penguin, 1972).

McManus, J. C. (1972), 'The Theory of the International Firm', in G. Pacquet (ed.), *The Multinational Firm and the Nation State* (Galt, Ontario: Collier-Macmillan).

Magdoff, H. (1972), 'Imperialism without Colonies', in R. Owen and R. B. Sutcliffe (eds), *Studies in the Theory of Imperialism* (London: Longman).

Malik, R. (1975), *And Tomorrow . . . The World? Inside IBM* (London: Millington).
Mansfield, E. (1974), 'Technology and Technological Change', in J. H. Dunning (ed.), *Economic Analysis and the Multinational Enterprise* (London: Allen and Unwin).
Marris, R. (1964), *The Economic Theory of 'Managerial' Capitalism* (London: Macmillan).
Mason, R. H. (1973), 'Some Observations on the Choice of Technology by Multinational Firms in Developing Countries', *Review of Economics and Statistics*, pp. 349–55.
Miliband, R. (1969), *The State in Capitalist Society* (London: Weidenfeld and Nicolson).
Mill, J. S. (1902), *Principles of Political Economy* (London: Longmans, Green and Co.).
Moore, B. (1966), *Social Origins of Dictatorship and Democracy: Lord and Peasant in the Making of the Modern World* (Harmondsworth, Middx: Penguin).
Morawetz, D. (1974), 'Employment Implications of Industrialisation in Developing Countries: A Survey', *Economic Journal*, pp. 491–542.
Morley, S. A., and Smith, G. W. (1974), 'The Choice of Technology: Multinational Firms in Brazil', Rice University Program in Development Studies, Paper no. 58 (mimeo).
Müller, R. and Morgenstern, R. D. (1974), 'Multinational Corporations and Balance of Payments Impact in LDCs: An Econometric Analysis of Export Pricing Behaviour', *Kyklos*, pp. 304–21.
Mundowsky, M., and Sell, A. (1976), 'Auswirkungen unterschiedlicher Patentsysteme auf die wirtschaftliche Entwicklung von Entwicklungsländem: Eine empirische Untersuchung am Beispiel der pharmazeutischen Industrie in Lateinamerika', University of Kiel, Discussion Papers of the Institut für Wirtschaftspolitik, no. 1 (mimeo).
Murray, R. (1971), 'The Internationalisation of Capital and the Nation State', *New Left Review*, May–June, pp. 84–109. Reprinted in H. Radice (ed.), *International Firms and Modern Imperialism* (Harmondsworth, Middx: Penguin, 1975).
Murray, R. (1972), 'Underdevelopment, International Firms and the International Division of Labour', in *Towards a New World Order* (Rotterdam: Rotterdam University Press).
Musgrave, P. B. (1974), 'International Tax Differntials for Multinational Corporations. Equity and Efficiency Considerations', in UN Department of Economic and Social Affairs, *The Impact of*

Multinational Corporations on Development and on International Relations, Technical Papers: Taxation (New York: United Nations, ST/ESA/11).

Myrdal, G. (1953), *The Political Element in the Development of Economic Theory* (London: Routledge and Kegan Paul).

Myrdal, G. (1968), *Asian Drama: An Enquiry into the Poverty of Nations* (London: Allen Lane).

Nath, S. K. (1973), *A Perspective on Welfare Economics* (London: Macmillan).

National Science Foundation (various dates), *Research and Development in Industry* (Washington, DC: US Government).

Nayyar, D. (1975), 'The Impact of Transnational Corporations on Exports of Manufactures from Developing Countries', (Geneva: UNCTAD), mimeo.

NCAER (1971), *Foreign Technology and Investment: A State of Their Role in India's Industrialisation* (New Delhi: National Council for Applied Economic Research).

Needleman, L., Lall, S., Lacey, R., and Seagrave, J. (1970), *Balance-of-Payments Effects of Private Foreign Investment: Case Studies of Jamaica and Kenya*, (Geneva: UNCTAD, TD/B/C.3/79/Add.2).

Negandhi, A., and Prasad, B. (1975), *Frightening Angels: A Study of US Multinationals in Developing Countries* (Kent, Ohio: Kent State University Press).

New Internationalist, The (1975), 'Kicking the Bottle', Mar, pp. 13–15.

Newfarmer, R. S., and Mueller, W. F. (1975), *Multinational Corporations in Brazil and Mexico: Structural Sources of Economic and Non-Economic Market Power*, Report to the Subcommittee on Multinational Corporations of the Committee on Foreign Relations, US Senate (Washington, DC: US Government).

Nowshirvani, V. F., and Bildner, R. (1973),'Direct Foreign Investment in the Non-Oil Sectors of the Iranian Economy, *Iranian Studies*, Spring–Summer, pp. 66–109.

O'Brien, Peter (1975), 'Foreign Technology and Industrialisation: The Case of Spain', *Journal of World Trade Law*, pp. 525–52.

O'Brien, Philip (1975), 'A Critique of Latin American Theories of Dependency', in I. Oxaal et. al., *Beyond the Sociology of Development* (London: Routledge and Kegan Paul).

O'Connor, J. (1970), 'The Meaning of Economic Imperialism', in R. J. Rhodes (ed.), *Imperialism and Underdevelopment* (New York: Monthly Review Press).

OECD (1970a), *Gaps in Technology: Analytical Report* (Paris: Organi-

sation for Economic Co-operation and Development).
OECD (1970b), *Investing in Developing Countries* (Paris: Organisation for Economic Co-operation and Development).
Orr, D. (1974), 'An Index of Entry Barriers and its Application to the Structure Performance Relationship', *Journal of Industrial Economics*, pp. 39–49.
Owen, R., and Sutcliffe, R. B. (eds) (1972), *Studies in the Theory of Imperialism* (London: Longman).
Pack, H. (1976), 'The Substitution of Labour for Capital in Kenyan Manufacturing', *Economic Journal*, pp. 45–58.
Palloix, C. (1973), 'The Internationalisation of Capital and the Circuit of Social Capital', translated from the French and reprinted in H. Radice (ed.), *International Firms and Modern Imperialism* (Harmondsworth, Middx: Penguin, 1975).
Parker, J. E. S., (1974), *The Economics of Innovation: The National and Multinational Enterprise in Technological Change* (London: Longman).
Parry, T. G. (1974), 'Technology and the Size of the Multinational-Corporation Subsidiary: Evidence from the Australian Manufacturing Sector', *Journal of Industrial Economics*, Dec, pp. 125–34.
Patnaik, P. (1972). 'Imperialism and the Growth of Indian Capitalism', in R. Owen and R. B. Sutcliffe (eds), *Studies in the Theory of Imperialism* (London: Longman).
Pavitt, K. (1971), 'The Multinational Enterprise and the Transfer of Technology', in J. H. Dunning (ed.), *The Multinational Enterprise* (London: Allen and Unwin).
Paxson, D. A. (1973), 'The Territorial Diversification of Multinational Enterprises', Reading University, Discussion Papers in International Investment and Business Studies, no. 6 (mimeo).
Pearce, I. F., and Rowan, D. C. (1966), 'A Framework for Research into the Real Effects of International Capital Movements', in J. H. Dunning (ed.), *International Investment* (Harmondsworth, Middx: Penguin, 1972).
Penrose, E. T. (1956), 'Foreign Investment and the Growth of the Firm', *Economic Journal*, pp. 220–35. Reprinted in J. H. Dunning (ed.), *International Investment* (Harmondsworth, Middx: Penguin, 1972).
Penrose, E. T. (1959), *The Theory of the Growth of the Firm* (Oxford: Blackwell).
Penrose, E. T. (1968), *The Large International Firm in Developing Countries: The International Petroleum Industry* (London: Allen and Unwin).

Penrose, E. T. (1971), 'The State and Multinational Enterprises in LDCs', in J. H. Dunning (ed.), *The Multinational Enterprise* (London: Allen and Unwin).

Penrose, E. T. (1973), 'International Patenting and Developing Countries', *Economic Journal*, pp. 768–86.

Perlmutter, H. V. (1969), 'The Tortuous Evolution of the Multinational Corporation', *Columbia Journal of World Business*, Jan–Feb, pp. 9–18.

Pickering, J. F. (1974), *Industrial Structure and Market Conduct* (London: Martin Robertson).

Posner, M. V. (1961), 'International Trade and Technical Change', *Oxford Economic Papers*, pp. 323–41.

Poulantzas, N. (1973a), *Political Power and Social Classes* (London: New Left Books).

Poulantzas, N. (1973b), 'Marxism and Social Classes', *NewLeft Review*, no. 78.

Poulantzas, N. (1975), *Classes in Contemporary Capitalism* (London: New Left Books).

Prachowny, M. F. J., and Richardson, J. D. (1975), 'Testing a Life Cycle Hypothesis of the Balance-of-Payments Effects of Multinational Corporations', *Economic Inquiry*, Mar, pp. 81–98.

Radice, H. (ed.) (1971), *International Firms and Modern Imperialism* (Harmondsworth, Middx: Penguin).

RBI (1968), *Survey of Foreign Collaboration in Indian Industry* (Bombay: Reserve Bank of India).

RBI (1974), 'Survey of Foreign Financial and Technical Collaboration in Indian Industry – 1964–70 – Main Findings', *Reserve Bank of India Bulletin*, June, pp. 1040–83.

RBI Bulletin (Reserve Bank of India, monthly).

Reddaway, W. B., Potter, S. J., and Taylor, C. T. (1967–8), *Effects of UK Direct Investment Overseas* (London: Cambridge University Press).

Reuber, G. L., with Crookel, H., Emerson, M., and Gallais-Hammonno, G. (1973), *Private Foreign Investment in Development* (Oxford: Clarendon Press, for the OECD Development Centre).

Rhodes, R. J. (ed.) (1970), *Imperialism and Underdevelopment* (New York: Monthly Review Press).

Robbins, S. M., and Stobaugh, R. B. (1974), *Money in the Multinational Enterprise: A Study in Financial Policy* (New York: Basic Books).

Robinson, J. (1972), *Economic Philosophy* (London: C. A. Watts; and

Harmondsworth: Penguin).
Rosenberg, N. (1976), 'On Technological Expectations', *Economic Journal*, Sep, pp. 523–35.
Rowley, C. K., and Peacock, A. T. (1975),*Welfare Economics: A Liberal Restatement* (London: Martin Robertson).
Rowthorn, R. (1971), in collaboration with S. Hymer, *International Big Business, 1957–1967: A Study of Comparative Growth* (London: Cambridge University Press).
Rumelt, R. P. (1974), *Strategy, Structure and Economic Performance*, (Boston: Harvard Univeristy Graduate School of Business Administration).
Salehkhou, G. (1974), 'Commercialisation of Technology in Developing Countries: Transfer of Pharmaceutical Technology to Iran', Ph.D. thesis, New School for Social Research, New York.
Sauvant, K. P. (1976), 'The Potential for Multinational Enterprises as Vehicles for the Transmission of Business Culture', in K. P. Sauvant and F. G. Lavipour (eds), *Controlling Multinational Enterprises* Boulder, Col.: Westview Press.
Scherer, F. M. (1970), *Industrial Market Structure and Economic Performance* (Chicago: Rand McNally).
Sen, A. K. (1972), 'Control Areas and Accounting Prices: An Approach to Economic Evaluation', *Economic Journal*.
Sen, A. K. (1973), *On Economic Inequality* (Oxford: Clarendon Press).
Sen, A. K. (1975), *Employment, Technology and Development* (Oxford: Clarendon Press).
Servan-Schreiber, J. J. (1968), *The American Challenge* (London: Hamish Hamilton).
Severn, A. K., and Lawrence, M. M. (1974), 'Direct Investment, Research Intensity and Profitability', *Journal of Financial and Quantitative Analysis*, Mar, pp. 181–90.
Sharpston, M. (1975), 'International Sub-Contracting', *Oxford Economic Papers*, pp. 94–135.
Shoup, C. B. (1974), 'Taxation of Multinational Corporations', in UN Department of Economic and Social Affairs, *The Impact of Multinational Corporations on Development and on International Relations, Technical Papers: Taxation* (New York: United Nations).
Shubik, M. (1959), *Strategy and Economic Structure* (New York: Wiley).
Shulman, J. S. (1969), 'Transfer Pricing in the Multinational Firm', *European Business*, Jan, pp. 46–54.
Singer, H. (1950), 'The Distribution of Gains between Investing and

Borrowing Countries', *American Economic Review*, pp. 473–85.
Singh, A. (1971), *Take-overs* (Cambridge: Cambridge University Press).
Singh, A., and Whittington, G. (1975), 'The Size and Growth of Firms', *Review of Economic Studies*, pp. 15–26.
Stephenson, H. (1972), *The Coming Clash: The Impact of the International Corporation on the Nation State* (London: Weidenfeld and Nicolson).
Stevens, G. V. G. (1974), 'The Determinants of Investment', in J. H. Dunning (ed.), *Economic Analysis and the Multinational Enterprise* (London: Allen and Unwin).
Stewart, F. (1974), 'Technology and Employment in LDCs', *World Development*, Mar, pp. 17–46.
Stewart, F. (1975), 'A Note on Social Cost–Benefit Analysis and Class Conflict in LDCs', *World Development*, Jan, pp. 31–9.
Stewart, F., and Streeten, P. P. (1972), 'Little–Mirrlees Methods and Project Appraisal', in *BOUIES* (1972), pp. 75–91. Reprinted in *The Frontiers of Development Studies* (Macmillan, 1972).
Stewart, F., and Streeten, P. P. (1976), 'New Strategies for Development: Poverty, Inequality and Growth', *Oxford Economic Papers*, pp. 381–405.
Stikker, D. U. (1971), 'The Impact of Foreign Private Investment', in Asian Development Bank, *Southeast Asia's Economy in the 1970s*, (London: Longman).
Stilwell, F. J. B. (1975), *Normative Economics* (Oxford: Pergamon Press).
Stinchcombe, A. L. (1974), *Creating Efficient Industrial Administrations* (New York: Academic Press).
Stobaugh, R. B. (1971), 'The Neotechnology Account of International Trade', *Journal of International Business Studies*, Fall, pp. 41–60.
Stobaugh, R. B. (1974), 'A Summary and Assessment of Research Findings on US International Transactions Involving Technology Transfers', in National Science Foundation, *The Effects of International Transfers of Technology on the US Economy* (Washington, DC: US Government).
Stoneman, C. (1975), 'Foreign Capital and Economic Growth', *World Development*, Jan, pp. 11–26.
Stopford, L. M., and Wells, L. T. (1972), *Managing the Multinational Enterprise: Organisation of the Firm and Ownership of the Subsidiaries* (New York: Basic Books).
Streeten, P. P. (1971), 'Costs and Benefits of Multinational Enterprises in Less-Developed Countries', in J. H. Dunning (ed.), *The Multi-*

national Enterprise (London: Allen and Unwin). Reprinted in *The Frontiers of Development Studies* (Macmillan, 1972).

Streeten, P. P. (1972), 'Technology Gaps between Rich and Poor Nations', *Scottish Journal of Political Economy*, pp. 213–30. Reprinted in *The Frontiers of Development Studies* (Macmillan, 1972).

Streeten, P. P. (1973), 'The Multinational Enterprise and the Theory of Development Policy', *World Development*, Oct, pp. 1–14.

Streeten, P. P. (1975a), 'Policies towards Multinationals', *World Development*, June, pp. 393–7.

Streeten, P. P. (1975b), 'The Dynamics of the New Poor Power', in *Resources Policy*, June 1976.

Streeten, P. P., and Lall, S. (1973), Summary of UNCTAD Studies (Geneva: UNCTAD), in three parts: (a) 'The Methodology Used in Studies on Private Foreign Investment in Developing Countries' (TD/B/C.3(VI)/Misc.6); (b) 'Main Findings of a Study of Private Foreign Investment in Selected Developing Countries' (TD/B/C.3/111); (c) 'Some Reflections on Government Policies concerning Private Foreign Investment' (TD/B/C.3(VI)/Misc.7).

Subrahmanian, K. K. (1972), *Imports of Capital and Technology: A Study of Foreign Collaborations in Indian Industry* (New Delhi: People's Publishing House).

Sunkel, O. (1969–70), 'National Development Policy and External Dependence in Latin America', *Journal of Development Studies*, pp. 23–48.

Sunkel, O. (1971), 'Underdevelopment, the Transfer of Science and Technology, and the Latin American University', *Human Relations*, February, pp. 1–18.

Sunkel, O. (1973), 'Transnational Capitalism and National Disintegration in Latin America', *Social and Economic Studies*, Mar, pp. 132–76.

Survey of Current Business (1975): 'Foreign Direct Investment in the United States in 1974', Oct, pp. 36–42; 'US Direct Investment Abroad in 1974', Oct, pp. 43–64.

Taylor, C. T., and Silberston, Z. A. (1973), *The Economic Impact of the Patent System* (London: Cambridge University Press).

Tharp, P. A. (1976), 'Transnational Enterprises and International Regulation: A Survey of Various Approaches in International Organisation', *International Organisation*, Winter, pp. 47–73.

The Times (1974), 'Devious Routes for Nixon Funds', 1 July.

Tomlinson, J. W. C. (1970), *The Joint Venture Process in International Business: India and Pakistan* (Cambridge, Mass.: MIT Press).

Turner, L. (1973), *Multinational Companies and the Third World* (London: Allen Lane).

U.K. Government, Department of Industry (1974), *Business Monitor: Overseas Transactions* (London: HMSO).

UN (1964), *The Role of Patents in the Transfer of Technology to Developing Countries* (New York: United Nations).

UN (1973), *Multinational Corporations in World Development* (New York: United Nations).

UN (1974), *The Impact of Multinational Corporations on Development and on International Relations* (New York: United Nations).

UNCTAD (1971a), *Policies Relating to Technology of the Countries of the Andean Pact: their Foundations* (Santiago: United Nations Conference on Trade and Development, TD/107).

UNCTAD (1971b), *Restrictions on Exports in Foreign Collaboration Agreements in India* (by the Indian Investment Centre) (New York: United Nations).

UNCTAD (1972), *Guidelines for the Study of the Transfer of Technology to Developing Countries* (New York: United Nations).

UNCTAD (1974), *The Role of the Patent System in the Transfer of Technology to Developing Countries* (Geneva: united Nations Conference on Trade and Development, TD/B/AC.11/19), and Addendum on Laws of Selected Countries.

UNCTAD (1975), *International Subcontracting Arrangements in Electronics between Developed Market-Economy Countries and Developing Countries* (New York: United Nations, TD/B/C.2/144/Supp.1).

UNCTAD (1976), *Transfer of Technology* (Nairobi: United Nations Conference on Trade and Development, TD/190).

UN Economic and Social Council (1976), *Measures against Corrupt Practices of Transnational and Other Corporations, Their Intermediaries and Others Involved* (New York: United Nations Economic and Social Council, E/5838).

UNIDO (1972), *Guidelines for Project Evaluation* (New York: United Nations).

UNIDO (1973), *Manual on Investment Promotion Centres* (New York: United Nations).

US Tariff Commission (1970), *Economic Factors Affecting the Use of Items 807.00 and 806.30 of the Tariff Schedules of the United States* (Washington, DC: US Government).

US Tariff Commission (1973), *Implications of Multinational Firms for World Trade and Investment and for US Trade and Labour* (Washington, DC: US Government).

Vaitsos, C. V. (1971), 'The Process of Commercialisation of Technology in the Andean Pact' (Lima), mimeo.
Vaitsos, C. V. (1973), 'Patents Revisited: Their Function in Developing Countries', in C. Cooper (ed.), *Science, Technology and Development* (London: Frank Cass).
Vaitsos, C. V. (1974a), 'Policies on Foreign Direct Investment and Economic Development in Latin America', Institute of Development Studies, University of Sussex, Communication no. 106.
Vaitsos, C. V. (1974b), *Intercountry Income Distribution and Transnational Enterprises* (Oxford: Clarendon Press).
Vaitsos, C. V. (1975), 'Power, Knowledge and Development Policy: Relations between Transnational Enterprises and Developing Countries', in G. K. Helleiner (ed.), *A World Divided: The Less Developed Countries in the World Economy* (London: Cambridge University Press).
Vaitsos, C. V. (1976), 'The Revision of the International Patent System: Legal Considerations for a Third World Position', *World Development*, Feb, pp. 85–102.
Vaupel, J. W., and Curhan, J. P. (1969), *The Making of Multinational Enterprise* (Boston: Harvard Graduate School of Business Administration).
Vaupel, J. W., and Curhan, J. P. (1973), *The World's Multinational Enterprises* (Boston: Harvard Graduate School of Business Administration).
Verlage, H. C. (1975), *Transfer Pricing for Multinational Enterprises* (Rotterdam: Rotterdam University Press).
Vernon, R. (1966), 'International Investment and international Trade in the Product Cycle', *Quarterly Journal of Economics*, pp. 190–207.
Vernon, R. (1971), *Sovereignty at Bay: The Multinational Spread of US Enterprises* (New York: Basic Books).
Vernon, R. (1974a), 'Multinational Enterprises in Developing Countries: An Analysis of National Goals and National Policies' (Vienna: UNIDO), mimeo.
Vernon, R. (1974b), 'The Location of Economic Activity', in J. H. Dunning (ed.), *Economic Analysis and the Multinational Enterprise* (London: Allen and Unwin).
Watanabe, S. (1972), 'International Subcontracting, Employment and Skill Promotion', *International Labour Review*, pp. 425–49.
Wedderburn, K. W. (1973), *'Industrial Relations'*, in H. R. Hahlo *et al.* (ed.), *Nationalism and the Multinational Enterprise* (Dobbs Ferry, NY: Oceana Publications).

Weichmann, U. L. (1974), 'Integrating Multinational Marketing Activities', *Columbia Journal of World Business*, Winter, pp. 7–16.

Weisskopf, T. E. (1972), 'Capitalism, Underdevelopment and the Future of the Poor Countries', in J. Bhagwati (ed.), *Economics and the World Order* (New York: Macmillan).

Weisskopf, T. E. (1973), 'Dependence and Imperialism in India', *Review of Radical Political Economics*, Spring, pp. 53–96.

Weisskopf, T. E. (1974), 'American Economic Interests in Foreign Countries: A Survey', University of Michigan, Center for Research on Economic Development, Discussion Paper no. 35 (mimeo).

Wells, L. T. (1972) (ed.), *The Product Life Cycle and International Trade* (Boston: Harvard Graduate School of Business Administration).

Wells, L. T. (1973), 'Economic Man and Engineering Man: Choice of Technology in a Low Wage Country', *Public Policy*, Summer, pp. 319–42.

White, L. J. (1976). 'Appropriate Factor Proportions for Manufacturing in Less Developed Countries: A Survey of the Evidence (Princeton: Woodrow Wilson School, Research Program in Development Studies).'

Wilkins, M. (1974), 'The Role of Private Business in the International Diffusion of Technology', *Journal of Economic History*, pp. 166–88.

Willmore, L. (1976), 'Direct Foreign Investment in Central American Manufacturing', *World Development*, June, pp. 499–578.

Winslow, J. F. (1973), *Conglomerates Unlimited: The Failure of Regulation* (Bloomington, Ind.: Indiana University Press).

Wionczek, M. (1973), 'New Mexican Legislation on Technological Transfers', *Development Digest*, Oct. pp. 92–7.

Wionczek, M., Bueno, G. M., and Navarrete, J. E. (1974), *La Transferencia Internacional de Technologia–El Caso de México* (Mexico City: Fondo de cultura Económica).

Wolf, B. N. (1975), 'Size and Profitability among US Manufacturing Firms: Multinational versus Primarily Domestic Firms', *Journal of Economics and Business*, Fall, pp. 15–22.

Index

Aaronovitch, S., 12n, 14n, 18n, 25n, 41n
Accounts, analysis of sample firms' 62, 99–129 *passim*, 130, 216
Adam, G., 30n
Adelman, I., 50n
Adler, M., 20n
Advertising, 25–6, 28, 31, 50, 52, 75–7, 105, 112–13, 123, 126, 128, 129, 157, 197, 210, 211
Africa, 6, 7, 134
Agarwal, J. P., 72n, 107n, 109n
Age, of sample firms, 122, 123, 136–7, 173, 174
Agriculture, 26, 196n
Aharoni, Y., 37n
Ahluwalia, M. S., 96
Aid, international, 3, 27, 54, 55, 84, 165n, 194, 222
Alavi, H., 221n
Aliber, R. Z., 20–1
America: Central, 6, 13, 30n, 32n, 63n, 99n, 107n, 122n; Latin, 6, 7, 36n, 55, 57, 64, 69n, 76n, 92, 138, 149, 153, 154n, 223n, 224
Amin, S., 16n
Andean Pact, 61, 97, 136, 137n, 153n, 198, 213, 216, 222n
Arbitration, 193n, 209
Argentina, 6n, 13, 14n, 99n, 153n
Asia, 6, 7, 13n, 30n, 57n
Asset/liability management, 42
Assets: current, 102–11, 116–17, 121, 122n, 136; fixed, 99, 102, 103, 106–11, 113, 115, 121; liquid, 14
Audit, 193
Aurora, G. S., 73n
Australia, 36n, 101, 104
Autonomy, 40, 44, 58

Bacha, E. L., 83
Bagchi, A., 36n
Bain, J., 18n, 123n
Balasubramanyam, V. N., 105n, 110n
Baldwin, R. E., 83
Ball, G. W., 44n

Balogh, T., 82n
Banking, 14, 20, 54, 94, 114, 116–20, 127, 128
Baran, P. A., 16n
Baranson, J., 35n
Bargaining, 12, 27–9, 38, 43, 44, 51, 61, 66–8, 70, 77–9, 85, 98, 137n, 138, 145, 146, 149, 150, 156, 158, 159, 163, 166, 177, 180, 183, 185, 191–3, 196n, 199, 201–18, 222, 224
Barnet, R. J., 39n, 45n, 58n, 75n
Barratt Brown, M., 16n, 32n
Batra, R., 83n
Baumann, H. G., 19, 20n, 25n, 35n
Behaviour, corporate, 16–46, 86, 166, 198
Behrman, J., 44n, 79n
Benefits, of TNCs, 12, 47–80, 82–5, 160–5, 172–7, 182–5, 191, 197, 200–2, 206–9, 211, 212, 218
Bergsten, F., 45n, 61n
Bhagwati, J., 152n
Bhalla, A. S., 72n, 105n, 110n
Bildner, R., 91n
Birnberg, T. A., 36n
Blair, J. M., 12n, 18n, 27n
Blumberg, P. I., 12n, 18n, 45n
Borrowing by TNCs: by countries 82–4; domestic, 54, 113–20, 128–9, 199, foreign, 40, 41, 54–6, 116, 118–20, 128, 129, 165, 178, 182
Bos, H. C., 83, 84n
BOUIES, 160n, 184n
Bradshaw, M. T., 13n
Brand names, *see* Promotion
Brash, D. T., 101
Brazil, 6n, 13, 14n, 32n, 59n, 63n, 105n, 194
Brems, H., 83
Bribery, 78, 79, 207, 222, 223
Brock, G. W., 24n, 65n
Brooke, M. Z., 39n, 41n, 56n
Buckley, P. J., 11n, 16n, 18n, 23n, 28n, 32n

Canada, 6, 20n, 26n, 36n, 62, 64, 207n
Capacity utilisation, 100, 105
CAPFI, 91n

274   Index

Capital: abundancy, 17; access to, 199; assets, 20n, 162, 172, 174; availability of, 20, 26–8, 36n, 51, 53, 54, 100, 165, 166, 192, 198; costs, 72, 162, 164–5, 172, 211; diversion of, 165; domestic, 44, 55, 83, 157, 162, 163, 165, 167n, 169, 170, 172, 174, 177, 178, 182, 199, 212, 213; equipment, 140, 210, 211; equity, 10, 21, 92, 121, 130, 140, 141; fixed, 102, 103; flow, 10, 20, 49, 55, 63, 64n, 68, 80–6, 94, 95, 130, 140–2, 162, 164, 177n, 193; foreign, 13, 54, 68, 71, 82–4, 92–5, 122, 136, 141n, 142, 157, 162, 164, 165, 177, 178, 180, 182, 183, 193–5, 200; intensity, 26, 71, 72, 84, 104–6, 108–11, 196; labour ratios, 106–10; markets, 20, 21, 54; output ratios, 3, 84, 106–9, 111, 121, 165, 172; productivity, 105, 108, 110–12; provision of, 53–6; raising of, 20, 53, 54; use of, 99, 105–10, 111, 121, 126, 161–3, 172, 174, 205

Capitalist system, 13, 18, 32, 44–5, 60, 65, 73, 79, 80, 83, 104, 153, 194, 196, 200, 221, 222

Caribbean countries, 30n, 134

Carlsen, J., 56n, 91n, 145n

Cartel agreements, 24, 63, 138, 151, 200, 213–16

Casson, M., 11n, 16n, 18n, 23n, 28n, 32n

Caves, R. E., 12n, 18n, 19, 26n

Centralisation of authority, 39, 40, 43, 44, 46, 57, 59, 62, 217

Chenery, H., 50n, 79n, 96, 221n

China, 196n

Chipman, J., 83

Chudnovsky, D., 123n, 127

Chudson, W. A., 64n

Class conflict, 49–52, 187, 188, 220–3

Cohen, B., 13n, 28n, 77n, 135n

Colombia, 13, 56n, 59, 75n, 89–93, 95–129 *passim*, 130–57 *passim*, 170–3, 175, 176, 178, 179, 182, 203, 205

Comanor, W. S., 25n, 123n

Commonwealth, 92

Communication factors, 14n, 18, 39, 40, 56–8, 62

Comparisons between TNC and non-TNC firms, 72, 99–129 *passim*, 134, 135, 137, 140–2, 144–8, 150, 151, 166, 171, 173, 175–8, 182

Competition, oligopolistic, *see* Oligopolistic theories

Competition, perfect, 17, 80

Concentration, 12, 18, 22n, 26, 27, 32, 198

Confrontation, inter-state, 45

Consumption patterns, 3, 50n, 58, 70, 72, 76, 143, 161, 170, 174, 195–7, 221, 222

Contracts, technological *see* Technology

Control, *see* Regulation

Cooper, C., 73n, 196n

Corden, W. M., 17n, 29n, 83n

Corrupt practices, 200n, 217, 224

Cost: benefit analysis, 85, 86, 159–64, 169–77, 182–8, 192, 207, 211; to host countries, 47–80 *passim*, 84–5, 140–2, 143, 146, 151, 191–3, 200, 210–12; levels of TNC, 23, 24, 28–33, 57, 60, 61, 73, 75, 76, 85, 143, 146, 152, 196, 197, 199, 208

Courtney, W. H., 72n, 105n

Crawford, M., 152n

Credit, access to, 20, 54–6, 107, 118–20, 199, 207

Culture, effects on, 18, 21, 44, 48, 57, 58, 63, 75, 166, 187, 194, 195

Curhan, J. P., 54n, 99n

DANE, 91n

Dasgupta, A. K., 160n

Data: availability of, 13, 158, 163, 175, 181, 184, 185, 204; collection, 6, 14, 43, 90–6, 99–129 *passim*, 163, 171;

Davis, E. W., 120n

Decision-making: by firms, 10, 21, 29, 31, 37, 40, 57, 62, 137, 211; by governments, *see* Regulation

de la Torre, J., 76n, 135n, 137

Demand: creation of, 25, 52, 75, 158; patterns, 31, 47, 70, 72, 73, 186;

Dependency, 57, 64, 142–5, 154, 167, 200, 221

Depreciation, 40–1, 99, 102, 113–17, 150, 153, 161n, 174

Devaluation, 63n, 117, 118, 126, 171

Development, industrial, 39, 63, 95, 144, 150, 194

Disputes, 200, 201

Distribution: of product, 26, 43, 75, 76; of income, *see* Income

Divestment, 198

Dividends, 121, 122, 146, 151n, 162

Dobb, M., 47n

dos Santos, T., 28n

Dunning, J. H., 16n, 25n, 37n, 38, 54n, 135n

Duty-free zones, 30

East African Common Market, 134

Index

Economics, development, 3, 5, 15, 16, 191, 220
Education, 21, 52, 73, 196
Edwards, C., 91n
Efficiency, 21, 29, 32, 39, 41, 57, 63, 64, 104n, 106–8, 111, 112, 143, 166, 185, 208, 223, 224
Elek, A., 4
Employment, 4, 71, 74, 97, 98, 100, 106, 193, 196, 199, 209
Enterprise, domestic, 80, 174, 179, 185, 197–9
Entrepreneurial factors, 10, 21, 39, 48, 56, 57, 62, 63, 143n, 158, 167, 179, 185, 198, 203
Entry barriers, 75, 123, 137, 193, 197, 198
Environment, for foreign investment, 95–8, 104, 167, 194, 197, 216
Equity, 21, 55, 56, 67, 91, 92, 94, 113, 116–18, 121, 126, 130, 137n, 140, 141, 164, 193–4, 212; domestic, 92, 94, 114, 199, 207; foreign, 92, 94, 114, 116–17, 121, 140, 143n, 150, 179, 198
Eurodollar markets, 20
Europe, 30, 33, 36n, 44, 61, 63, 194, 224n; East, 30n, 54, 73n, 194n
EEC, 38, 61n
Evaluation techniques, *see* Cost-benefit analysis
Exchange: foreign, 21, 48, 54, 55, 74, 82, 130, 136, 138, 142, 143, 152n, 156, 159–64, 193; rates, 20, 29, 37n, 42, 59, 60, 63, 100, 136, 152, 161, 164, 171
Expansion, overseas, 16, 25–8, 34, 36, 41, 44n, 70, 74
Export: performance, 134–9 *passim*; restrictions, 63, 135, 137–9, 200, 201
Exports: level of, 13, 74, 77, 130, 134–9, 145, 150, 167, 179, 180, 185, 197, 199; manufactured, 13, 14, 19, 29–34, 51, 69, 76, 77, 90, 209; sourcing, *see* Sourcing
Expropriation, 96
Externalities, 48, 51, 63, 85, 157, 184, 185, 207
Fees, 41, 130, 145–7, 150, 151, 154, 216
Finance, patterns of, 40–1, 99, 100, 113–20, 122, 123, 128, 172; international, 14
Financial Times, 24n, 42n
Finger, J. M., 30n, 32n, 74n
Fleck, F. H., 59n
Foster-Carter, A., 48n, 53n
France, 6, 10n
Franchise, 76

Frank, A. G., 28n, 63n
Frankena, M., 76n, 105n
Franko, L. G., 43n, 44n, 67n
Freeman, C., 14, 22n, 23, 24n
Funds, flow of, 113, 116, 119
Furnish, D. B., 97n

Galbraith, J. K., 37, 45n
Gearing, 55, 56, 116, 118–20, 128, 129
George, K. D., 12n
Germany, West, 6, 8, 10n, 12, 31
Gibrat's Law, 28n
Gilpin, R., 44n, 45n, 222n
Gintis, H., 52n
Girvan, N., 91n
GNP, 4, 12, 62, 82, 84, 95, 96, 101
Gold, D., 45n
Goods: capital, 68, 74n, 130, 143, 144, 154; intermediate, 143, 144; resale of, *see* Resale by sample firms
Goodsell, C. T., 79n
Green, R. H., 205n
Greer, D. F., 68n
Griffin, K. B., 64n, 84n
Grubel, H. G., 23n, 27n, 32n, 34n
Grundmann, H. C., 68n

Hart, P. E., 100n
Harvard, Multinational Enterprise Project, 10
Heckscher–Ohlin theory, 17, 83
Helleiner, G. K., 13n, 30n, 64n, 70n, 74n, 75n, 76n, 105n, 222n
Hirsch, S., 18n, 31n, 32, 135, 136n
Hone, A., 76n,
Hollis, M., 52n
Hong Kong, 13, 30
Horst, T., 8n, 16n, 17n, 19, 25n, 28, 54n, 59n, 65n, 101n, 122n, 123n
Howe, R., 194n
Hufbauer, G. C., 16n, 32n, 156n
Hymer, S., 12n, 18n, 19, 32, 39n, 44n, 58

IBM, 24, 30
IBRD, 96
ILO, 91n, 193n, 224
IMF, 118, 194n
Import: dependence, 142–5; prohibition, 152, 170, 176, 199, 208; quotas, 97; substitution, 30, 82, 143, 173
Imports, of manufactured goods, 13, 60, 69, 90, 118, 130, 143–5, 151, 153, 154, 159, 170, 192, 197n
Incentives, fixed, 38, 96, 136, 193, 194, 207,

Income: distribution of, 50–2, 71, 160, 161, 183, 187, 194, 195–7, 199, 215, 221, 223; inequalities, 4, 50, 71, 194, 195; per capita, 95, 96, 104, 212; social effects, 156–88 *passim*
Independence, economic, 4, 58
India, 6, 13, 28n, 32n, 36n, 43n, 56n, 60n, 69, 73n, 76n, 77, 90–129 *passim*, 134–53 *passim*, 157, 167, 171–9 *passim*, 182, 198, 201; Reserve Bank of, 91n, 102n, 105n, 106n, 107n, 120, 122n, 138n, 141n, 143n, 146n, 151n
Indonesia, 194
Industrialisation, levels of, 98, 194, 198, 221
Industry, manufacturing, 7, 8, 12n, 14, 18, 23, 27, 30, 65, 91–5, 123, 142, 143, 157, 183
Inflation, 5, 99, 102, 107, 164, 165n, 171, 172, 181
Information 24, 25, 193, 202–5, 213, 216, 217
Ingham, K. P. D., 21n
Innovation, 21–6, 32–4, 57, 61, 64, 65, 68, 69, 73–5, 105n, 143n, 197
Inputs, 26, 143, 159–77 *passim*, 184, 199, 208
Institutions, and *see* Banking, 55, 199
Insurance, 192
Interest, 17, 18, 41, 54, 55, 81, 116–21, 126, 129, 130, 140–2, 150, 151, 154, 162, 177, 178, 206, 211, 216
Invention, *see* Innovation
Investment: alternatives to foreign, 48, 157–68, 169–80, 181–8; cash, 140, 141; direct, 6–8, 10, 16–38, 54, 66, 67, 69, 75, 83, 92, 94, 165, 167, 178, 179, 183, 192, 195; domestic, 8, 78, 83, 85, 90, 143n, 158–64, 177; flows, 38, 81; import-substituting, 77; manufacturing, 6–8, 11–13, 28, 36n, 83, 91n, 92, 95, 96, 142, 173, 184–5, 193, 194; patterns, 8–10, 12, 34, 37, 57, 84; planning, 39; portfolio, 10, 17, 20, 28n, 81; servicing of, 55, 140–2; smaller firms, 19, 20; social value of, 160–4;
Investors, other than TNCs, 49, 62, 92, 207
Invoicing, *see* Transfer pricing
Iran, 89–98, 101, 134, 136, 137, 140–4, 146–8, 150, 151, 153, 171–6, 178, 179, 194
Ishikawa, S., 73n, 196n
Italy, 69

Jacquemin, A., 28n
Jamaica, 89–98, 101, 134, 137, 138, 140–4, 146–8, 150, 151, 167, 171–3, 178, 179
Japan, 6, 8, 10n, 12n, 14, 31, 138n
Jobs, export of, 193
Johnson, H. G., 17n, 22n, 23n, 32n, 44n, 64n, 66n
Johnson, P. S., 24n

Kamien, M. I., 14n, 24n
Katz, J., 99n, 153n
Keegan, W. J., 61n
Kemp, M. C., 83
Kenya, 89–98, 101, 134, 137, 140–4, 146–8, 150, 151, 153, 171–3, 178, 179, 220
Kidron, M., 28n, 73n, 91n, 140n, 145n
Kindleberger, C. P., 12n, 18n, 26n, 29n, 40n, 47n, 51n, 64n, 78n
Klein, R. W., 32n
Knickerbocker, F. T., 18n, 31n, 32, 101n, 213n
Knowledge, 18, 21, 23n, 28, 56, 66, 67, 69, 74n, 135, 140, 141, 152, 166, 211, 216, 217
Kochanek, S. A., 28n
König, W., 74n, 193n

Labour, 72, 74, 77, 83, 94, 152, 161, 163, 185, 192, 198–200, 207, 212; export of, 74n; intensity, 72, 73, 76; productivity, 72, 105, 110–12; scarcity, 169–71, 174, 175; skilled/unskilled, 50, 74, 95, 136, 143n, 158, 176, 183, 184, 194, 212; surplus, 71, 196
Lal, D., 51n, 78n, 160n, 174n, 183
Lall, S., 4, 16n, 23n, 47n, 48n, 59n, 60, 64n, 68n, 73n, 75n, 85n, 112n, 150n, 152n, 153n, 160n, 164n, 175n, 203n, 204
Langdon, S., 75n
Language, differences in, 18, 44, 215
Lawrence, M. M., 22n, 25n, 28n
Leads and Lags, 42
'Learning by doing', 78, 179, 181, 184
Ledogar, R. J., 75n, 76n
Leftwich, R. B., 119n, 122n, 123n
Legal aspects, 196–8, 200–2, 205, 207
Leipziger, D. M., 72n, 105n
Leverage, 116, 118–20
Levitt, K., 63n
Leys, C., 91n, 97, 220, 221n
Liabilities, 106, 113, 114, 116–18, 126, 127
Licensing, 19, 34–6, 66–8, 70, 97, 105n,

136, 138, 145, 179, 197, 203
Liquidity, 37, 113
Little, I. M. D., 85n, 160n, 174n, 183, 185, 186
Little—Mirrlees method, 85, 159–88 *passim*
Loans, 55, 56, 106, 107, 113–18, 120, 127, 129, 130, 140, 143n, 150, 164, 182, 199, 211
Lonsdale, J. E., 75n
Lupo, L. A., 100n

Mabro, R., 205n
MacDougall, G. D. A., 83
McManus, J. C., 35n
Macro-economic approaches, 83–4, 157, 164, 192, 194–9
Magdoff, H., 32n
Malaysia, 89–93, 95–8, 101, 134, 136–44, 146–8, 150, 151, 153, 170–3, 175, 176, 178, 179
Malik, R., 24n
Management, 9, 11, 17, 21, 27, 28, 34–6, 39–40, 42, 51, 54, 56–64, 74n, 108, 122, 145, 164–6, 192, 195, 202, 207–12, 217
Manipulation, financial, 62, 99, 152, 154n, 162n
Mansfield, E., 14n, 18n
Market: access to, 26; allocations, 138; black, 152n; power, 25–9, 35, 55, 69, 70, 104n, 112, 137n, 152, 154, 177; research, 25, 76; sharing, 138, 216; structure, *see* Oligopolistic competition
Marketing factors, 17, 23–8, 31–4, 36, 39, 41, 43, 45–6, 51, 54, 65, 66, 69, 75–7, 112–13, 135, 137, 158, 166, 186, 187, 192, 195, 197, 198, 203, 208, 210, 211, 221
Markets: domestic, 18, 57, 68, 95, 96, 101, 166, 192; export, 67, 68; world, 10, 30, 40, 51, 77, 152n, 153, 185, 186, 195, 199, 203, 204, 206
Marris, R., 18n
Marxism, 16n, 19, 22, 23n, 29n, 32, 45n, 49, 52, 64, 65, 79, 218, 221
Mason, R. H., 72n
Mayhew, K., 4n
Mergers, 18, 20
Mexico, 6n, 13, 30, 32n, 59n, 63n, 74, 99n, 135n, 194, 201
Micro-economic approaches, 82, 84–6
Middle East, 7, 54
Miliband, R., 45n
Mill, J. S., 214
Mirrlees, J. A., *see* Little—Mirrlees method.

Monopolistic elements, 17–19, 33, 34, 44, 45, 51, 66, 67, 69, 70, 76, 82, 97, 122n, 123, 145, 167, 177, 199, 201–4, 214–16
Morawetz, D., 64n, 70n, 72n, 105n
Morehouse, W., 73n
Morgenstern, R. D. 59n, 154n
Morley, S. A., 72n, 105n
Morris, C. T., 50n
Motivation of Corporations, 11, 16, 18, 28n, 36–8
Mueller, W. F., 32n, 59n, 63n, 74n
Müller, R., 39n, 45n, 58n, 59n, 154n
Mundowsky, M., 69n
Murray, R., 16n, 29n, 45n, 222n
MPEs, 10, 11
Musgrave, P. B., 59n, 193n, 205n
Myrdal, Gunnar, 4, 47n, 49n, 79

Nath, S. K., 47n, 160n
Nationalisation, 35n, 37, 63, 79
Nationalism, 11, 63, 64
Nayyar, D., 13n, 74n, 77n
NCAER, 91n
Negandhi, A., 21n, 57n
Negotiation, 91, 150, 152, 213–18
Nell, E., 52n
Neoclassical theories, 17, 19, 49–53, 64n, 81, 83, 85, 159–64
Netherlands, 6
New Internationalist, 75n
Newfarmer, R. S., 32n, 59n, 63n, 74n
Nicaragua, 135n
Nigeria, 194
Nowshirvani, V. F., 91n

O'Brien, P., 68n
OECD, 6
Offshore processing, *see* Sourcing
Oil money, 14, 216
Oligopolistic theories, 4, 9, 17–29, 31–2, 34, 36, 38, 40, 43, 45–81, 83, 84, 101, 138, 152, 156, 186, 192, 198, 200, 204, 213n, 216
OPEC, 205, 213, 216
Opportunity costs of local capital, 162, 165, 172, 174, 177, 178, 182, 183, 186
Organisation, industrial, 10, 16, 19, 21, 36, 39–46, 56–64, 72, 75, 123, 143, 166, 195, 199
Orr, D., 123n
Output, industrial, 12n, 72, 82, 94, 134, 137, 143n, 147, 158, 159–77 *passim*, 184, 195, 208, 221
Owen, R., 16n

Ownership, 9, 11n, 37, 38, 46, 67, 70, 91, 120, 146, 147, 149; changes in, 37; foreign, 92–4, 97, 98, 122, 123, 135, 146, 147, 149, 153, 166, 173–5; joint, 42–4, 93, 94, 97, 121, 122, 146, 147, 175, 212; local, 147, 175, 208, 212, 224; patterns, 43, 91, 93, 94, 135
Oxford University, 89

Pack, H., 72n, 196n
Pakistan, 13, 43n
Palloix, C., 16n
Paris Convention, 68, 97, 196
Parker, J. E. S., 10n, 11, 14n, 22n, 23n, 25n, 28n, 35n, 92, 93
Parry, T. G., 104
Patents, 22, 23n, 24, 33, 34, 65, 67–9, 97, 196, 197, 203, 211, 213
Pavitt, K., 22n, 64n
Payments: balance of, 4, 60, 82, 85, 89–188 *passim*; direct, 89, 130–55, 156, 165, 169; total, 89, 156–80; personnel, 105, 106, 108–11, 161; technological, 5, 97, 120–2, 126, 142, 145, 146, 151, 179, 202–3, 206–8
Peacock, A. T., 47n, 49n, 50n, 78n
Pearce, D. W., 160n
Pearce, I. F., 83
Penrose, E. T., 18n, 28, 68n, 69
Performance, sample firms', 99, 105–13, 185
Perlmutter, H. V., 11
Personnel, expatriate, 130
Personnel payments, *see* Wages and salaries
Philippines, 6n
Pickering, J. F., 24n, 27n
Pitchford, J., 83
Planning, global, 77, 137
Policy: co-ordination of, 216; Corporate, 11, 28, 94, 120, 147, 150, 210, 214; economic, 4, 15, 44, 63n, 78, 79, 173, 184, 200; fiscal, 63, 193, 205, 209; government, 5, 20, 23, 29–38 *passim*, 43, 45–7, 50, 51, 53, 56, 60, 61, 70, 71, 77–83, 85, 95, 96, 98, 120, 135, 136–9, 143, 145, 152, 157, 160, 162, 170, 177, 183–8, 191–224; implementation of, 74, 191–224; LDC, 43, 174; remittance, 37; staffing, 44
Political factors, 9, 11n, 12, 27–9, 37, 38, 40, 44, 46–8, 50, 52, 58, 60, 62, 63, 71, 77–80, 84, 95, 96, 143, 146n, 152–4, 187, 188, 191, 192, 194, 197, 202, 203, 205, 219, 222, 223

Portfolio, *see* investment
Posner, M. V., 32n
Poulantzas, N., 16n, 45n, 222n
Power; distribution of, 39, 44–6, 194, 221
Prachowny, M. F. J., 137n
Prasad, B., 21n, 57n
Predictability, importance of, 37, 193
Preferences, 52, 71, 186, 187
Price: controls, 153; index, consumer, 118; levels, 24, 29, 30, 51, 53, 57, 59–62, 76–8, 82, 118, 144, 147, 151, 153, 157, 174–5, 201, 211, 214
Prices: export, 60n, 154, 204; import, 60n, 68, 143, 153, 197, 204; shadow, 85, 86, 159–77 *passim*, 183–5, 187, 192; transfer, 41, 47, 51, 54, 56, 59–63, 68, 74, 80, 85, 91, 97, 118, 143–5, 146n, 177, 180, 200, 202–6, 208, 216; world, 85, 153, 171, 175, 176, 187
Pricing, over-, *see* Transfer prices
Privilege, distribution of, 194
Product: cycle, 32–4; differentiation, 23, 25–7, 31, 33, 63, 65, 71, 75–7, 85, 113, 135, 137n, 195, 197, 208, 221; maturity, 33, 34; necessity of, 191, 192; quality of, 29, 143, 148, 184, 199
Production: costs, 29, 30, 32, 199, 208; domestic, 158, 159, 192, 208; international, 11, 12, 15, 19, 29, 32, 43, 46, 51, 74n, 135, 142, 147, 195, 196, 200, 205, 208, 234; levels of TNC, 12, 13, 33, 99, 105; mass, 71, 212
Products, appropriateness of, 70, 85, 187
Profitability of sample firms, 100, 105, 120–9, 137, 141, 145, 150, 152–4, 178, 208, 210
Profits: declaration of, 11n, 62, 120, 147, 150–4, 163, 204; domestic, 28n, 162, 175, 199; foreign, 83, 121, 140–2, 144, 151, 162, 174, 175, 204, 207; level of, 55, 67, 83, 97, 99, 113, 121, 123, 126, 128–30, 136, 146n, 150–5, 164, 169, 177, 202, 205; remission of, 59, 118, 119, 140, 146–8, 151, 154, 162, 177, 202; repatriation of, 60, 62, 63, 140, 207, 209, 213
Progress, technical, *see* Technology
Promotion, 25–6, 33, 50, 52, 70, 71, 75, 76, 112, 113, 123, 128, 165, 166, 197, 198, 200–2, 206; wasteful, 76, 77, 197
Property rights, 207
Protection, by host country, 30, 51, 62, 78, 122, 123, 146, 152, 162, 171, 175–7, 182–4, 192n, 193, 204, 207, 208

Index

Raw materials, 26, 144, 174, 204
Recruitment, 11n, 21, 57
Reddaway, W. B., 6, 99n, 156n
Regulation, 148, 150, 156, 191, 192–207, 217, 218, 223, 224
Reinvestment, 55, 59, 62, 113, 122
Remmers, H. L., 39n, 41n, 56n
Rent, oligopolistic, 36, 42–4, 55, 70
Replacement: financial 159, 164–9 *passim*, 177–9; local, 159, 160, 166–8, 172, 179–80, 181–3, 185, 207
Resale, by sample firms, 130, 174–5
Research, 89–91, 99, 129, 151, 156, 171, 196, 211; and development, 7–8, 14, 22–5, 27, 31, 33, 40, 46, 47, 61, 68, 72–4, 123, 196, 201, 210, 211; expenditure on, 28n, 57, 61, 65, 72, 105, 205, 210
Resnick, S. A. 36n
Resources: allocation of, 29, 215; natural, 36n
Restrictions, 28, 30, 77, 79, 97, 135–9, 167, 200
Restrictive practices, 24, 51, 68, 69, 70, 91, 97, 137–9, 200, 149, 201–3, 213, 222
Retailing, 26, 30, 31, 76
Reuber, G. L., 6, 37n, 38n, 43n, 51n, 64n, 72n, 73, 78n, 99n, 105n, 143n, 145, 193n
Richardson, J. D., 137n
Risk, 14, 17, 20–1, 23, 24, 28, 28n, 34–7, 41–4, 54, 60, 66, 81, 138, 151, 166, 184, 193, 207
Robbins, S. M., 40n, 41n, 42n, 59n, 118n, 147n, 150n
Robinson, J., 47n, 49n
Rowan, D. C., 83
Rowley, C. K., 47n, 49n, 50n, 78n
Rowthorn, R., 12n, 32, 49n
Royalties, 36, 41, 56, 67, 97, 130, 141, 145–51, 153, 162, 169, 177, 179, 203, 216
Rumelt, R. P. 39n

Salary, *see* Wage
Saez, W., 28n
Salehkhou, G., 153n
Sales: commissions on, 123, 126; level of sample firms', 94–5, 100–6
Sanctions, 214
Sauvant, K. P., 40n
Savings, 3, 48, 54, 55, 70, 82–4, 161, 212
Sawyer, M., 12n, 14n, 18n, 25n, 41n
Scale: economies of, 26–7, 50, 54, 83, 107, 108, 136, 152, 180; factors, 17, 20, 24, 32, 72, 101, 167, 179, 181
Scherer, F. M., 18n

Schwartz, N., 14n, 24n
Science policy, 73, 196n
Sen, A. K., 50n, 100n, 160n, 187n
Servan-Schreiber, J. J., 63n
Services, sale of, 59, 67, 206
Severn, A. K., 22n, 25n, 28n
Shareholding, *see* Equity
Sharpston, M., 30n, 74n, 76n, 193n
Shoup, C. B., 193n, 205n
Shubik, M., 18n
Shulman, J. S., 59n
Silberston, Z. A., 68n
Singapore, 13, 30n, 135n
Singer, H., 82n
Singh, A., 18n, 28n, 41n, 199n
Size of firms, 17, 18, 24, 27, 28, 45, 57, 100–4, 110, 111, 120, 136, 158, 192
Skill, 3, 7, 8, 21n, 26–8, 33, 41, 48, 50, 51, 62, 67, 74–6, 83, 135, 137, 143n, 158, 192, 200, 203, 205, 212, 217, 223
Smith, G. W., 72n, 105n
Socialism, 37, 60, 63, 64, 66, 194n
Solidarity, 213–16
Sourcing, 29–30, 34, 74–6, 193
South Korea, 13, 135n
Speculation, 63n
Sri Lanka, 197n, 204
Stability, 26, 28n, 32, 35, 37–9, 43n, 46, 54, 60, 65, 74, 77, 95, 96, 138, 192–4, 208, 215
State, theory of, 50, 78–9, 187, 220–3
Stephenson, H., 44n
Stevens, G. V. G., 16n, 19, 28n, 37n
Stewart, F., 49n, 50n, 64n, 70n, 72n, 73, 85n, 105n, 184n, 196n, 212
Stikker, D. U., 91n
Stilwell, F. J. B., 47n, 50n
Stinchcombe, A. L., 223n
Stobaugh, R. B., 33n, 40n, 41n, 42n, 59n, 72n, 105n, 118n, 147n, 150n
Stock, changes, 115, 174, 175
Stoneman, C., 84n
Stopford, L. M., 35n, 39n, 40n, 43n
Storage, 75
Strategy of firms, 10, 39, 40–2, 46, 59, 86, 137n, 143, 191, 192, 194
Streeten, P. P., 4, 28n, 45n, 47n, 48n, 50n, 64n, 66n, 72n, 74n, 79n, 184n, 202n, 213n
Subcontracting, 36
Subordination, 57, 58
Subrahmanian, K. K., 32n, 91n
Subsidies, government, 97, 136, 138
Sunkel, O., 28n, 73n, 196n
Sutcliffe, R. B., 16n

280 Index

Sweden, 13
Sweezey, P., 16n
Switzerland, 6, 8

Taiwan, 13, 30, 135n, 194
Takeovers, 18, 20, 25, 41, 46, 76, 198–9, 207
Tariffs, 30, 38, 50, 59, 61, 75, 83, 97, 136, 152, 154, 162, 164, 177, 181, 193, 204, 208, 216
Taxes, 28, 37, 40, 42, 50, 51, 59–61, 67, 74, 83, 96, 97, 102, 120–2, 126, 130, 146, 150–3, 162, 164, 167, 169, 175, 181, 192–4, 199, 202, 204, 205, 207, 209, 213, 214, 216, 222
Taylor, C. T., 6, 68n
Technology: adaptability of, 71–3, 80, 105; advanced, 34, 108, 110, 165, 195, 196, 198; age of, 149, 196, 201; appropriateness of, 70–3, 105, 167, 187, 196, 212; availability of, 165, 166, 179, 182, 185, 208; changes in, 33, 43, 67, 192, 202–3; choice of, 105–8, 110, 112, 137, 223; cost of, *see* Royalties; dependence, 73, 74, 196; domestic, 56, 63, 70, 73n, 74, 108, 179, 196, 197; high, 72, 205n; intermediate, 73, 196; international, 11, 14, 15, 17, 21–6, 27, 28, 30–2, 34, 35, 37–9, 41, 43, 45, 46, 48, 51, 54, 57, 58, 60–75 *passim*, 77, 83, 85, 110, 145, 150, 164, 167, 179, 182, 183, 192, 195–8, 200, 203, 208, 210; low, 72, 148; sale of, 34–6, 56, 59, 63, 66–70, 91, 138, 139, 159, 198, 200, 201, 203, 206; stolen, 72; transfer of, 3–5, 22, 29, 64–75, 77, 105n, 135, 146, 149, 150, 185n, 196, 197, 201, 202, 217n
Tharp, P. A., 43n
Times, The, 41
Tomlinson, J. W. C., 43n
Trade: international, 3, 10–13, 15, 17, 29, 32n, 34, 46, 51, 75, 81–3, 85, 102, 105n, 145, 151, 152, 157, 161, 163, 169–71, 175, 176, 187, 195, 196, 206, 214, 224; intrafirm, 59, 60, 147, 150, 151, 204, 211; tradable/non-tradable inputs, 161–3, 169–7, 176, 183, 184; trade theory, 17, 81–4; Unions, 60, 74, 77, 192–4, 199, 224
Training, 21, 40n, 57, 72, 97, 199, 212, 217, 223
Transfers, financial, 39, 41–2, 83
Transfer-pricing, *see* Prices
Transnational Corporation, definition of, 8, 10, 11, 16

Transport, 7, 26, 30, 75
Turner, L., 222n
United Kingdom, 6–9, 10n, 12, 13, 21, 28n, 31, 42, 92, 138n, 199n
United Nations, 6, 7, 8n, 11n, 12n, 13n, 15, 42, 43n, 59n, 93, 224; UN Conference on Trade and Development, 22n, 24n, 30n, 64n, 68, 72, 74n, 82, 85, 89–188 *passim*, 193n, 196, 200, 201, 224; UNIDO, 170n, 184n, 193n
United States, 6–8, 10, 12–14, 20–3, 26n, 28, 31, 32n, 33, 35n, 37n, 38, 40–3, 55, 57n, 61, 63n, 64, 65n, 75, 92, 99, 100, 113n, 117, 119, 121, 122, 138n, 194, 198, 205, 222, 223; Tariff Commission, 6, 8, 10, 13, 14n, 15, 22n, 24n, 28n, 41, 43n, 61n, 99n, 113n
University of Sussex, 90

Vaitsos, C. V., 56n, 59n, 64n, 66n, 68n, 69n, 72n, 85, 91n, 97n, 118n, 137n, 139, 140n, 145n, 147n, 149n, 150n, 153n, 196, 217n
Valuation problems, 56, 140
Value-Added, by sample firms, 100, 105, 108, 110, 111, 175
Vaupel, J. W., 54n, 99n
Verlage, H. C., 59n, 61n, 151n, 205
Vernon, R., 4, 10, 12n, 18n, 22n, 24n, 25n, 30n, 31n, 32, 34, 35n, 39n, 40n, 43, 44n, 99n

Wage: costs, 30n, 31, 33, 162, 163; policy, 199; salary levels, 30, 62, 72–4, 83, 109, 105n, 161, 174, 194, 199, 212
Watanabe, S., 30n
Watergate, 41
Wedderburn, K. W., 224n
Weichmann, U. L., 40n
Weisskopf, T. E., 12n, 84n, 221n
Welfare: arguments about, 47–53, 79; effects on, 4, 5, 11, 15, 23n, 29, 47–86, 160, 162n, 163–5, 170, 172, 173, 175–7, 181, 182, 184–8, 194, 195, 222, 223
Wells, L. T., 32n, 35n, 39n, 40n, 43n, 64n, 72n
Wilkins, M., 67n
Willmore, L., 32n, 63n, 72n, 99n
Wilson, T. A., 25n, 123n
Wionczek, M., 99n, 201n
Wolf, B. N. 28n, 101n, 122n

Xerox, 24

Yeomans, K. A., 120n